The Descent of Bath UNIVERSITY COLLEGE
WINCHESTER

'4

The ascent of Babel explores the ways in which the mind produces and understands language: the ways in which the sounds of language evoke meaning, and the ways in which the desire to communicate causes us to produce those sounds to begin with.

The Tower of Babel has come to represent the diversity of language. But the ascent of Babel symbolises the quest to understand the mental processes which underlie our use of language. It also represents the progression from sound to meaning, and the ascent that we each undergo, from birth onwards, as we learn our mother tongue.

'*The Ascent of Babel* discusses fascinating questions on especially the origins and development of language, with answers based on a very wide range of experiments. It is highly readable, with a useful bibliography of original papers on the key findings, and general reading on language, mind and understanding.'

Professor Richard Gregory, University of Bristol

The Ascent of Babel

An Exploration of Language, Mind, and Understanding

Gerry T. M. Altmann

Illustrations by
Andrea Enzinger

OXFORD
UNIVERSITY PRESS

OXFORD

UNIVERSITY PRESS

Great Clarendon Street, Oxford OX2 6DP

Oxford University Press is a department of the University of Oxford.
It furthers the University's objective of excellence in research, scholarship,
and education by publishing worldwide in

Oxford   New York

Athens Auckland Bangkok Bogotá Buenos Aires Calcutta
Cape Town Chennai Dar es Salaam Delhi Florence Hong Kong Istanbul
Karachi Kuala Lumpur Madrid Melbourne Mexico City Mumbai
Nairobi Paris São Paulo Singapore Taipei Tokyo Toronto Warsaw
with associated companies in Berlin Ibadan

Oxford is a registered trade mark of Oxford University Press
in the UK and in certain other countries

Published in the United States
by Oxford University Press Inc., New York

© G. Altmann (text), A. Enzinger (illustrations), 1997

First published 1997
First published in paperback 1998
Reprinted 1999

A catalogue record for this book is available from the British Library

Library of Congress Cataloging in Publication Data
(Data applied for)

ISBN 0 19 852377 7

Printed in Great Britain by
Bookcraft Ltd.,
Midsomer Norton, Avon

for Sam

Preface

Most people I meet stop to think about language for no longer than it takes them to notice that the instructions on how to program their CD-player have been written in a language that defies understanding. They care more about how their CD-player *should* work than how their language *actually* works. When I started writing this book I wanted to rise to what I saw as a challenge: to write the equivalent of a manual that would explain not the insides of a CD-player, and how it turns thousands of little indentations on the surface of the CD into sound, but the insides of the human mind, and how it turns thousands of little vibrations on the surface of the ear-drum into meaning. The difference is, CD-players are simple, even if their instruction manuals are not. Minds are complex, and they do not come with instructions. That, of course, is what makes them so challenging, and so exciting.

I wanted to write this book so that it would be readable by non-specialists. I wanted to convey to them the excitement and challenge of *psycholinguistics*—the study of how the mind turns language into meaning, and back again. I am mindful of the preface to Doris Lessing's *The golden notebook*, where she invites the reader to skip as much of the book as is necessary in order to maintain interest. The reader of this book should also skip as necessary. Or at least, skip any chapters that seem less interesting. The first chapter, 'Looking towards Babel', is an attempt to convey the excitement of psycholinguistics, and the mysteries that are on offer. Probably, it should not be skipped, except in emergency. The other chapters fill in the details. I have written each chapter so that it is self-contained, although occasional pointers are given, both forwards and backwards, if there is relevant material in other chapters. Inevitably, because different chapters are about different topics, some may seem, to different readers, more interesting than others.

I have also written this book for my students, who are a good example of a non-specialist, although admittedly captive, audience. Many students find psycholinguistics a mysterious and impenetrable subject. So I have designed this book so that it could in principle accompany the kinds of psycholinguistic courses they may take. It is not written like a textbook (nor is it written in textbook-speak). There are no references in the text, just at the end, in the chapter-by-chapter bibliography. There are pointers there to general non-specialist reading matter and, separately, to the academic articles that contain the original material I have described in the main text. I have tested out the manuscript when teaching both introductory and advanced courses (as a supplementary text), and am grateful for the positive feedback I received.

I have been necessarily selective with the material I have chosen to describe. It is impossible to write a single comprehensive chapter on topics which deservedly fill entire shelves (and more) in our academic libraries. I have, however, attempted to identify the current issues and the state-of-the-art. Some of the chapters inevitably reflect my own interpretation of that state-of-the-art. The chapter on meaning, for example (my personal favourite), contains a very different perspective on that topic than the one to be found in the psycholinguistic textbooks. That is primarily because the textbooks borrow heavily from work in logic, philosophy, and linguistics. I doubt very much that the human mind should be described using logical formulae, philosophical speculations, or linguistic idealizations. Instead, I have borrowed from insights that have been developed in the field of artificial neural networks—computer-simulated systems that bear some superficial resemblance to the simplest workings of interconnecting neurons. The penultimate chapter, 'Wiring-up a brain', reflects these insights quite explicitly. The final sections in that chapter are pure speculation on my part. But where the material is speculative, I have said so.

There are, inevitably, a whole host of people without whom this book would not have been written. First and foremost, my psycholinguistic colleagues who have made the field what it is, and provided the raw materials that I have worked with here. My more immediate colleagues, at the Universities of Sussex (where I worked until Chapter 9) and York (Chapter 10 onwards) provided much support and encouragement, as well as useful advice. The first four chapters were in fact written whilst I was on sabbatical at the Department of Psychology, University of Melbourne, Australia. Chapters 7 and 8, as well as the final draft, were written whilst I was a visiting scientist (on two separate occasions) at the Max Planck Institute for Psycholinguistics in Nijmegen, The Netherlands. Both places provided a rich environment within which to think about the issues I was writing about.

Various chapters have been tested out on different people (not just my students), and I should like to thank them for their valuable comments. And many other people responded to requests for further information, or made useful suggestions. They are: Simon Altmann, Edith Bavin, Heike Behrens, Holly Branigan, David Caplan, Rachel Clifton, Stephen Crain, Anne Cutler, Zoltán Dienes, Andrew Ellis, Caroline Gale, Alan Garnham, Simon Garrod, Esther Grabe, Geoffrey Hall, Shaun Hellman, Glynn Humphries, Matt Lambon Ralph, Peter Jusczyk, Willem Levelt, William Marslen-Wilson, Joanne Miller, Jane Oakhill, Gavin Phillips, Philip Quinlan, Ardi Roelofs, Eleanor Saffran, Dan Slobin, Maggie Snowling, Lesley Stirling, Michael Tanenhaus, Ian Walker, and, of course, everyone at Oxford University Press. Andrea Enzinger's creativity kept us smiling.

Finally, there are a number of psycholinguists (some were on that list, some were not) who have, over the years, played a significant part in my own psycholinguistic upbringing. They have inspired me through the psycholinguistics they did, their enthusiasm, or simply their personal encouragement and friendship. I consider myself fortunate to know them. But even more fortunate to know Sue, and of course Sam.

September, 1996   G.T.M.A.

Contents

In the beginning

According to Biblical legend, God saw that the people of Earth were building a tower in order that they might reach His Heaven. To prevent this, He spread chaos and confusion amongst them. He scattered them throughout the Earth, and forced on them different languages so that they would be prevented from communicating with one another and building another Babel.

Stories such as this caused the tower at Babel (there really was such a tower) to symbolize not just the origins and diversity of the world's many languages, but language itself. The *ascent* of Babel symbolizes something else. In part, it symbolizes a quest, not for a glimpse of Heaven, but for a glimpse of those facets of the human mind that enable us to produce and understand language. But it also symbolizes the progression that we each undergo, from birth onwards, as we learn our own mother tongue. As babies and infants we play at the base of the tower. As adults, we stand at its summit. And when we hear a language, the sounds of that language enter our ears and evoke an ascent of yet another kind—the progression from sound to meaning. And when we study language, we discover that, like the tower at Babel, it is built upwards, with one structure resting on another, and another. The foundations of that structure are cast in sound. The summit of that structure is cast in meaning. And in between are syllables, words, and sentences.

In the chapters that follow, we shall attempt the *psycholinguistic* ascent—to understand better the mental processes that underlie our use of language. The first few chapters are structured according to the infant's ascent from the *in utero* world of the unborn baby, and what can be learned even there, to what older infants have to learn so that they can pick up the rudiments of a vocabulary and the rudiments of a grammar with which to use it. From Chapter 5 onwards, we leave behind, temporarily, what has to be learned, and examine how a vocabulary can reside in the mental structures of the brain. We go on to consider the conventions we share that enable us to convey meaning, not simply with individual words, but with those words ordered in particular ways. We explore the nature of grammar—what it is good for, and what it is not. We then examine the nature of language understanding, and what that involves. In Chapter 9, we reach a plateau, as we explore what understanding actually *is*—what meaning is, and how it can reside not just in the *mental* structures, but also in the *neural* structures of the brain.

Extracting meaning from language as we listen to it is only half the story—we also convey meaning as we speak it. How we do that is the subject of Chapter 10. After that, we consider language not as it is spoken, but as it is written. Finally, in Chapters 12 and 13 we consider brains (again): what happens to language when real brains go wrong, and what happens with language when artificial, computer-simulated, brains go right. Chapter 14 is mercifully short, on the evolution and diversification of human language. We end our ascent with a final view from Babel—a look at the true significance of language.

So where, amongst all of this, shall we discover Babel's summit? Perhaps surprisingly, its summit lies at its foundations, amongst the chaos and confusion of the infant's first steps up through Babel. There lies the secret of language, and there can be found the key that unlocks the final mystery. For that mystery, as we shall discover, is not about language, but about learning. About how babies learn. About how children learn. And most of all, about how *brains* learn. But that is for later. First, and before we even start our ascent, we need to understand better the nature of the mysteries that await us on Babel's slopes.

1

Looking towards Babel

Someone once said that a good title for a book about language would be *Teach your dog to talk*. It has all the ingredients necessary for instant mass appeal; dogs are popular, and teaching them to do just about anything at all is a challenge. So teaching a dog to talk would really be something. The title would convey instant mystery; how could *anyone* teach a dog to do that? The trouble is, another title that would be at least as appealing would be *Teach your dog to juggle*. Who really cares about talking? We all manage pretty well at it, without even being taught how to do it. So a whole book about talking, and how we do it, sounds about as interesting as an entire book on walking, and how we do that. Juggling, on the other hand, is something else.

Language, unlike juggling, is a human faculty that we take for granted, like having two legs, two arms, one head. Nobody taught us to have two legs, just as no one taught us to listen, to understand, to make sense of a whole jumble of sounds. Imagine what it must be like, worldwide, for the 180 or so babies born each minute to suddenly hear such a cacophony of noise. Obstetricians say that the reason a newborn baby cries when naked is that it is cold. It has never felt that before. It has never seen bright lights. It has never heard the sound of a human voice, the sound of its own voice, a dog's bark, the cars outside, the aeroplane overhead. And yet somehow, it manages to make sense of the different sounds it hears; it learns to hear patterns in those sounds, and associate meanings with those patterns, and even produce new patterns itself. It learns to *communicate*. As adults, we carry around knowledge about tens of thousands of different words: what they mean, how they should be spelled, how they sound, how to move the muscles in the lips and tongue to pronounce them, how to join them up to form sentences; in short, how to *use* them. As infants, we acquire that knowledge. How?

No one questions that incredible feat. But learning to juggle, that really *is* something, apparently, to write home about.

We take our ability as a species to speak and hear (and understand) so much for granted that, more often than not, we fail to see the real mystery surrounding how we manage to do this. How is all that information about all those words stored in the brain? How do we use that information? We can hardly open up a brain like a book and look up the words in the same way that we thumb through a dictionary. Even using a simple dictionary that you *can* thumb through involves knowledge about the way the dictionary is organized, the nature of the alphabet, the shapes of individual letters, and so on. So if we could thumb through a brain, and look up the information that it contains, where would all this other knowledge, about how to use the brain-dictionary, be? And wherever it is, where did it come from?

We rarely appreciate how overworked our babies are; they have to do much more than just use their brain-dictionaries, they have to create them in the first place, and figure out a way of using them. And who helps them? Making sense of the spoken language we provide them with is hardly an easy task. Speech is quite unlike writing. Its words are quite different:

≡   *therearenospacesbetweenthembutthatisprobablytheleastoftheproblems.*

The majority of the spoken language that we hear around us is one long continuous, changing sound—just listen to someone speaking a language you have never heard before. Basically, language is a nightmare. Yes, da Vinci and Einstein were clever, but your average baby is not that far behind.

So the mystery is there, and like any mystery, it has its fair share of intrigue, excitement, discovery, argument, and counter-argument. Just as cosmologists and quantum physicists search for a unified theory of the universe, so psycholinguists search for a unified theory of how we produce and understand language. The scientific methods used in their search can be just as rigorous and scientific, and the theories just as plausible (or implausible). The excitement is just as great. When scientists discovered that the background radiation in the universe was not uniform, but had ripples in it (much like ripples in water), it made front page news in many of the world's major newspapers; the excitement this news generated arose because it told us something about how the universe was constructed. That knowledge alone was worth telling to the world. And yet, language, like ripples in the radiation bathing the universe, can tell us something about the mind, and how it is constructed. At the end of the day, it comes down to simple aesthetics; you may be excited by the mysteries of the cosmos, or the mysteries of the mind. Psycholinguists are excited by the mysteries of language.

Intellectual origins

Psycholinguistics, like most of psychology, can trace its origins as far back as the Greeks, and probably even before. More recently, psycholinguistics experienced an intellectual growth spurt in the mid 1960s, just as the study of linguistics, in its contemporary form, got under way. Noam Chomsky, a linguist at the Massachusetts Institute of Technology, had developed a new way of describing the rules that determine which sentences are grammatical and which are not. It is not too surprising that psycholinguistics would depend substantially on advances in linguistics. Although psycholinguists are predominantly interested in how language is produced and understood, linguists were, at the time, more interested in ways of describing the language itself. What psycholinguistics needed was a vocabulary with which to talk about language, and that is exactly what linguistics provided. In effect, linguists provided the equivalent of a periodic table of the elements, and a set of rules for predicting which combinations of the elements would be explosive. The parallel between chemistry and linguistics is not that far-fetched, and is yet another indication of how much we take language for granted; whereas we wonder at the good fortune we had in the discovery (or invention) of the periodic table, we rarely consider the fact that linguistics has developed a system of almost equal rigour. And just as chemistry is a far-reaching subject concerned with the simplest of atoms and their combination into the most complex of molecules, so linguistics is concerned with the simplest of sounds and their combination into, ultimately, the most complex of sentences.

But if linguistics provided the equivalent of a periodic table and rules for combining the elements (whether sounds, words, or sentences), what was left for psycholinguistics to do? The answer to this question is pretty much the same as the answer to another question: if architects can provide a complete description of a building, in the minutest of detail, what is left for builders to do? Architects design things. The finished design is simply a description of a building. It does not necessarily describe how the building materials are made, or why ceilings are put up after walls, or why windows tend not to be in floors. It does not necessarily describe how the building functions. When Bruegel painted his tower of Babel, did he start painting from the top or from the bottom? In principle he could have started from the top, and the finished painting would have ended up exactly the same. The point is, he did not need to know how such a tower would be built. So the answer to the original question, about what else there was for psycholinguistics to do, is simple. Linguistics provides a vocabulary for talking about the ways in which sentences are constructed from individual words, and the ways in which words are themselves constructed from smaller components (right down to the individual sounds and the movements of the muscles that create those sounds). By contrast, psycholinguistics attempts to determine how these structures, whether sounds, words, or sentences, are produced to yield utterances, or are analysed to yield meaning. If linguistics is about language, psycholinguistics is about the brain.

Despite the close relationship between linguistics and psycholinguistics, the latter has generally been considered to be affiliated not to linguistics, but to psychology. Psychology encompasses just about every facet of human behaviour, whether it concerns the workings of individuals or the workings of groups of interacting individuals. But psycholinguistics comes under a branch of psychology called *cognitive psychology*, which is concerned primarily with how the mind represents the external world—if it did not somehow manage this, we would be unable to describe that world using language, recall it using memory, interpret it through what we see, learn about it through experience, and so on.

Tools of the trade

Because of the disparate nature of the different subdisciplines within psychology, it should come as no surprise that they each have their own set of tools to aid in their investigations. Few people realize that there are disciplines within psychology which are amenable to empirical science. In psycholinguistics, we do not just *think* that certain things may go on within the mind, we *know* they do, in just the same way as a physicist knows that mass is related to gravity. We know, for instance, that newborn babies are sensitive to the intonation (changes in pitch, rhythm, and intensity) of their maternal language; they can tell their own language apart from other languages. We know also that very young infants (just weeks old) are sensitive to sounds which may not occur within their own language, but may occur in other languages. We know that they lose this sensitivity within about eight to nine months. We know that when adults hear a word such as 'rampart', not only do they access whatever representation they have in their minds of this word, they also access the representations corresponding to 'ramp', 'part', 'art' and probably 'amp' as well. We know also that this does not happen only with single isolated words, but that it also happens with words heard as part of normal continuous speech; if you hear 'They'll ram part of the wall', you will access the individual words that are intended, but also other spurious words, such as 'rampart'.

With knowledge such as this, the next step is to consider the implications of these facts for the way in which the mind works; how could babies possibly be aware of distinctions between one language and another when they have only just been born? If babies lose their sensitivity to speech sounds which are absent from their language simply because they have never heard those sounds, how could they be sensitive to any sounds in the first place? And if adults spend all this time accessing spurious words, how do we ever manage to figure out which words were intended, and which were not? And never mind us adults, how do babies manage? So the empirical science side of psycholinguistics necessarily informs its theoretical side.

Of course, like any science, one has to be able to validate the tools available, and trust them. For instance, how can we know that a baby can distinguish between one language and another? We cannot ask it, and it certainly cannot tell us. In fact, it is relatively easy to understand, if less easy to do. One thing babies do pretty well is suck. And there exists a technique called *non-nutritive sucking* in which a normal rubber teat is placed in the baby's mouth. The teat is filled with fluid and connected by a thin tube to a pressure-sensitive device that can tell whether the teat has been compressed or not— i.e. whether the baby has sucked or not. This in turn is connected to a computer which, whenever there is a suck, plays a sound over a loudspeaker to the baby. Babies learn very quickly that each time they suck, they get to hear a sound (not surprising, as babies are used to getting what they want when they suck). They start to suck more in order to hear more. But babies get bored very quickly, so after a short while they start to suck less. At this point, the computer senses a decrease in sucking, and changes the sound being

played. If the babies can tell this new sound from the old one, they perk
up, and get interested again and start to suck more. Of course, if they do
not perk up, they might either have failed to distinguish the new sound
from the old, or have failed to stay awake (a common problem with this
technique!). But crucially, if sucking rate does go up, they must have
been able to distinguish the two sounds. Importantly, you can play more
than just single sounds to the babies; you can play whole sets of sounds,
and after they get bored, you play a new set of sounds, to see if the
babies can tell that there is some difference between this new set and the
old set.

This example demonstrates just one of many experimental tools that
psycholinguists have at their disposal. It is relatively simple, and we
understand pretty much how it works, and why. On occasion, however, the tools may work, and we may be able to validate them, but
without necessarily understanding why they work as they do. This is
partly true of one of the tools psycholinguists use to study the ways in
which the meanings of words are accessed on the basis of the sounds
making up the speech input. A commonly used technique is based on a
phenomenon called *priming*. The basic version of this technique is
simple: it involves presenting people with words on a computer screen.
Each time a word comes up, the person has to decide whether it is a real
word in their language, or a *nonword*—e.g. 'boat' vs. 'loat'. They have
two buttons in front of them, and they simply press the yes-button or

the no-button as quickly as possible. So the task is easy and straight-forward, and typically people take just a few hundred milliseconds to press the appropriate button. Perhaps one of the earliest findings in psycholinguistics was that people take less time to decide that 'boat' is a real word if they have just seen (or heard) a related word such as 'ship'. If beforehand they see or hear 'shop', there is no such advantage. This priming effect also works between words like 'bat' and 'ball'— they are not related in meaning, but are simply common *associates*.

We can only speculate as to how the priming effect actually comes about, although it is the subject of much theoretical discussion, and there are a number of plausible hypotheses. But even without a proven theory of how it works, we can use priming as a tool to find out about which words are *accessed* during spoken language recognition. For instance, Richard Shillcock (a psycholinguist at Edinburgh University, who first speculated about the merits of the title *Teach your dog to talk*) played people recordings of words like 'bat', then, immediately after the word stopped, he presented 'ball' on a computer screen. The basic priming effect was there. But he also found that words like 'wombat' decreased decision times to 'ball' as well. 'Wombat' is completely un-related to the word 'ball', so we have to assume that 'bat' was somehow accessed, and that this is why 'ball' was responded to faster. This is a simplified account of the experiment (which we shall return to in Chapter 6), but the basic idea is there.

On the impossibility of proving anything

Empirical tools are all well and fine, but they are of little use without having theories to test. As with any scientific endeavour, the purpose of experimentation in psycholinguistics is to narrow down the range of hypotheses that could explain the phenomena of interest. Much experi-mentation in any science is to do with disproving alternative theories. This is not because scientists are bloody-minded and want only to prove their colleagues wrong; it is a necessary property of science. The out-come of any single experiment may well be incompatible with any number of different theories. But it may still be compatible with many more (and they cannot all be right). In fact, it will be compatible with an infinite number more, ranging from the reasonable to the totally unreasonable (such as, 'This result only happens when the experiment is run in a leap year'—clearly absurd but, unless tested, it has not been shown to be false). Fortunately, we tend to ignore the unreasonable. Unfortunately (for the scientists concerned), there have been cases where what turned out to be right was previously judged totally unreasonable, such as that the Earth is round, and the planets revolve around the Sun.

So experiments cannot, logically, prove a hypothesis to be true; they can only prove other hypotheses to be false. The paradox, of course, is that even if a hypothesis is in fact true, by the generally accepted definitions of scientific investigation, it is unprovable . . . On the whole, we can safely ignore this paradox, because there are few theories which are completely uncontroversial (and this is true in just about every branch of science). Psycholinguistics is certainly not exempt from controversy, but it is a fortunate and inevitable consequence of such controversy that theoretical advances are made. In fact, psycholinguistic theory is becoming so sophisticated that computer programs can be written which embody that theory. Computer simulations exist which mimic even the earliest learning of babies and infants. Perhaps it is no surprise that these programs are modelled on properties of the human brain (we shall come back to these properties in Chapter 13). For now, it is simply enough to be reassured that psycholinguistics is a science like any other; it has its empirical tools, its testable theories, and its unsolved mysteries. Perhaps juggling—even a dog juggling—is not so interesting after all. A child learning to speak? That really *is* something worth talking about.

The ascent of Babel takes many forms. The psycholinguistic ascent attempts to understand not language itself, but language as it is used by the mind. A mind that begins to develop even before birth. Our ascent of Babel must therefore begin where we begin, *in utero*.

Babies, birth, and language

It used to be thought that babies, before they were born, did little more than lie back and mature. They would occasionally move around or have a stretch, but would otherwise do little else. This view of the unborn baby as a passive, almost dormant inhabitant of an isolation tank is certainly wrong. There are countless anecdotes about unborn babies and their likes and dislikes—even *in utero*, babies are remarkably responsive to the right kinds of external stimulation.

No one doubts that babies are good at learning and, as we shall see later, we know that they are capable of learning even a few hours after birth. But there is also evidence to suggest that they can learn *before* birth. This is hardly surprising. It would be unlikely that the ability to learn suddenly switched on at birth. Just when it develops is unknown. However, it may be long enough beforehand to allow the baby to learn something useful about the sounds it hears *in utero*.

It is generally agreed that the auditory system, or the sense of hearing, is functional by around seven months (from conception), although that figure is really only an approximation to the truth. Certainly, by around seven months, we can be fairly confident that the baby can hear. Just what it hears is another matter. The baby is immersed in fluid, surrounded by membranes, muscle, and skin. Much of the sound around the mother never even makes it through, and what little does get through is distorted by all that tissue and fluid. Because the sounds that the baby hears *in utero* are the first sounds it hears, they may kick-start the whole process which leads, ultimately, to the ability to interpret and recognize different sounds. It is therefore important to understand the nature of the distortion that the sound undergoes as it reaches the baby. And to understand the distortion, and why it may be significant that the sound is distorted in a particular way, it is necessary to acquire a basic understanding of what sound is and how it is produced.

Sound is heard (or *perceived*) when vibration of the air causes a membrane in the inner ear to vibrate. Changing the frequency of the vibration leads to a change in the sense of pitch; a soprano sings at a higher pitch than a baritone, by causing his or her *vocal folds* to vibrate at a higher frequency (faster) than the vocal folds of the baritone. The vocal folds function in just the same way as the neck of a balloon when you let the air out; the noise is caused by the vibration of the rubber in the neck (the equivalent of the vocal folds) which is itself caused by the air flow from the body of the balloon (the equivalent of the lungs) up through the neck. If you stretch the neck of the balloon, the noise goes up in pitch, and if you loosen it, it goes down. Pitch and frequency are different things—frequency is a physical property of the signal, whereas pitch is what we perceive (the same note played on different instruments contains different frequencies, but will be perceived as having the same pitch). Jargon aside, sounds are just complex vibrations transmitted through the air. And if the air is in contact with something else, the sound gets transmitted through that as well because the vibrating air causes it to vibrate too, whether it is water, skin, muscle, or amniotic fluid. But not everything vibrates as easily as air. Skin and fluid are a little more sluggish, and very high frequency vibrations do not pass through so well. So what the baby hears *in utero* is distorted.

What babies hear is a lot worse than simply turning down the treble and turning up the bass on a stereo to accentuate the low frequencies in the music, and de-emphasize the high frequencies. It is more like the sound that you get from covering your mouth with your hand and talking through that. In physical terms, although a young adult with normal hearing can hear frequencies in the range of around 20 to 20 000 vibrations, or cycles, per second, the frequencies produced by the human voice are only in the range of 100 to 4000 cycles per second (one cycle per second is one Hertz, or Hz). A telephone tends to eliminate any frequencies above 3000 Hz; the reason it is sometimes hard to identify the caller is that people differ mainly in the higher frequencies that they produce, and some of these are lost over the telephone. None the less, most of the information above 3000 Hz is largely redundant. The quality of speech over a telephone line is still vastly superior to that experienced by the unborn baby; only frequencies up to about 1000 Hz get through to the baby. If you could only hear frequencies up to 1000 Hz, you would recognize the tune of a well known song because of the changing pitch, rhythm, and duration of the notes, and perhaps the relative intensity, or loudness, of individual notes, but you would be unable to make out the individual words or even the individual sounds; they would be too muffled. So how much use could this input be? What information is contained in the lower frequency range which the baby could learn and which would also be useful?

There is actually a substantial amount of information contained within the lower frequencies. For instance, most sentences are spoken with a particular melody, or *intonation*. Statements such as 'She went to the shop' are spoken with a different intonation from questions such as 'She went to the shop?' The difference is that in the statement, the pitch tends to go down at the end, whilst in the question, it tends to go up. Different languages put different intonation on their sentences. Australian speakers, for instance, differ characteristically from English speakers, putting more prominent rises in pitch at the ends of their sentences. Rhythm is another feature that is present in the lower frequencies of the speech, and that can change depending on which language you speak. English has a particular kind of rhythm that is exemplified by limericks; the rhythms are determined by where the *stress* falls; the beat falls on each stressed syllable. French, on the other hand, has a slightly different rhythm, where the beat tends to coincide with every syllable (French speakers do not apply the same stressed/unstressed distinction to their syllables as English speakers do). Irrespective of which language is spoken, rhythm can be picked up from just the first 1000 Hz—it is present in the speech that the baby is exposed to prenatally.

On babies' sensitivity to rhythm and intonation

Intonation (variation in pitch) and rhythm are properties of a language which may differ depending on the precise language being spoken. They are also properties of the language to which babies are exposed very early, primarily in the form of the mother's voice, which travels through bone and tissue to the uterus and, although still muffled, is louder than any speech sounds coming in from the outside. The variation in the physical signal that gives rise to the perception of varying intonation and rhythm is generally referred to as *prosodic* variation—the variation in pitch, amplitude (which is perceived as loudness), and duration (how long the sounds are, how quickly they vary, and so on). In fact, prosodic variation is just about the only variation in the language that the baby has exposure to before it is born.

In the mid–1980s, a research group in Paris headed by Jacques Mehler demonstrated that very young babies (just four days old) already know enough about their own language to be able to tell it apart from another language. At such an early age, one might expect that the baby is doing all it can to distinguish speech sounds from other sounds (whether doors shutting, dogs barking, dishwashers washing, and so on). To distinguish between different languages is surely overkill. Why should the baby want to distinguish between languages? The answer, of course, is that it does not. If babies are sufficiently sensitive to changes in, for instance, the prosodic characteristics of the speech they hear, it follows that they should be able to distinguish between speech exhibiting different prosodic characteristics. And if the speech from two languages differs with respect to prosody, then babies should be able to distinguish between the languages.

Mehler used the same non–nutritive sucking technique described briefly in Chapter 1. Speech from one language (French) was played to four-day-old babies each time they sucked on their teat until they *habituated*—that is, until the novelty wore off and they started to suck less. Once their sucking rate fell below some pre-determined amount, speech from another language (Russian) was played to them each time they sucked (the speech was recorded from a single French–Russian bilingual speaker so that the voice characteristics remained the same). Mehler found that the babies, all of whom had French-speaking parents, sucked more when the different language was played to them (because of the novelty of this new stimulus, the infants had *dishabituated*). It did not matter whether the babies were first given French or Russian; if the language was changed after the babies had habituated, they sucked faster. If the language did not change, they sucked the same.

In a related experiment, Mehler and his colleagues wanted to be sure that the babies were not simply discriminating between the languages on the basis of the different sounds that they use. So they *filtered* the speech so as to remove the higher frequencies (recall that one cannot make out the different sounds in a language without those higher frequencies). In effect, they artificially simulated the kinds of speech that the babies would have heard *in utero*, and gave the babies just the prosodic content of each language. But still the babies could distinguish between them.

Finally, if babies were given language pairs that they had had no experience of (for instance, playing English and Italian to the French babies, or French and Russian to babies who were neither French nor Russian), the habituation/dishabituation pattern was *not* found. The babies were therefore discriminating between the languages on the basis of prior familiarity.

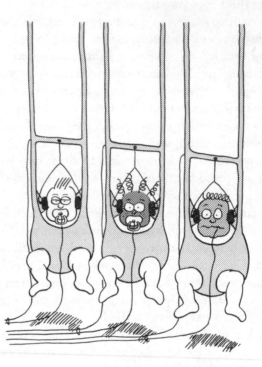

Prenatal learning

So infants as young as just four days are sensitive to the kinds of prosodic variation that is normal for their maternal language. It is unlikely that in this short time they hear enough of their own language to develop such a high degree of sensitivity; it is more likely that some learning has taken place prenatally. But although Mehler and his collaborators' studies are suggestive, they do not actually prove that the learning took place *in utero*. However, there are a number of findings, notably by Anthony DeCasper and his colleagues at the University of North Carolina, which can only be explained in terms of prenatal learning.

In one study, DeCasper and his associates arranged for a group of pregnant women to read aloud the same short story each day for the last six weeks of their pregnancy. After the babies were born, DeCasper used a non-nutritive sucking technique to establish whether the babies would prefer to hear the same story that they had, in effect, already heard, or whether they would prefer a new story. In fact, they preferred the story they had already heard (although all they could have heard of it, *in utero*, was the prosody with which it was spoken).

DeCasper used a slightly different technique to the one used by Mehler's team. He took advantage of the fact that babies will quickly learn to modify their sucking rate in order to receive some pleasurable stimulation. They will suck faster than normal, or slower than normal, depending on which way ensures they get what they want. So to find out whether babies prefer to hear one thing or another, you set things up so that they have to suck one way to hear one thing, and the other way to hear the other. And whichever way they suck (faster than normal, or slower than normal) will indicate which thing they preferred. In DeCasper's experiment, they sucked whichever way ensured that they would hear the familiar story, as opposed to a new story.

The babies in this experiment preferred the familiar story even if the recordings used to establish the preference were made by someone other than their mother. But several studies have shown that newborn babies prefer to hear their mother's voice when given the choice. So this last finding, coupled with the DeCasper result, suggests that babies manage to do two things when listening prenatally; they can learn about the specific prosodic characteristics of the voice that they hear most of *in utero*, and they can learn about the general prosodic characteristics of a sequence of sounds (making up a story, for instance) uttered by that voice.

Testing babies in utero

The studies so far have found postnatal responses to prenatal experience. In a further study, DeCasper and his colleagues wanted to go one step further, and find a prenatal response to prenatal experience. They arranged for pregnant mothers to read aloud a short story every day between the 34th and 38th week of pregnancy. At the end of the 38th week, that same story and a different story were played to the fetus, through the mother's abdomen. The mother was not aware of which story was being played when, so that any response in the fetus could not be due to some sensitivity to the mother's response to the story. Fetal response was judged on the basis of changes in the fetal heart-rate. One story was played for 30 seconds, then there was a 75-second period of silence, after which the other story was played for 30 seconds. DeCasper found that fetal heart-rate decreased when the familiar story was played, irrespective of whether the familiar story was played first or second. Apparently, therefore, the fetuses distinguished between the two stories, and did so on the basis of what they had learned previously. Although further work remains to be done to corroborate these results, the evidence all converges on the view that babies *are* able to learn about the sounds they hear prenatally.

It was research of this kind that led to the practice, prevalent mainly in the USA, of talking to babies prenatally through the mother's abdomen (a device called a 'pregaphone' was marketed for this very purpose). There is no evidence that prenatal stimulation other than that normally experienced has any beneficial effects. In fact, it is unclear whether any prenatal learning, even under normal circumstances, is necessary. For instance, children with normal hearing who are born of deaf parents in communities where sign language is the more usual form of communication do not seem to suffer from the lack of prenatal exposure to spoken language; their spoken language skills develop within normal limits so long as they have sufficient exposure to (and social interaction using) the spoken language. This does not mean that prenatal learning is of no use. It may well be useful (more of this shortly), but it may not be necessary for normal language development. A baby born without any prenatal language experience may be able to learn, subsequently, everything it needs to know about the prosody of the language.

So the next question is simply this: how could knowing about the prosody of the language (whether from pre- or postnatal experience) possibly have any *use*? Being able to distinguish statements from questions, or another language from its own, is hardly something that the newborn infant has to worry about, and would be of little help when it comes to figuring out where, in all the jumble of sounds it hears, the actual *words* are.

The importance of being prosodic

As a step towards at least a partial answer to this question, we need to detour slightly and consider a further ability of very young infants. The problem for a newborn baby is similar to the problem faced by an adult when listening to speech uttered in an unknown foreign language.

Where do words begin and end? At least the adult knows about words, and that the speech he or she can hear probably contains some. And knowing about words, even in principle, is likely to be a big help when learning to understand a new language. After all, if the task, when learning that language, is to associate meanings with words, then identifying the words is half the task. But knowing about words may also help the adult distinguish the noise coming from the speaker's mouth (or radio, or wherever else it may be coming from) from all the other noises that can be heard. How? Because spoken words have (at least) one property that is not shared with other kinds of noise.

A fundamental property of spoken words is that they are formed by opening and closing the mouth in subtly different ways, which include changing the shape of the lips, moving the tongue in certain ways, and opening or closing the velum (the flap of skin that allows air to go through the mouth or through the nose or through both). The result of this opposition between the mouth being open and the mouth being closed (perhaps only partially) is that we produce *syllables*.

Syllables are, of course, the fundamental building blocks of words. Some languages combine syllables together to make words even though the individual syllables themselves may have no meaning of their own (English, for instance). In other languages (Chinese, for instance) each syllable has a distinct meaning, and the meaning of a word made up of more than one syllable need not be related to the individual meanings of its component syllables. In each case, though, the syllable is a fundamental unit of spoken language. So knowing about syllables, and being able to spot them, would be a useful ability to have if one were trying to learn a language. Not only would it help in terms of an initial attempt to identify words, but it would also be useful because non-speech sounds tend not to consist of identifiable syllables.

After a number of studies, Jacques Mehler and his colleagues Josianne Bertoncini and Peter Jusczyk concluded that the ability to perceive speech in terms of syllables exists at birth. In a series of experiments with babies ranging in age from just four days to a few months, these researchers found that newborn babies could discriminate between certain sequences of sounds but not between certain others. For instance, they can distinguish between different sounds such as [p] and [t][1], and not surprisingly, therefore, between different syllables such as [pat] and [tap].

---

[1] The square brackets mean that the item they enclose should be taken to be a sound (or sequence of sounds)—'pat' would refer to an actual word, while [pat] would refer to the corresponding sounds.

What is surprising, though, is that despite this ability, they do not easily distinguish between [pst] and [tsp]. This could be because these sounds, when put together, make a noise that is very hard to tell apart. Alternatively, it could be because these sequences are not real (or *legal*) syllables.

In order to test this, Mehler and his associates added a vowel to each side of the sequences, to create [upstu] and [utspu] (the [u] being pronounced as in the word 'put'). Although the [pst] and [tsp] sounds remained identical, the addition of a vowel on either side meant that each sequence could now be interpreted as a sequence of two legal syllables. If [pst] and [tsp] were hard to discriminate simply because they were difficult sounds, then the addition of the extra vowels should make no difference. If, on the other hand, they had been hard to discriminate because they violated some sort of expectation of what a proper syllable should sound like, then the additional vowels should help, as they turn the sequences into proper sounding syllables. And sure enough, this is exactly what happened; the addition of the vowels did make the sounds much more discriminable.

What was so ingenious about this experiment was that the infants' sensitivity to syllables was not tested by having them discriminate between different syllables, but by having them discriminate, in effect, between *legal* and *illegal* ones. The same sounds in one context were

indiscriminable ([pst] vs. [tsp]), but in another context were discriminable ([upstu] vs. [utspu]). But despite the ingenuity of the lateral
thinking that went into the design of these studies, we are now faced
with a new dilemma: how can infants possibly know what is a legal or
illegal syllable? It is obviously a useful ability to have, for the reasons that
were mentioned before, namely that being able to interpret the
incoming sounds in terms of (legal) syllables is a big help when it comes
to learning a language and discriminating between the sounds of that
language and other non-language sounds. But where does this knowledge come from? Is it genetically programmed in our DNA? Probably
not. After all, if knowledge about syllables could be preprogrammed, or
innate, why not other knowledge as well? In fact, some researchers take
the view that other knowledge is innate, but we shall come to that in
another chapter. For the moment, we shall stick to syllables, and
although there is currently no absolute proof that knowledge about
syllables is not innate, there is an alternative explanation for the
extraordinary abilities that the newborn infant appears to have.

It is at this point that we can return to an earlier question, namely
whether knowledge about prosody could be at all useful to the newborn
language learner. On first asking this question we side-tracked slightly
and discovered that babies seem to organize what they hear in terms of
syllables. But how can babies do this? The answer, or at least, one of a
range of answers, is that babies do not organize what they hear
syllabically—they organize it *prosodically*. Neither [pst] nor [tsp] qualify as
legal syllables because syllables generally require a vowel in them
somewhere. But putting a vowel in amongst a sequence of consonants
necessarily changes the prosody. That is, changes are introduced which
influence the pitch, rhythm, and relative intensities of the different
sounds. And the reason [pst] and [tsp] may not be easily distinguished
may not be because the newborn knows that there should be a vowel in
there, but because they cannot recognize the prosody; it is not one of
the prosodic patterns that the baby has come to expect. With [upstu]
and [utspu], on the other hand, the baby can recognize the sounds as, in
some sense, conforming—they each have prosodic 'tunes' which are
familiar on the basis of the baby's prior experience. And because they
conform, the baby can make sense of them, and tell them apart.

Sensitivity to prosody might do more, though, than just help identify
legal syllables. An analogy may help: many popular songs are structured
so that the music accompanies the words quite precisely; each time a
new word (or even syllable) is sung, a new note (or collection of notes)

is played. The drummer may even provide a beat that closely accompanies the singing of each word or syllable. If someone were listening to such a song in a language they did not know, they could listen to the changing notes, and the beat, without knowing anything about the words that accompanied the music. But the changing notes and the different beats would most likely be accompanied by different words. After listening to only a little of the song, it would be possible to attend less to the notes and the beat, and more to the words that fell on the different notes and different beats. In short, being able to recognize structure in the *music*, would allow someone listening to the song to discern structure in the *vocals*. If the same words were sung in monotone, with no backing music, it would sound like a continuous jumble of uninterpretable sounds. But because the words are not sung in monotone, and have backing music which has some recognizable structure to it, the words themselves can be disentangled from one another. And although they would have no meaning (if in an unknown language), it would at least be possible to separate one from the other (or at least, one syllable from another syllable). The important point about this analogy is that the equivalent to the backing music and the beat in the human voice is prosody.

For the newborn, listening to the human voice is perhaps a little similar to someone listening to a song in a language they know nothing about. The newborn already knows something about the structure of the music, including the beat. The other sounds that accompany the music (that is, the actual syllables) are differentiated from one another simply because the music itself has structure. Of course, this is a very simplified account, but it gives some of the flavour of what may really be going on. The key question is this: how easy would it be for a child to acquire a language that was identical in all respects to spoken English (or any other language) except that it was spoken in monotone? Presumably, not easy at all, although we shall never know for sure—we can only conjecture. But at least we would have a solid empirical basis for that conjecture.

Passing the buck

It might be tempting, at this point, to sit back and think that psycholinguists now know how babies come to recognize words. Certainly, the evidence is sufficient for us to begin to understand how the process gets under way. Babies are clever, and know quite a bit even by the time they are born. But whereas we may now understand better how the baby comes to develop some sort of knowledge about syllables, and hence words, we have simply attributed the acquisition of this knowledge to the acquisition of some other, perhaps more fundamental knowledge concerning prosody. And how did *that* knowledge develop? It is not enough to say that it developed simply because the information was there *in utero*. Why is that, just by hearing a bunch of sounds, the baby should learn about the structure of those sounds?

A theory that says babies learn everything they need to know about their language *after* they are born is no different, really, from a theory that says they learn some of it *before* they are born. Even if they do not learn anything prenatally, and instead they learn about the prosodic characteristics of the language postnatally, the problem is still the same; how do they learn, and why do they learn what they do? After all, put a computer with a microphone in a roomful of people, and unless it contains a relevant program (and how did that get there?), it will not do much at all, let alone learn about the language that the people speak.

Psycholinguistics itself does not have a ready answer to these fundamental questions. Fortunately, what look like the beginnings of some answers have developed in the field of *computational modelling*—using computers to mimic the learning process. In Chapter 13 we shall explore some of the advances made in this field, and the ways in which they can shed light on some of the fundamental questions that remain to be answered.

⬟

We have failed so far to consider a question which bears fundamentally on all these issues: is there something about our ability to perceive speech that is uniquely human? Do we have some sort of genetic predisposition to understand speech in a certain way? The next chapter considers this question in the context of our ability to distinguish not between syllables, but between the sounds that they are composed of.

Chinchillas do it too

In a review of infant speech perception work written in the early 1980s, Peter Jusczyk suggested that instead of trying to find out what babies *can* do, we should instead try and find out what adults can do that babies *cannot* do. One big difference between adults and babies is that adults have acquired knowledge about individual words; they have a mental dictionary, or *lexicon*. And obviously, not having any experience of the specific words in the language will severely limit the babies' abilities. But are there any other limitations on babies' abilities that have nothing to do with this lack of a lexicon? At the time of Jusczyk's review, it was beginning to look as if, in terms of speech perception abilities that do not require a lexicon, babies could do most things that adults could do. This caused a number of researchers to wonder whether this remarkable ability might not be due to innate knowledge about the language. Even before it was discovered that newborns seemed to be able to organize what they heard in terms of syllables, a much more fundamental ability had been discovered which, it seemed, could only be explained by assuming a genetic component. So fundamental is this ability that we take it even more for granted than probably any other feat of human speech perception; it is simply the ability to tell one sound apart from another.

The fact that babies can distinguish between [p] and [t] is surely uninteresting—is this ability any more remarkable than the ability to tell colours apart, or to see different shades of grey? Being able to discriminate colour is a property of our visual perceptual system that occurs because we have cells in the retina of the eye which are sensitive to different wavelengths of light. This does not mean that we have innate knowledge of colour, but it does mean that there has probably been some evolutionary pressure that has selected for, and favoured, mutations which enabled organisms to discriminate between different kinds of light. So why is the ability to discriminate between [p] and [t], or [p] and [b], any different? What is there about this ability that could possibly be interesting?

These sounds, or *phonemes*, differ from one another in very subtle ways. Phonemes are the smallest parts of spoken words which, if changed, can lead to the creation of new words. So 'bat' and 'pat' differ by just one phoneme. As do 'speech' and 'peach'. But it is the subtlety of the differences that makes it all the more remarkable that we can tell phonemes apart.

The phonemes /b/ and /p/[2] are almost identical; both are produced at the lips (they start closed and finish open), but in producing the first, the vocal folds vibrate, and in producing the second, they do not. So the sounds [ba] and [pa] differ in that the vocal folds start to vibrate sooner in [ba] than in [pa]. The difference is small; in [pa] the vocal folds start to vibrate around 40 milliseconds after the lips open, whereas in [ba] they start to vibrate within around 20 milliseconds after the lips open. This difference in the onset of vibration of the vocal folds is normally referred to as a difference in the *voice onset time*.

So far, nothing has been said that makes it surprising that either adults, or infants, can tell these different sounds apart; all we need to suppose is that our perceptual system is sufficiently finely tuned that we can tell that there are tiny differences between the sounds. But it is not quite so simple. First of all, what we think we hear is not necessarily what we have actually heard. In a now classic demonstration of this, Harry McGurk, whose interests in social issues and child development led him to become Director of the Australian Institute of Family Studies, and a student of his, Janet MacDonald, showed people a video recording of a speaker saying the sound [ba]. However, they replaced the original sound with the sound [ga]. So what people saw in this experiment was a lip movement compatible with [ba], but what they were played was the sound [ga]. Would they report hearing [ba] or [ga]? In fact, they reported neither. What they said they heard was [da]—a sound which is midway between [ba] and [ga]. In effect, people experiencing the 'McGurk effect' take the two sources of evidence, visual and auditory, and combine them to perceive an illusory sound that is between the originals.

---

[2] There is a convention to refer to phonemes by enclosing the appropriate symbol in slashes. Just as one can distinguish between a word and the sound of that word, so one can distinguish between a phoneme (e.g. /p/), and the sound of that phoneme (e.g. [p]).

Of course, most of what we perceive *is* determined by the sounds entering the ear (even the illusory sounds in the McGurk effect are determined, in part, by the actual sounds played on the video). But the McGurk effect demonstrates that on occasion we hear something that is not in fact in the speech signal. This can be contrasted with occasions when we fail to hear something that is. It is this failure that allows us to recognize speech as effortlessly as we do.

Different sounds, same sensation

Different versions of /b/ may have different delays between the opening of the lips and the onset of vocal fold vibration (the voice onset time). This difference in voice onset times between the two versions can be as great as the difference between a /b/ and a /p/, or between two versions of /p/. Despite this, we do not think of the two versions of the /b/ as being any different. More importantly, as Al Liberman and his colleagues first discovered in the late 1950s at the Haskins Laboratories in Connecticut, we cannot even perceive the two versions of the /b/ as being any different. As we shall see, this finding has some puzzling, and important, consequences.

The effects studied by Liberman involved the creation of artificial versions of /b/ and /p/ which differed in voice onset time by varying degrees. In fact, a whole continuum of sounds can be created, with sounds at one extreme having a voice onset time of zero and sounds at the other extreme having a voice onset time of, for instance, 60 milliseconds. When sounds taken from this continuum are played to people, they can easily say which sounds belong to the /b/ category, and which belong to the /p/ category. Generally, anything with a voice onset time less than 20 milliseconds is classified as a /b/, and anything with a voice onset time greater than around 40 milliseconds is classified as a /p/. The important part of the experiment is that if pairs of sounds are presented one after the other, and people are asked to say whether the two sounds are at all different, they can only spot a difference if the sounds are from either side of the boundary. If the pairs are from the same side of the boundary (i.e. both are between 0 and 20 milliseconds or between 40 and 60 milliseconds), they cannot tell that there is any difference in the sounds. In fact, there can be a bigger difference in voice onset time between sounds taken from the same side of the boundary, which cannot be distinguished, than between sounds that straddle the boundary and which can be told apart. This phenomenon is called *categorical perception*; only speech sounds that are perceived as belonging to different phoneme categories can be discriminated.

This result has been replicated many times, and with different phonemes; including, for instance, a continuum of phonemes with /p/ at one end, /t/ towards the middle, and /k/ at the other end, as well as the continuum /b/–/d/–/g/. There is no vocal fold vibration in the /p/–/t/–/k/ continuum whereas there is in the /b/–/d/–/g/ continuum. In other respects, the two continua are identical. The different sounds along each continuum do not differ in terms of voice onset time, but in terms of subtle differences in the changing frequencies at the beginnings of each sound. These differences reflect the different positions at which the mouth is closed off when the phonemes are uttered.

Again, nothing has been said that is too surprising; we need simply assume that adults have somehow learned which sounds are relevant to their language and have learned to ignore differences in sounds that are irrelevant. So in English, phonemes with voice onset times less than around 20 milliseconds are /b/s and phonemes with voice onset times more than around 40 milliseconds are /p/s, and any other differences are irrelevant; that is, any other differences do not discriminate between different words in the language. Whereas [bat] and [pat] are different words, [bat] with voice onset time of 0 milliseconds and [bat] with voice onset time of 20 milliseconds are both 'bat'. This view, based on a notion of *relevance*, is corroborated by the finding that the speakers (and hence hearers) of different languages may find different differences relevant. For instance, English speakers have only two categories (that is, one boundary) along the voice onset time continuum. Thai speakers, on the other hand, have three categories (and therefore two boundaries). Similarly, Japanese speakers do not have a clear boundary at all in the /l/–/r/ continuum, while English speakers do. These differences across languages reflect the fact that whereas in one language, a difference in two sounds may not indicate a different word, in another language it might.

The most obvious explanation for why we perceive phonemes categorically is that we simply learn, on the basis of what we hear around us, which differences (in voice onset time, or in frequency, or whatever) should be attended to, and which differences should be ignored. It is so obvious, that it came as quite a surprise to discover, as

Peter Eimas and colleagues did in the early 1970s at Brown University, Rhode Island, that the same phenomenon can be found to occur with one-month-old infants. Could infants learn enough about the sounds in their language that they could already, by the time they are just one month old, ignore irrelevant differences? And how could the infant possibly know which differences are relevant if it has not yet acquired knowledge about which are the different words in its language?

The puzzle was all the more intriguing when it was found that infants were sensitive not only to differences relevant to their own language, but to differences relevant to other languages as well. So an English baby would be able to discriminate between sounds relevant to Thai which adult English speakers would not be able to discriminate between. However, the baby would not be able to discriminate between *any* two sounds; it would still only be able to discriminate sounds that straddled the relevant boundaries. Not surprisingly, many researchers concluded on the basis of these findings that humans are born with some special apparatus that is geared not simply to recognizing only phonemes (and in so doing, ignoring irrelevant differences), but to recognizing any phoneme that could potentially occur in any language.

The ability to discriminate between differences relevant to other languages, but irrelevant to the mother language, is lost after around 10 months. It is at this stage that infants become 'adult' with respect to how they recognize phonemes. Presumably, we learn in those first 10 months to ignore the differences which, although recognizable in principle, are irrelevant and unused in the environment around us.

A uniquely human ability?

Recognizing phonemes is apparently as fundamental and predetermined as recognizing, for instance, movement. In the late 1950s and early 1960s it was established that when the eye sees a moving image, cells in the brain respond to the movement of the object, irrespective of the size or shape or colour of whatever it is that is moving (their response is measured in terms of what is basically electrical activity). This led to the notion that these cells were specialized for detecting motion. A wide range of visual phenomena were subsequently investigated which supported this hypothesis (including certain kinds of visual illusion). The relevance to phoneme detection is that various phenomena concerning the perception of phonemes were discovered that were analogous to these visual phenomena. And because, in the visual system, these phenomena were taken as indicating that we have specialized motion detectors, the equivalent phoneme perception data were taken as indicating that we have specialized phoneme detectors, that respond to certain sounds and not to others in much the same way as the different cells in the retina respond to different wavelengths of light. And because speech is a uniquely human characteristic (other animals communicate vocally, but they do not do so with human speech sounds), it was supposed that evolution had somehow equipped humans with a perceptual apparatus that was specifically pretuned to human speech.

It soon transpired, however, that this view of a pretuned, pre-programmed perceptual mechanism was unlikely to be right. First, certain non-speech sounds can be perceived categorically (for example, musical tones), so categorical perception is not limited to speech sounds. However, the fact that non-speech sounds are perceived categorically may simply mean that we use whatever apparatus we have for perceiving speech for perceiving other kinds of sound as well. Also, and perhaps more importantly, not all phonemes are perceived categorically; vowels, for instance, tend to be perceived non-categorically, and slight differences between two versions of the same vowel *can* be perceived. Finally, in 1975 at the Central Institute for the Deaf in St. Louis, Missouri, Pat Kuhl and Jim Miller found that chinchillas do it too.

Like many animals, chinchillas can be trained to move from one side of a box to another when they hear one sound (the *target sound*) but not when they hear any other sound. If the animal moves to the other side when a sound similar, but not identical, to the target sound is played, one can assume that the two sounds sounded the same to the chinchilla. If it stays put, they must have sounded different.

The finding that what is essentially a rodent can perceive phonemes categorically was a severe setback to any theory which supposed that categorical perception was a uniquely human ability resulting from the existence of phoneme-specific detectors. It did not help that certain kinds of monkey, and even certain kinds of bird, also perceive phonemes categorically! Subsequent analysis of what was going on suggested that the reason that within-category sounds (such as two different version of /b/) could not be discriminated was not due to specialized detectors (chinchillas are unlikely to have phoneme detectors), but was instead due to some particular property of the auditory system, shared by other non-human species.

The human ear, in fact *any* ear, is not a perfect channel for sound; what gets through is actually a distorted version of the original signal, and the signals that the brain receives reflect that distortion (in part due to the ear's physical properties, and in part due to distortions introduced within the nervous system that connects to the ear). Consequently, the inability to detect certain differences may reflect these distortions (the two different signals are distorted to the point of becoming the same). What may then have happened is that speech evolved to take advantage of differences that could be perceived. The chinchilla does not distinguish between certain sounds because they happen to be phonemes, but because they happen to sound different. As a species, we have learned to ensure that if we want two sounds to be perceived as different (for the purposes, perhaps, of distinguishing between different words), we should ensure that we use just those sounds, or a subset of them, that *can* be distinguished.

Unfortunately, even this account cannot quite explain everything. There is a substantial fly in the ointment which places a complete, water-tight theory slightly out of reach.

Fast talking

The boundaries that we find in categorical perception should be relatively fixed if they reflect properties of the 'hardware'. And yet Quentin Summerfield, at Queen's University in Belfast, demonstrated that the boundaries that separate one phoneme from another are not fixed. His basic finding is relatively simple. Recall that a phoneme on the /ba/–/pa/ continuum with a voice onset time of 40 milliseconds is perceived as [pa], and with a voice onset time of 20 milliseconds it is perceived as a [ba]. It was found that, if these sounds were heard in the context of speech uttered at different rates, then the boundary would shift. For instance, at a very fast speaking rate, something with a short voice onset time that should be perceived as a [ba] is in fact perceived as a [pa]. The perceptual system 'knows', somehow, that everything is speeded up, and that what should normally be a longish time interval will now be a shorter interval. So a shorter interval is treated as if it were a longer one, and consequently a shorter voice onset time is treated as if it were a longer voice onset time. Similar effects have been found using other continua, with stimuli that vary not in terms of voice onset time (as on the /ba/–/pa/ continuum) but in terms of other subtle differences in timing (between the start of one frequency component and another).

Again, this result looks as if it can be explained simply in terms of learning; as adults we learn to adapt to speech at different rates, and so we learn to be flexible in our interpretation of perceivable differences. But things are never that simple, and it turns out that babies do it too. Peter Eimas, with Joanne Miller at Northeastern University in Boston, found that babies also differentially interpret the relative durations of the different frequency components depending on the rate of the speech. It is probably just as well that babies can adjust to, or correct for, different rates of speech; otherwise they would hear two versions of the same syllable, uttered at different rates, and assume that they were different when in fact they were supposed to be the same.

We are left with a puzzle. The problem is that a word spoken quickly is not just a speeded-up version of a word spoken slowly. The actual sounds change: voice onset times differ, and slight changes in the frequencies occur which, were it not for the change in rate, would ordinarily be interpreted as different sounds. If the difference between fast and slow speech were the same as the difference between a tape played faster or slower, the problem would be easily solved, because although the absolute speed changes, the *relative* changes that occur between the individual sounds on the tape would be the same, irrespective of the speed. But in naturally produced speech, the difference between two sounds changes depending on the rate at which they were uttered. So being able to compensate for speaking rate is a complex process, and it would not be unreasonable to assume that it would require some considerable experience of spoken language. How could a baby manage this? It cannot be due to any knowledge about what words actually exist, as the baby does not yet have this knowledge.

We do not know whether babies are as adept at compensating for speech rate as adults are. Are babies and adults basically doing the same thing? The information we have so far suggests that the answer is 'yes', but there are likely to be subtle differences that we have yet to discover. If the answer continues to be 'yes', then perhaps this is the uniquely human ability that categorical perception was once thought to be. So the next obvious question is this: what about chinchillas? Do they compensate for speech rate? We do not know. But Macaque monkeys do, so probably chinchillas do too.

Whether babies, monkeys, chinchillas, and other inexperienced users of language all do the same thing as adult humans when compensating for speech rate is unknown. And whether these inexperienced language users can, like adult humans, compensate for different voices and different accents is also unknown. If they do not, then we need to explain how babies cope with so much variation between different speakers (and between the same speaker on different occasions). If they do, we need to explain how the hardware of the ear, and the wetware of the nervous system, allow such compensation to take place. Whatever the answers, the mystery remains. But at least we shall have a better idea of just how severe the problems are for the newborn baby and its speech recognition apparatus.

Phonemes and syllables are the building blocks of words. To communicate, the developing infant has to learn about words—what they mean, and how they are combined into meaningful sentences. It is to that mystery that we now turn.

4

Words, and what we learn
to do with them

Qua ngôn ngũ' chúng ta co' thê' hiêu' du'o'c ý nghí cu'a con ngu'o'ì. Unless you read Vietnamese, that sentence will mean nothing to you. Being able to distinguish between the different letters and the different words is of little use if you are unable to extract any meaning from those words. And even if you had the appropriate dictionary, you would still need to know something about the grammar of Vietnamese to be sure that you had understood the sentence in the way that was originally intended. But getting hold of the appropriate dictionary, and asking someone about the grammar of the language, is not an option for your average infant. So how do infants manage?

A problem with figuring out how children learn about words is that you just cannot ask an 18-month-old child what words it knows, or what it knows about those words, or how it came to know whatever it knows. And as any parent knows, even when children act as if they understand, they quite often do not.

One of the first words that my son Sam Altmann used was 'yeah'. But the following is an example of a typical dialogue with him (aged around 20 months):

Question:	*Do you want a yoghurt?*
Answer:	*yeah* [and he proceeds to eat it]
Question:	*Do you want a juice?*
Answer:	*yeah* [but he ignores it]
Question:	*Do you want to eat worms?*
Answer:	*yeah* [they were not offered!]

It looks as if he had learned to say 'yeah' in response to *any* 'Do you want . . .' question. But did the meaning Sam attached to 'yeah' bear no resemblance at all to the meaning that we adults attach to it? In fact, it did bear some resemblance. Sam would, unprompted, point to something he wanted and say 'yeah'. But only if it was out of reach. He would repeat it again and again, with increasing desperation, until he got what he wanted (or until he was removed from the object of his sudden affection). Presumably, then, 'yeah' functioned in much the same way as 'Give it to me'. But Sam could also sit in his toy car and say 'yeah' until someone came over and pushed him around in it. So 'Do this for me' would be a better translation. And the reason he might say 'yeah' in response to just about any 'Do you want . . .' question was probably that, like all children, he was simply being opportunistic; it is better to be offered something than to be offered nothing.

This example highlights two things. The first is that children do not learn by simple imitation, even though they often take great delight in imitating—Sam never saw anyone point at something and say 'yeah'. The second is a methodological problem with research into language acquisition; when interpreting the ability of a child to use and understand words, it is important to understand the intentions of the child itself. How to do that is quite another matter. Still, ultimately it matters little whether the child's first words mean the same thing as the adult's. As long as they mean something (to the child at least), the child has started on the path to adult language use.

Broadly speaking, research into early language acquisition has pursued two goals; one has been to understand the acquisition of knowledge about individual words, and the other has been to understand the acquisition of knowledge about how words combine to form meaningful sentences. These two goals serve as the background from which to view research into language acquisition.

Learning words

One question of practical concern is whether there is any definition of what constitutes normal development. Although infants demonstrate an ability to comprehend (and even produce) individual words between around eight and 10 months of age, and to comprehend or produce combinations of words between 20 and 36 months, different children proceed at different rates. At 12 months, for instance, the average infant may have a comprehension vocabulary of around 100 words. But some infants have a vocabulary less than half this number, and some have a vocabulary almost twice this number. Of course, these numbers are only approximate because even large scale studies (the largest having investigated more than 1800 infants) rely on parental assessments (aided by checklists and guidelines) which are sometimes prone to subjective impression rather than objective fact. None the less, the numbers give an indication of the scale of individual differences.

Although there is considerable variation in the number of words that infants comprehend at around 12 months, there is much less variation in the number of words that these infants produce. They produce a lot fewer, and so there is less scope for variation. Without comprehension, there could not be any production, so it is unsurprising that the expressive vocabularies of these infants (used for production) lag behind their comprehension vocabularies. In any case, a 10-month-old infant may well understand the meaning of a word without being able to articulate that word; it takes some time before infants have sufficient control over their tongue, lips, and so on. At 12 months, the average infant may produce just 10 words, with some infants not producing anything much until around 20 months. These late talkers seem to catch up in the vast majority of cases, and often their comprehension vocabulary is normal for their age (even before their expressive vocabulary has caught up). By 24 months, the average number of words produced goes up to in excess of 300 although, again, some toddlers produce less than half this number, and some produce almost twice as many.

Children know more words the older they get, and this is exactly what one would expect. However, although age is a relatively good predictor of vocabulary size, it by no means explains everything. There is so much variability across different infants that age cannot explain even the majority of this variation. Other factors play an important role in influencing the development of the child's vocabulary. These may include environmental factors (such as the degree to which it is necessary for the child to express what he or she wants) and biological factors. The first three years of a child's life are accompanied by significant changes in the structure of the brain (specifically, changes in the connections between individual nerve cells—*synaptogenesis*) which may influence the development of many of the child's abilities, including, of course, abilities not normally associated with language.

The fact that developments in brain function are correlated with developments in the child's more general abilities has led some researchers to look for, and find, correlations between the development of these other abilities and the development of language. Indeed, these researchers have argued that certain abilities may be prerequisites to early language development; that is, without the ability, language could not develop. Although a variety of abilities have been investigated, one that stands out as being particularly important is the ability to take part in *pretend play*, which involves one thing (for instance, a bath sponge) being used to symbolize another thing (for instance, a boat).

Pretend play, and the ability to represent one object with another, plays a central part in contemporary theories of how children's minds develop. The symbolic use of one object to represent another is also central to the development of language; after all, words are really just spoken symbols that represent whatever it is that the word means. If children could not represent one thing with another, they certainly could not use words to represent anything but the sounds they consist of. So what *do* words represent?

Acquiring meaning

The first words that a child tends to utter are the names of the observable objects in its environment; there are disproportionately more nouns than anything else in the early vocabulary (up until around three years). There are numerous anecdotes told by parents which suggest that the names of those first things are learned by simple association. More than one infant or young toddler has believed that the word for a telephone is a 'hullo'. It sounds a simple enough thing to do, but it is no mean feat to be able to associate sounds with objects, even when those objects are being waved close to the child's face, or they are being pointed to, or they happen to be growling ominously. Actually, associating sounds with objects is easy—the accomplishment is to associate the right sounds with the right objects. If children simply associated the sounds they heard with whatever was in their field of vision, or whatever they were attending to, what would happen as they looked around with the radio on, or their parents chatting? They would surely associate whatever sound they were hearing with whatever object they were seeing.

Fortunately, children (that is, their brains) do not associate, willy-nilly, whatever they happen to hear with whatever they happen to be looking at at the time. And this is the puzzle: what prevents them from doing so? One theory is that the exaggerated intonation in child-directed speech serves to attract the attention of the child—the radio will not grab the child's attention in the same way, nor will two adults speaking. This attention-grabbing tactic means, in principle at least, that the child will not associate irrelevant speech with the things it happens to be looking at at the time. But unfortunately, this is not quite enough. It fails to explain how children learn the appropriate associations in societies which do not distinguish between child- and adult-directed speech (there are, admittedly, only very few). And it cannot explain how, even if children are directed to the relevant speech, they know which is the appropriate bit to associate with what they see. How is the child to know which bit of the utterance 'Look how big that doggie is' corresponds to the furry beast in front of it? It is easy for us to say, because we already know what 'look', 'how', 'big', and so on, mean. But what about the child who has yet to master these other words?

So one problem for the child is to figure out which bit of the listened-to utterance is the important bit—the bit that is supposed to be associated with whatever is being looked at. But this is only half the problem, because there will be a whole myriad of things that are in the child's line of sight at any one moment. And which of these is to be associated with whatever is being heard? In general, there is no guarantee that the child will be attending to the right object when the speaker utters the word for that object. In fact, the object might not even be in the line of sight—a parent or carer might utter 'Look at the doggie' when the child is *not* looking at it. And by the time the child sees the dog, the sound corresponding to 'doggie' will be long gone. And the child would still need to figure out what it was supposed to be looking at—the dog? Its owner? Its fur? Its teeth?

It seems an almost impossible task to figure out which of several possible things, or things going on, should be associated with which of several possible sounds. Especially when different kinds of words-as-sounds require different kinds of association. So whereas some words (corresponding to nouns) tend to associate with objects, other words (corresponding to verbs) tend to associate with the events that those objects play a part in. But which aspect of the event? Is it Daddy kicking the ball, the ball flying through the air, the ball hitting the ground, Daddy running, panting, going red in the face, or what? What *constrains* the child's interpretation of each word it hears?

Questions such as these have been addressed in laboratory conditions which allow the range of things that a new word could be associated with to be tightly controlled. By showing children objects they have never seen before, or never heard the name of before, the experimenter can look at what children think the meaning of a new word is when it is given to them. Typically, these experiments involve a puppet who speaks in 'puppet talk', and the child is given the task of picking out the objects that the puppet wants. In effect, the child has to guess the meaning of a new word and demonstrate what that meaning is by picking out the appropriate object. The meanings of verbs can also be studied, by showing the puppet doing something (perhaps to another puppet), and giving that action a name, such as 'gorping'. The child then has to say when it sees the puppet gorping again. Puppets are used because children are generally quite inclined to help a puppet—the fun element maximizes the likelihood that the children will cooperate, something that they are often loath to do.

A number of studies by Ellen Markman and colleagues, carried out in the 1980s at Stanford University, looked at cases where children were given novel words for things that the puppet was pointing to (in fact, not all these studies used puppets, but the principle is the same). The child's task was made a little more difficult, and consequently a little more realistic, by ensuring that there were several things in the line of sight, or that one thing contained another. What would children do? How would they interpret the new words they heard in puppet-speak? Two findings stand out. The first is that if children hear a new word for something, they assume that it applies to the whole thing, and not to any of that thing's parts (it applies to the dog as a whole, and not to its teeth). And the second is that if they already know the name of something, they assume that a new word cannot apply to that same thing—it must either apply to a *part* of that thing (to the teeth and not to the dog as a whole), or to another thing. This is just as well, as otherwise children might end up with hundreds of words for one thing, and no words for a hundred others.

Markman's findings illustrate some useful assumptions for children to make—they allow each child to restrict the range of things that a new word could refer to. But where do these assumptions come from? How does the child know to make them? In fact, it is possible that the child is not doing anything that rats and pigeons (and other animals) cannot also do. If a rat, for instance, is trained to expect some event (call it 'A') when given some stimulus (call it 'B'), and then experiences A again when given both B and a new stimulus C, it will not ordinarily associate that new stimulus C with A. This is similar in some respects to the child assuming that if it already knows the name of something, a new name probably does not refer to that same something. And generally, whole things are more salient than their parts (so if something moves, all of its parts move too, and the whole assembly of moving things will be more salient than any individual part of that assembly). When a child associates words with whole objects rather than to those objects' parts, it may do so on the basis of very primitive perceptual sensitivities. So it looks as if at least some of the 'assumptions' that children make may have their origins in some very basic phenomena that can be seen in other animals—phenomena that have more to do with *associative learning* than with language.

The idea that the way in which we learn words has something in common with the associative learning exhibited by rats, pigeons, and, come to that, Pavlov's dogs has led to considerable controversy. There is certainly a superficial resemblance between associating the sound of a bell with the arrival of food and associating the sound of a word with the object to which that word refers. But did the sound of the bell have meaning for Pavlov's dogs in the same way that the word 'dinner' had meaning for Pavlov himself? Probably not, but this does not mean that the mechanism that underlies the dogs' learning plays no part at all in our own learning. Obviously, children are more sophisticated than other animals in terms of the kinds of things they can learn, and the circumstances in which they can learn them. This sophistication is nowhere more apparent than in our ability to communicate our beliefs and intentions, and to communicate not just the physical world around us, but also the mental world we inhabit. And whilst other animals (most notably the primates) do have intentions and beliefs, their ability to communicate these aspects of their mental world is severely limited. Although there is evidence that chimpanzees can communicate some of their intentions, and can be aware of another chimp's beliefs, there is little evidence that the chimp can communicate another chimp's intentions, or another chimp's beliefs.

The distinction between the mental world and the observable world is particularly important when we consider that we use language not simply to refer to things that we can see but to refer to things and events that we cannot see, or that happened in the past, or may happen in the future. Language is not simply a way of directing the attention of the hearer or reader to some part of his or her immediate environment. If it were, as more than one psycholinguist has observed, we could just point and grunt. So the task of mapping words onto their meanings is going to be pretty difficult if those meanings are not there. How is the child to know that the meaning of 'drink' in 'Drink your milk' refers precisely to the thing that the child is *not* doing? There are lots of things that a child is not doing at any one time, so which specific one is it supposed to be?

Analyses of the earliest speech spoken to infants and young children suggests that only the nouns used in that earliest speech tend to refer to things in the here-and-now. The verbs do not necessarily do so. This explains, in part, why nouns are acquired earlier than verbs. But there is another reason too. Verbs are very much more complex in their meanings. Nouns refer to things, whereas verbs refer to events that often involve more than one of those things. The meaning of 'drink' presumes that someone is doing the drinking and something is being drunk. Interpreting a verb requires an appreciation of the things that take part in the event that the verb refers to. Interpreting a noun requires an appreciation only of the single thing that it refers to.

Several theorists believe that the meanings of verbs can be acquired only once a core body of nouns, to which those verbs will apply (the something and the someone in the drink example), have already been learned. Experiments with young children show that if they see a video of a rabbit feeding a duck, and either hear 'The rabbit is zorking the duck' or 'The duck is zorking', they will interpret 'zorking' to mean 'feeding' (as in 'supplying food') in the first case, and 'eating' in the second. Why? Because the video shows two events; it shows the rabbit doing something to the duck (feeding it), and the duck doing something itself (eating). When the child hears the sentence 'The rabbit is zorking the duck' it knows that it should map this sentence onto the event that involves both the rabbit and the duck (hence the importance of knowing the meanings of 'rabbit' and 'duck'). When it hears 'The duck is zorking', it knows it should map this sentence onto the event that involves only the duck. Equivalent effects have been found by Letty Naigles at Yale University in children as young as two years. So what? It sounds obvious, so why care? There are at least two reasons why this is a very important result.

The first reason is that these children interpret the meaning of a novel verb-word on the basis of two things: the structure of the sentence they hear, and the structure in the world they see. They do not ignore the surrounding words and simply focus in on 'zorking', and map this onto a feeding event that is somehow isolated from who is doing the feeding and who is being fed. They use the structure of the events they see in the world to aid in their interpretation of the structure of the sentences they hear. Conversely, they use the structure of the sentence they hear to guide what they should be attending to in the world they see. It is a two-way process. This view of what is going on, developed by Lila Gleitman and colleagues at the University of Pennsylvania, is important because it means that children are not attempting to map individual words, somehow excised from the rest of the utterance, onto individual meanings somehow excised from the rest of the world. And yet this was the classical view of what word-learning involved.

The second reason why that Naigles result is important is that it means that verbs are learned in conjunction with a rudimentary knowledge of grammar. The meaning of a verb involves knowledge about the ways in which different things take part in the event described by that verb.

For 'eat': something does the eating, and something gets eaten. For 'give': someone does the giving, someone does the receiving, and something goes from one to the other. Adults, and indeed children, rarely confuse which things are doing what. When children hear that 'Daddy is eating the peas', they rarely assume (if they have been brought up in the English language) that the peas are doing the eating. Even children who have not progressed beyond uttering single words will be aware that Daddy tickling Mummy means something different from Mummy tickling Daddy. The point, quite simply, is that when a child knows what a verb means, it apparently knows who-does-what-to-whom.

So the acquisition of meaning is a complex process that depends, in part, on what kinds of words are being learned. Nouns are relatively easier to learn than verbs. Verbs require an appreciation of the fact that events in the world are structured—things cause those events to happen to other things. Consequently, the child, when learning the meanings of verbs, must also appreciate that the utterances it hears are also structured, so as to reflect the structure 'out there'.

The idea that the child learns about language through observing the way in which language maps onto the world (and vice versa) is certainly compelling. But it does present some problems for the child. For example, time, in the world, runs in just one direction, yet we can say things like 'Sam moved his bicycle after his mother cleaned it' even though the event that is mentioned *first* in the sentence happened *last* in the world. The temporal order of the descriptions of events does not necessarily map onto the temporal order in which those events happened. And, not surprisingly, this causes problems—it takes children until they are around six years old before they stop assuming that the first mentioned event happened first. Attempting to map structure in the language onto structure in the world is not without its problems.

One way or another, structure in the language is important. But when do children start to reflect it in their own language? When do they start producing grammatical sentences?

Learning grammar

Infants start combining words once they have an expressive vocabulary in the range of 50–100 words, and the more words they can produce, the more combinations they produce also. But infants need to know more than just a whole lot of words in order to produce multi-word utterances. They rarely produce random combinations. Instead, they somehow learn which combinations are meaningful. They also learn that certain combinations require particular *inflections* on certain words (e.g. 'I walk' but 'he walks'). This is particularly difficult in a language like English because its inflections are not the most salient, or noticeable, parts of words. In some languages they are more noticeable (Turkish, for example), and children brought up in languages like these acquire the use of inflections sooner. But somehow, children do learn what is required of them, and this requires the acquisition of knowledge that goes well beyond the meanings of individual words, and which is therefore quite different from the kind that can be learned simply by seeing a cow and hearing the appropriate word.

Since the late 1950s when Noam Chomsky first revolutionized the field of linguistics (he managed to revolutionize it several more times in subsequent years), a major concern for linguists has been to determine how children learn about word order and inflection, and specifically, the correct word order and the correct inflections for their language. Learning about grammar, and specifically, the correct grammar for a particular language, is no easy task. Chomsky had proposed that adults use rules to generate meaningful sentences, and that the task for the child is to somehow acquire these rules. For instance, there are specific

rules for transforming *active* sentences such as 'Children learn languages' into their *passive* form 'Languages are learned by children', and there are specific rules for creating the past tense of a verb. How children might acquire such rules is the subject of considerable controversy.

Children are not taught explicitly which rules apply to their language, and so they must presumably learn by example—another psycho-linguistic truth that is hardly surprising. But what is surprising is that no one tells their children that certain sentences are ungrammatical, and they certainly do not give their children examples of ungrammatical sentences. Yet the result of this learning process is an adult who knows that certain combinations of words are indeed ungrammatical. How can this be? When children do make errors, and produce ungrammatical sentences, the evidence suggests that, generally, no one corrects them; when children tell untruths, then they are corrected. Roger Brown, one of the pioneers of research into language acquisition, pointed out, slightly tongue in cheek, that this leads to an interesting paradox; if children are corrected for producing untruths, and are not corrected for producing bad grammar, how is it that the result of this regime is an adult who is adept at telling untruths but whose sentences are perfectly grammatical?

To summarize the problem: in order to learn a language one needs to be able to generate grammatical sentences, and to avoid generating un-grammatical ones. The fact that children learn to avoid ungrammatical sentences cannot simply be the result of never hearing any; what is so remarkable about language is that users of the language can generate sentences which they have never heard before. So never having heard an example of a particular sentence does not prevent it from being produced.

The concept of *grammaticality* is one that is defined not in terms of how to combine or inflect actual words, but in terms of how to combine or inflect *types* of words. A sentence such as 'The girl knew the language was beautiful' can be described as a sequence of *syntactic categories*: 'determiner noun verb determiner noun verb adjective'. Any word in a grammatical sentence can be replaced by any other word of the same syntactic category and the sentence will still be grammatical. However, the task for the child is not simply to learn about which sequences are grammatical, but to learn also about the *internal structure* of the sentence. It is the breakdown of a sentence into its internal (or *constituent*) structure that allows the sentence to be broken down into subjects, verbs, and objects. And in order to figure out who did what to whom (or the equivalent), we need to be able to identify the who, the whom, and the what in the internal structure of the sentence. In 'The girl knew the language was beautiful', what was beautiful was the language and not necessarily the girl. What was known by the girl was not necessarily the language itself, but that it was beautiful. So the internal structure of the sentence (shown below), broken down into its constituent parts ('the girl', 'the language', 'the language was beautiful', 'knew the language was beautiful', and so on), only licenses certain inferences to be made. That is what grammar is all about. (We shall come back to grammar, and how it is used, as opposed to learned, in Chapters 7 and 8.)

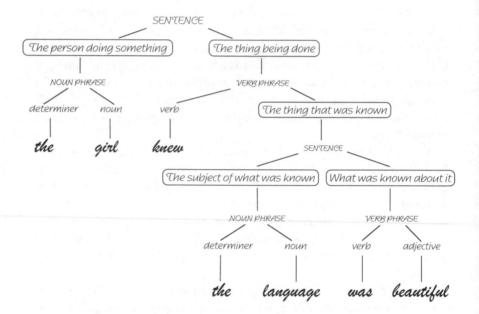

Learning about constituent structure, and specifically which is the correct breakdown of a sentence into these constituents, is not easy. In order to learn the right internal structure, the child needs to learn about both the different types of syntactic category (i.e. the different types of words), and their position in the sentence. But if the child does not know about syntactic categories, how can it learn about their position? And even if the child knew about different syntactic categories and wanted to calculate their relative positions, how could it do so if it did not know which words belonged to which syntactic category?

Arguments such as these, and the fact that children hardly ever get any feedback to tell them when they have made a grammatical error, have led linguists to suggest that languages would be unlearnable if the only input provided to the child was the language itself. But it is evidently the case that languages *are* learnable, and that adults know what is, or is not, grammatical. So where does this notion of 'grammatical' spring from?

Language in our genes

Noam Chomsky and, more recently, Steven Pinker, also at the Massachusetts Institute of Technology, have argued that the only viable explanation is that we are born with knowledge that aids in (and is necessary for) the task of learning language. Pinker's hypothesis is that the child is endowed, innately, with very crude knowledge about types of words (for instance, that there are types corresponding to nouns and to verbs) and about their role in the language (for instance, that there will be a word in the sentence that corresponds to its subject). This knowledge serves simply as a basis on which to determine (subconsciously, of course) which other types of words there are, and where they can be found relative to one another within the sentence. Moreover, this knowledge is supposed not to be specific to any one language, but is universal to all languages. For instance, young children apparently assume, when observing an event that is being described to them, that the thing causing the event (the rabbit who is supplying the food to the duck, for example) corresponds to the subject of the sentence. So all the child needs to figure out is which word is the subject (it varies depending on the language). If it knows the word for 'rabbit', sees the rabbit feeding the duck, and hears the sentence 'the rabbit is feeding the duck', it can learn that, in English at least, the first word (in fact, the first *noun phrase*) is the subject of the sentence. In this way, the child has learned a little bit about the grammar of English.

The fact that the speech addressed to young infants tends to be relatively uncomplicated means that the innate knowledge need only be very crude indeed. None the less, hypotheses such as these attract a high degree of controversy.

There are many abilities that *are* innate. As adults, for instance, we can tell which side of a room a sound might be coming from, and newborns can apparently do the same. And newly born babies will sometimes imitate facial expressions even though this requires that they somehow 'know' that the image on their retina, which is an image they have never seen before, corresponds to a part of their body that they also have never seen before. So the idea that there could exist innate abilities is not itself the source of the controversy. But the innateness hypothesis attracts a number of different controversies. For instance, a distinction can be drawn between different kinds of innate knowledge. If you place your finger in a newborn's hand, the baby will grasp it. This does not mean that the baby has innate knowledge of fingers. In fact, it will grasp anything placed in its hand although, again, this does not mean that it has innate knowledge of graspable things. Whatever it is that is innate here (a reflex) is very different from knowledge about the *structure* of objects that the baby could encounter in its new world. In one case, the innate ability does not require knowledge of the way in which the external world is organized, and in the other case, it does.

To suggest that infants are endowed with innate knowledge of the distinction between verbs and nouns may sound as extreme as suggesting that humans are born with the innate knowledge that their food should, if possible, be heated (there would be obvious evolutionary advantages if this improved the chances of survival for the species). But perhaps the noun/verb distinction is not so extreme after all. Perhaps what we are endowed with is the ability to distinguish between objects and the changes that can happen to those objects—in other words, to tell *states* from *changes in state*. Is this so very different from the distinction between nouns (which often refer to objects) and verbs (which often refer to actions, and hence, changes)? So one aspect of the controversy concerns the status of the innate knowledge that would be required in an account such as Pinker's—is the knowledge linguistic, concerning the nature of language, or is it something more general, concerning the nature of the world?

In some respects, Pinker's account is very similar to Lila Gleitman's account of how we acquire verb meanings, described earlier. There, a child would observe an event and map that event onto the sentence it was hearing. If a sentence included the names of two things that the child could see ('rabbit' and 'duck', for instance), and what was seen to be happening was that one thing was doing something to the other, then the child would interpret the sentence it heard as conveying exactly that information: that one was doing something to the other. So the child would learn about subject (the thing that is doing) and object (the thing it is being done to) by taking account of both the world *and* the sentence, and trying to map one onto the other. The only thing that would need to be innate would be the ability to map one thing (language) onto another (the world), and vice versa. The difference between the two accounts concerns the nature of the predisposition that is assumed to be innate. In Pinker's account, it is a predisposition that is supposedly specific to language (there are nouns, there are verbs, there are subjects); in Gleitman's, it is a predisposition that is specific to things which co-vary—that is, a predisposition to establish whether one kind of input (in this case, language) correlates with, and can therefore be mapped onto, another (the observable world).

Resolving these issues is difficult, and perhaps even impossible. It would be very hard to prove that a certain kind of knowledge was not innate. We would have to find a period when that knowledge was absent, perhaps by finding that the baby or infant lacked some ability that it should have if the knowledge were present. The problem then would be to be sure that our failure to find the ability did not come about simply because the experimental tools were not sensitive enough to what the baby was or was not able to do. And even if we believed the tools sensitive enough, the ability might be one that developed only after the infant had matured in some way (perhaps related to the process of synaptogenesis).

A further criticism that has been levelled against theories proposing an innate endowment is that they are perhaps too simple an explanation when no other way has been found to explain the phenomena being studied—perhaps there is an alternative explanation but it is yet to be found. It is unclear whether any rebuttal is really possible to criticisms such as this. Consequently, an important part of the debate has been concerned less with what may be innate, and more with what it is possible to learn from the language itself.

The rhythms of grammar

The innateness hypothesis has been around for as long as linguistics, in its modern form, has existed. And ever since linguists first suggested that the language input did not contain sufficient information by which to learn the language, there has been a search for alternative (non-innate) means by which the developing child could acquire the relevant knowledge. In the mid-1980s, James Morgan at the University of Minnesota suggested that the problem with existing theories of language learnability was that they assumed that children were exposed to sequence after sequence of grammatical sentences. On this view, each sentence (no matter how simple or complex) is simply an unstructured sequence of words, with the task being to somehow project structure onto this sequence for the purposes of interpreting the sentence—hence the problems outlined earlier. Morgan proposed that the input sequences are not unstructured, but in fact contain a number of clues (or, more properly, *cues*) to their internal structure. If so, part of the problem for the learning device would be solved; it would be presented with the very structure that (on the alternative accounts) it should be trying to find. In particular, Morgan, and others, proposed that one cue to the internal structure of sentences is their *prosodic* structure.

We have already seen that newborn infants are sensitive to the prosodic structure of their language, and that this may explain the sensitivity they demonstrate to syllabic structure. Studies have shown, in addition, that infants as young as just four and a half months are sensitive to the prosodic patterns that accompany some of the *boundaries* between the major constituents of a sentence. These patterns include durational changes (slight lengthening of vowels before such a boundary) and slight changes in pitch before and after a boundary (generally, a fall in pitch before, and a rise after). Morgan suggested that perhaps these cues to boundary location could help the child identify the internal structure of each sentence. Knowing where the boundaries were would be a first step to making sense of what could be found between them. For example, if 'the girl' in 'The girl knew the language was beautiful' was prosodically distinguished from the rest of the sentence, and so was 'the language', then the child could learn fairly easily the relative positions of determiner-type words ('the') and noun-type words ('girl', 'language'). It would not have to worry about the positions of the determiner words relative to any other words in the sentence. The child could also learn (if the appropriate boundary cues were present) about the relative positioning of *phrases*, such as 'the language', and 'was beautiful'.

As a test of this hypothesis, Morgan and his colleagues created a small artificial language composed of sequences of meaningless syllables ordered according to a set of rules that they made up and which specified which orders of the syllables were grammatical and which were ungrammatical—so 'Jix dup kav sog pel' might be grammatical, whereas 'Jix kav pel dup sog' might not be. This is little different from saying that 'The girl speaks many languages' is grammatical and 'The speaks languages girl many' is not. And in much the same way as 'The girl speaks many languages' can be broken down according to the grammar of English into its constituents as '(the girl)(speaks (many languages))', so 'Jix dup kav sog pel' could be broken down, according to its artificial grammar, as '(jix dup)(kav (sog pel))'. Morgan arranged for someone to speak these sequences either in monotone (in much the same way as one might simply list a sequence of syllables), or with the natural prosody (rhythm and intonation) that would convey the constituent groupings (imagine the difference between a monotone version of 'The girl speaks many languages', and one with exaggerated intonation). Adults listened to one or other of these two spoken versions of the language, and were shown, simultaneously, visual symbols that represented the 'objects' that the words in this language referred to. Morgan found that the language was learned more accurately when heard with its natural intonation. So prosody can, and according to this theory does, aid the learning process.

Despite the appeal of such a theory, it is unclear whether prosodic structure alone is sufficient to help the novice language user learn about internal structure. There is some suggestion that in everyday language constituent boundaries are not reliably marked by changes in prosody. On the other hand, in many languages the speech addressed to young children tends to have a much more exaggerated intonation than that addressed to adults. Moreover, the sentences spoken to young children

in these languages tend also to have very simple internal structure. So maybe after all prosody is useful. But is it necessary?

There exist languages, as we have already seen, in which the speech addressed to children is not particularly different from that addressed to adults (this is supposedly the case in Samoan and Javanese, for example). In some of these communities, the parents do not address their children until the children themselves start talking—the parents do not believe that their children are communicative beings until they can talk. Given the current state of the art, it is impossible to determine the effect this has on children brought up in these communities. Perhaps there are other cues to internal structure that these languages provide.

Morgan's account of early acquisition of syntactic information leaves one further puzzle unsolved. How does the child know to use the information provided by the prosodic cues? It may seem obvious to us that the melody and rhythm of a sentence defines natural groupings within that sentence, and that what we need to learn is the structure of each group, but in just the same way that a computer would not know to do this (unless programmed appropriately), how would an infant know? Is this some innate constraint? Or is it learned? And if so, how could it be learned?

The debate between advocates of, on the one hand, an innate basis for the acquisition of grammar, and on the other, a prosodic basis for its acquisition, is still ongoing. Both accounts appear to rely, one way or another, on something more than just the language input itself. So perhaps they are not so different after all. But as suggested earlier, this additional knowledge, if innate, may not be linguistic—it may instead reflect more generally the existence of human abilities that in turn reflect the way the world works.

Languages are not learned, they are created

The continuing controversies in language acquisition research arise because we still know too little about exactly how, and why, the infant learns to combine words. We also know too little, still, about how infants and young children learn to inflect their words. Do they inflect them by learning the mental equivalent of stand-alone rules, such as 'past tense = + ed'? Or do they inflect them by analogy to the other words they have already learned? The various debates are far from over (and it is impossible to describe them all in a single chapter). But one thing we do know is that to learn language, however that is done, requires the right kind of exposure; without sufficient external input early enough, infants are unlikely to acquire language normally.

Estimates vary as to the duration of the 'critical period' for language learning, but it is somewhere in the first six and 12 years (depending on which textbook, and which case study you read). The evidence suggests that the ability to learn a first language easily gradually tails off. There have been a number of distressing cases of children who have been brought up in isolation, with no language input to speak of. These children have generally emerged from their ordeal with nothing but rudimentary gestures. One girl was discovered when she was six, and went on to develop language pretty much as well as any other child who acquires a language at that age (as happens with, for instance, the children of immigrants). Another girl was discovered when she was around 12 or 13, and although she developed some language skills fairly quickly, she never progressed beyond the level expected of even a three year old. Just why the ability to learn tails off is the subject of considerable debate but, as Steven Pinker suggests, there just may not have been the selective pressure, during our evolution, to maintain our phenomenal learning abilities beyond an initial period. Indeed, what adaptive benefits could there possibly be? So long as we get to puberty, the species is safe.

So we need sufficient language input to acquire the language. But it is not quite that simple, because it seems to be the case that we do not simply acquire the language we are exposed to; rather we *create* a language consistent with what we hear. The evidence for this comes from the creation of the *creole* languages. In the early part of the 20th century, Hawaii was, in effect, one large sugar plantation, employing labourers from the Philippines, China, Portugal, and elsewhere. Although each ethnic group brought its own language, there was a need in the labouring community to break down the language barriers, and so a *pidgin* language developed: a mish-mash of words, mainly from English, which had the property that no two speakers of pidgin would necessarily use the same words in the same order. The pidgin languages (there are several around the world, not all based around English) were studied extensively by Derek Bickerton, based in Hawaii, who noticed that the children of pidgin speakers did not speak the same pidgin as their parents. What the children had learned was a language that shared the words of the pidgin they heard, but with none of the irregular word order of the different pidgins spoken by the different adults. It is as if the children imposed some order on what they heard, which was then subsequently reinforced during their interactions with one another. Most significant of all is the fact that creole languages (and again, Hawaiian Creole is just one example) can contain grammatical devices (that is, word order, inflections, and grammatical function words such as 'the' or 'was') which may not appear in any of the languages that had originally made up the pidgin of the parent generation.

The facts surrounding creole demonstrate that the ability to combine words is not dependent solely on exposure to other people's combinations of words. They argue against a learning mechanism which simply analyses what it hears, and argue instead for a more proactive mechanism that is driven by some fundamental (and perhaps innate) desire to describe the world using language, *in some form or other*. The emphasis here is required because it is becoming increasingly clear that whatever facility we have for learning language is not specific to spoken language; children brought up in communities where sign language is the predominant medium of communication learn it in a way that almost exactly mirrors the way in which other children learn spoken language (and this even includes the creation of the sign language equivalents of pidgin and creole). Indeed, the structures of the two languages, in terms of elements corresponding to words, rhythm, and even syllables, are almost equivalent. However, whether this means that there are innate constraints on what language can look like, or whether it means that language looks the way it does because of some early, possibly rhythmic, experience common to all infants, is at present unclear. Certainly, we appear to be born with a predisposition to learn, and if necessary, create language.

⩓

Learning is something that newborns, infants, children, and even adults, can do effortlessly. Theories of learning are becoming increasingly important in psycholinguistic theory; whereas we have some idea of what babies and infants are capable of, there are still gaps in our theories, and these gaps will most likely be filled by theories of how these early abilities are acquired. The puzzle is to work out which are acquired as part of some genetic inheritance, and which are acquired through learning. It cannot all be innate. And if there is a genetic component, no matter how substantial, the challenge is to understand how that component matures—how the innate predispositions provided to the child become realized, through exposure to their language, as actual abilities.

We shall reconsider the issue of learning, and what learning may involve, when we consider, in Chapter 13, computational accounts of the learning process. However, not all psycholinguistic research is necessarily concerned with learning; identifying adults' abilities, and attempting to understand on the basis of those abilities the representations and processes underlying adult language usage, is an important prerequisite to understanding the route that the human language device pursues from birth through to adulthood.

Organizing the dictionary

The average one-year old knows approximately 100 words. The average adult knows between around 60 000 and around 75 000 words, not including variants of the same one. The average one-year-old will select from around just 10 words when speaking; the average adult will select from around 30 000. To put this in perspective, this book contains only around 5500 different words, including variants of the same word. As adults, then, we have ended up knowing an awful lot of words (some of which we might use just once in our lifetimes). And when we hear just one of those words, we must somehow distinguish it from each of the other 60 000 to 75 000 words we know. But on what basis do we distinguish between all those words? If they are contained within the mental equivalent of a dictionary, how is that dictionary organized?

The dictionaries that we are perhaps most familiar with are arranged alphabetically. To find a word you start off with its first letter and go to the section of the dictionary containing words sharing that first letter. You then go to the section containing words with the same first two letters as your word, then the same first three letters, and so on, until you have narrowed down the search to a single dictionary entry. But not all dictionaries are arranged this way. Rhyming dictionaries, for instance, are organized not in groups of words sharing beginning letters, but in groups of words which rhyme. 'Speech' would appear grouped with 'peach' and 'beach'. 'Language' would appear grouped with 'sandwich'.

We tend to think that an alphabetic arrangement makes most sense, but only because we are used to the way that our spelling is organized. What does a Chinese dictionary look like? In a language like Chinese, the symbols do not represent words as such, instead they represent the meanings or ideas themselves; the symbols do not constitute a spelling in the sense that English speakers are most familiar with. The English alphabet is essentially a phonetic alphabet, where the order of the letters loosely represents the order of the sounds making up the word (we return to this issue in Chapter 11). But Chinese characters are not made up of subparts in this way; the characters give very little clue as to the sound of the word. Parts of some characters do relate to parts of the sound they should be spoken with, but only to parts—many characters give no hints at all. This has its advantages; the same character can have the same meaning in different dialects, even though the actual words that are spoken may differ. The disadvantage is that learning the set of characters required to read a novel or newspaper is no easy task.

So a dictionary of Chinese characters cannot be organized according to any alphabet. At best it could be organized by shape (which would be independent of the word's sound or meaning), or by meaning (independently of sound or shape). The point is this: the most natural organization of a dictionary depends on the nature of the script that can be used to access the dictionary. Most dictionaries of English access words according to the alphabetic sequence of letters, but some do so according to what they rhyme with, and some use other criteria (crossword dictionaries access by length, for instance). So given our own knowledge about the different words in the language that we hear and speak, how do we access words in that body of knowledge? What is the *access code* for the mental dictionary?

Different languages, different codes?

There are two phases to looking up a word in a written, alphabetically arranged dictionary. The first involves establishing a range of entries within which the word is assumed to appear, and corresponds to flicking through the pages until one reaches the page containing all the words that share the first few letters of the word that is being looked up. The second phase involves narrowing down the search and eliminating from the search all words which, although sharing the same beginnings, deviate later on in the spelling. In both phases, the crucial elements that we focus on, and on which basis we narrow down the search, are letters. So when accessing the mental dictionary, or *lexicon*, and narrowing down the search for a spoken word, what equivalent element do we focus on? What kinds of element do we use to retrieve words from our lexicons?

We might at first be tempted to assume that we retrieve words according to the phonemes they contain, if only because this fits most readily
with our experience of letter-by-letter look-up in a written dictionary.
But the fact that infants apparently organize what they hear in terms of
syllables (see Chapter 2) offers an alternative account of the access code;
perhaps as adults we break down what we hear into syllable-sized
chunks, and perhaps the lexicon is organized in terms of these chunks.

The lexicon must be organized, as it develops through infancy,
according to those aspects of the speech input to which the infant is
sensitive. But infant sensitivities may not be the only thing to determine
lexical organization. If properties of the written form of the language
can determine the nature of the access code used with written
dictionaries (different codes for English and Chinese), then properties of
the spoken form of the language should determine the nature of the
access code used with mental lexicons. But if different languages exhibit
different properties with respect to their spoken structure (e.g. rhythmic
structure, syllabic structure, and melodic structure), they may cause
infants brought up in those different languages to develop different
access procedures. And one does not have to look too far afield to find
such differences. English and French are a good example.

In French, the syllable has a rather more distinctive role in terms of defining the rhythmic properties of the language than it has in English. In English, the beat coincides with the stressed syllables. A good test of which is the stressed syllable in a word with more than two syllables is to attempt to insert an *infix* into the word—the word 'bloody' is an infix in 'fan-bloody-tastic'. Infixes of this type tend to occur immediately before the stressed syllable, which is why 'fantas-bloody-tic' is pretty bad! French is quite different from English; the beat tends to coincide with every syllable. So in French, the syllable is a rhythmic unit. The syllable is the smallest thing that is repeated regularly, rhythmically, with each beat. In English, the rhythmic unit is a sequence of syllables, with just one stressed syllable occurring in each such sequence. This rhythm is especially obvious in limericks. The thing that repeats on each beat is not the syllable in this case. This means that the syllable is generally more salient in French than it is in English. So perhaps French babies latch on to syllables in a way that English babies do not.

There is another important difference between English and French which also conspires to make the syllable more salient in French than it is in English. In French, the words 'balcon' and 'balance' (meaning 'balcony' and 'balance', respectively) start with different syllables. In 'balcon' the first syllable is /bal/, whereas in 'balance' it is /ba/. We could write these words, in order to highlight this difference, as 'bal-con' and 'ba-lance'. But the English word 'balance' is not quite the same as the French word 'balance'. Whereas the /l/ clearly belongs to the second syllable in the French word, it is less clear which syllable it belongs to in the corresponding English word. If people are asked to judge which syllable it belongs to, they cannot do so reliably; in effect, the /l/ belongs to both syllables. This phenomenon is particularly predominant when the first syllable is stressed and the second is unstressed (a very common pattern in English). This means that the break-down into distinct syllables is much harder in English than it is in French.

So do adult speakers of French make use of their syllables in a way that adult speakers of English do not?

A variety of experimental studies have explored this question, and not just with English and French—other language pairs also differ in theoretically interesting ways and these have also been studied. The research has largely been conducted by Jacques Mehler and colleagues, as part of their research into the acquisition and nature of the mental lexicon. The original motivation for the research was to discover whether, in French at least, the syllable functions as a *perceptual unit*—that is, as the chunk that is used to both access and organize the mental lexicon.

Mehler investigated this issue by devising a *syllable-monitoring task*, in which French speakers were asked to press a response button as soon as they heard a word containing a particular target syllable, for instance /ba/. He would then play them either a word like 'ba-lance' or a word like 'bal-con' (the hyphen is used here, again, simply to indicate the syllabic structure of the word). If the syllable is indeed a basic unit of perception, then this task should be relatively easy when the first syllable of the word matches the target syllable they have to listen out for. It should be easy to match the target /ba/ against 'ba-lance', or the target /bal/ against 'bal-con'. On the other hand, it should be harder, and should therefore take longer, if the word does not contain the target syllable (so it should be harder to match /ba/ against 'bal-con' and /bal/ against 'ba-lance'). In fact, this is exactly what was found, supporting the hypothesis that adult French speakers organize what they hear into syllable-sized chunks. If they simply broke down what they heard into sequences of individual phonemes, for instance, one would not be able to explain this effect—the phoneme sequence in /ba/ exists in both words, so no difference would have been found in the time taken to match it against these two words.

So much for French. What about English? When equivalent experiments are performed with English speakers the pattern is very different; the time it takes them to respond in the syllable-monitoring task is not dependent on the relationship between the target syllable and the syllable structure of the word they hear. English speakers are not sensitive to syllabic structure in the same way that French speakers are. Apparently, French speakers break down what they hear into syllable-sized chunks, whereas English speakers do not. On the face of it, then, it looks as if English and French adults do quite fundamentally different things when processing their respective languages.

Much of the evidence on infant speech perception leads to the view that babies and infants will organize what they hear according to the rhythms of their language (see Chapter 2 for more discussion of this theme). And if different languages have different rhythms, and so emphasise different aspects of the speech that the baby or infant hears, it follows quite naturally that adult speakers of these languages may organize what they hear according to these different aspects. They may process the speech they hear in fundamentally different ways. In other words, their minds will work (with respect to this aspect of speech pro-

cessing) in fundamentally different ways. But *do* they? There is another possibility, and it concerns the ways in which sounds are spoken.

Exploiting the smallest details

Different sounds are produced by changing the shape of the vocal tract (changing the position of the tongue, changing its shape, changing the position and shape of the lips, and so on). The vocal tract changes shape continuously during the utterance of a word—it does not change, stop, change again, but changes shape in a more 'fluid' manner; the shape at any one time is a function of what the shape was beforehand, what the intended shape is (given the sound to be produced) and what the shape will become in order to produce the next sound. Consequently, at any one moment, the sound that is produced reflects not simply the intended sound, but also the previous sound, and the sound that is to follow. To give an example: the vowel sound in the word 'worm' is different from the vowel sound in 'word', because in the former, the sound is influenced by the following /m/ (the 'r' is silent, and appears only in the spelling), whereas in the latter, it is influenced by the /d/. This phenomenon is termed *co-articulation*. So the speech that we hear does not consist of sequences of simple, individually identifiable, phonemes. In this respect it is rather different from the way in which a written word consists of a sequence of letters.

One can think of the process by which we produce speech (discussed in more detail in Chapter 10) as the stringing together of articulatory movements, or *gestures*. The position of the articulators (the tongue, lips, and other parts of the vocal apparatus) is determined by where they are heading within that particular articulatory gesture. Each of these gestures corresponds, more or less, to a syllable. So co-articulation is largely restricted to the speech contained within a single syllable. In a word like 'balderdash', there will be significant co-articulation of the /l/ on the preceding vowel, whereas in a word like 'balloon', there will be much less (if any at all), because the /l/ belongs to the following, stressed syllable. But what has this to do with the differences between English and French?

The fact that the syllabic structure in French is very clear means that in a French word like 'ba-lance' there will be little co-articulation of the /l/ on the preceding vowel—the /l/ falls in a different syllable. In 'bal-con' it falls in the same syllable and co-articulation on the vowel will occur. In English, on the other hand, the fact that in 'balance' the /l/ belongs to both syllables means that the vowels in both syllables will be co-articulated with the /l/—the first one because the /l/ is where the articulators are heading, and the second one because that is where the articulators have just been. So the differences in syllabic structure between the two languages are reflected in differences in co-articulation. But again, so what?

Imagine that both English speakers and French speakers (and speakers of every other language) are able to use the smallest possible details in the speech input to help distinguish between the different words in their lexicons. When French speakers hear the sequence /bal/ from 'bal-con', they hear (even if they are unaware of it) the co-articulation on the vowel of the following consonant. They, or more correctly their perceptual systems, should therefore be able to eliminate from the search any words like 'ba-lance' which would require the vowel to be free of co-articulation (recall from Chapter 3 that vowels are not perceived categorically, so small differences between vowels can be detected). They would in fact be able to eliminate any words whose first syllable was not /bal/. English speakers hearing the /bal/ of 'bal-cony' would also be able to eliminate any words whose first syllable was not /bal/. But they would not be able to eliminate words like 'balance' because both 'balcony' and 'balance' are compatible with co-articulation of the /l/ on the preceding vowel.

In the early 1990s, William Marslen-Wilson and Paul Warren, working in Cambridge, devised an ingenious experiment to test whether co-articulated information is used in this way. Imagine taking off the final /d/ from 'word' and replacing it with a /g/. When the perceptual system hears the first consonant and vowel it will think that it is hearing a word in which the next consonant is a /d/—that is what the co-articulation on the vowel indicates. It will therefore rule out words like 'worm', 'work', and so on, leaving just 'word'. When it then encounters the final /g/, it will have to rule out 'word'. Imagine now that the /g/ had replaced the last /b/ of the made-up word 'worb'. In this case, the perceptual system, on hearing that first consonant and vowel would rule out *all* words, as none is compatible with a following /b/. When it then encounters the /g/, there will be nothing left to rule out. Marslen-Wilson and Warren recorded someone saying 'word', 'worb', and 'worg' (in fact, they used other examples but the principle is the same), and then replaced the final phonemes in 'word' and 'worb' with the final phoneme spliced from 'worg'. They then asked people to listen to these composite words and to decide as quickly as possible whether or not what they were hearing was a real word. In both these cases, of course, they were not. But in the case created from 'word', as opposed to the case created from 'worb', as the nonword unfolded, co-articulation would lead them to think that they were hearing a real word, so they should take longer to say, subsequently, that it was not a word after all. This is exactly what was found.

So it looks as if we *do* use the smallest detail possible to distinguish between alternative words in the mental lexicon. And because, in French, words like 'bal-con' and 'ba-lance' can be distinguished on the basis of these (co-articulation) details, whereas in English words like 'bal-cony' and 'balance' cannot, it might look as if French speakers are doing something quite different from what English speakers are doing. In fact, they might all be doing just the same—they might both be using co-articulated information if it helps. In French it does, a lot. In English it does, but not so much.

Interpreting the dip-stick

As with any scientific endeavour, controversies exist not only in respect of the alternative theories concerned with the processes underlying language understanding, but also in respect of the utility of the different tasks that have been used in order to uncover these processes. No task is totally immune to controversy, and the syllable-monitoring task is no exception. Part of the problem concerns our assumptions about what the task taps into—cynics say that if the human mind is like an engine, then any experimental tool used to investigate that engine is a little like a dip-stick, except that we can never be sure that we are sticking it in the right place, and we can therefore never be sure about how to interpret the sticky mess that we subsequently find.

The original motivation for the syllable-monitoring task was that it would be sensitive to the processes that convert the acoustic input into a form that can then be matched against the mental lexicon—the equivalent of analysing a printed word in terms of its individual letters for the purpose of matching those letters against a written dictionary. But perhaps the syllable-monitoring task is instead sensitive to information that is in fact contained within the lexicon itself. After all, when we access a word in the lexicon, we must retrieve all sorts of information about that word, including some representation of the articulatory gestures required to utter that word. And perhaps people's responses in the syllable-monitoring task are determined by the availability of that information. If the auditory signal is compatible with many words whose first-syllable-gestures are the same as the target syllable-gesture (and few whose first-syllable-gestures are different), people may be able to respond quickly. If the auditory signal is compatible with many words whose first-syllable-gestures are not the same as the target syllable-gesture, people may respond more slowly.

There is one further piece in the jigsaw. If the French sensitivity to syllabic structure is no more than a consequence of the presence or absence of co-articulation, what happens if people respond so fast that they could not yet have encountered the co-articulated information on the vowel before initiating their response? In this case, they might hear the consonant–vowel sequence /ba/ but not so much of the vowel that they could hear any co-articulation from a subsequent /l/. At this very early stage, it would not be possible, if listening to 'bal-con', to eliminate from the search 'ba-lance'. In effect, they would find the relevant page in the dictionary, but would not have yet reached the information that would allow any finer discriminations within that page. So both words would be compatible with the input so far. Consequently, this input would be compatible both with the target syllable /ba/ and with the target syllable /bal/. In fact, subsequent analyses of the French data found exactly this—the faster responses did not vary as a function of syllabic match or mismatch.

What should we now make of the syllable's role in French? Is the syllable represented mentally only for the purposes of speech production (see Chapter 10)? Does it have no direct role in the processes that match the acoustic input against the mental lexicon? Currently, it is impossible to tell. Whether we say that French speakers can exploit syllables whereas English speakers cannot, or that French speakers can exploit co-articulation in ways that English speakers cannot, is really the same. Co-articulation reflects syllabic structure. The two are, in many respects, inseparable.

So what should we now conclude? What progress has been made in our attempts to unlock the access code? The evidence is far from clear, and mainly circumstantial. But what would count as progress? We could have unambiguously discovered, for instance, that the speech input is broken down into a sequence of syllables which are then matched against the lexicon. Or we could have discovered that the input is broken down into sequences of phonemes, and that these phonemes are matched against the lexicon. Instead, we have discovered that even more subtle information than that can influence which words stay in, or are eliminated from, the lexical search. Of course, this does not tell us whether this (co-articulated) information is used directly in the lexical search, or whether it is used simply to anticipate the next phoneme, or the end of the syllable. These other units may none the less form the basis for the lexical search. But crucially, the system *acts* as if the smallest detail is mapped directly onto the lexicon. We know the currency that we are dealing in, we just cannot guarantee what denomination the notes come in.

There is nothing incompatible between the finding that infants are sensitive to syllabic structure, and the supposition that adults (even French adults) do not break down what they hear into syllable-sized chunks before matching these against the mental lexicon. If infants develop gradually more refined sensitivities to the structure of the speech that they hear, perhaps being able to make finer and finer discriminations, and learning which discriminations are useful and which are not (see Chapter 3), it follows that the access code used in the construction of the lexicon, and in the retrieval of information from that lexicon, may itself develop and, in effect, evolve. We can in fact only guess at what the initial organization of the lexicon might be, and how it may change as infant sensitivities themselves change. The goal of much current research into the acquisition and organization of the early lexicon is to map out these changes.

≜

In the following chapter, we leave behind the question of what, if anything, constitutes the access code, and consider instead what 'recognizing' a word actually means. In terms of the analogy with searching through a written dictionary, at what point (in time) do we read off the information contained within the lexical entry, and what determines when we reach this point? In addressing this issue, we can remain agnostic with respect to the nature of the access code. At the end of the day, more important than the denomination of the notes is what you can buy with them.

Words, and how we (eventually) find them

The history of science is littered with examples of analogies that do not work. Often, they are simply inappropriate, simply wrong, or simply confusing. But even when inappropriate, they can prove useful. For instance, it is not unnatural to think of our knowledge about the words in our language as residing in some sort of dictionary. The *Oxford English Dictionary* (*OED*), all 20 volumes of it, is as good an example as any—its purpose is to provide, for each entry, a spelling, a pronunciation, one or more definitions, general knowledge about the word itself, and perhaps a quotation or two. Getting to this information is relatively efficient. You scan down the page, ignoring the definitions of the words you are uninterested in until you come to the word you want. Of course, if you are lucky enough to possess the dictionary on CD-ROM, you do not even need to scan down the page (let alone pull the appropriate volume off the shelf); just type in the word, and up pops everything you ever wanted to know about it. But so what? Why should anyone care about how the *OED* works, CD-ROM or no CD-ROM? In the last chapter we saw that the analogy between accessing a

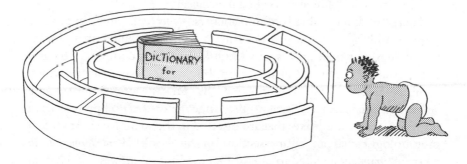

written dictionary and accessing the mental lexicon is at best fragile. So why carry on with it? The answer to this is simply that it provides a useful starting point from which to proceed, using a vocabulary that is easily understood to describe a process (accessing the mental lexicon) that is easily misunderstood.

Describing the mental lexicon as 'something like you've never imagined' is probably accurate, but certainly useless. At least a conventional dictionary can be imagined, and is therefore a useful place from which to start our exploration of the mental equivalent. Most importantly of all, the questions one can ask of a dictionary such as the *OED*, and the questions one can ask of the mental lexicon, are remarkably similar. The answers, though, can be surprisingly different.

Before delving into the mental lexicon and looking at how we retrieve words, we need first to address an important, if basic, question: what, exactly, are these things we call 'words'?

Words and what they contain

The purpose of language, and communication in general, is to convey meaning. In spoken language, the word is the smallest stand-alone thing that can do this. It is not, however, the smallest verbal gesture capable of expressing meaning. An 's' added onto the end of 'fact' also expresses meaning; namely that we are dealing with more than one fact. So words can generally be broken down into even finer units, called *morphemes*. This last sentence contains 13 words, but 21 morphemes—the word 'units', for instance, consists of the morpheme 'unit' and the morpheme 's', and the word 'morphemes' consists of 'morph'+'eme'+'s'. Figuring out which kinds of morpheme can be stuck onto which other kinds, and how this affects the meaning of the resulting word, has been studied within a branch of linguistics called *morphology*.

There are different kinds of morphemes: *stems* (e.g. 'unit', 'word', or 'speak') and *affixes* (e.g. '-s', or '-ing'). Languages differ in terms of where they put their affixes—in English, the most common affix is a *suffix*, coming at the end of the word, but we also have *prefixes* which come at the beginnings of words (e.g. the 'pre-' in 'premature'). Some languages (for instance, Tagalog, the language of the Philippines) have *infixes* too; these are affixes that are inserted in the stem. Mark Aranoff, a morphologist, has an entire section in his book *Word formation in generative grammar* devoted to one of the few English infixes—'fuckin' as in 'fan-fuckin'-tastic'. But affixes are not the only device we can use for modifying the meanings of words; the irregular past tense in English— 'run–ran', 'speak–spoke', and so on—is a remnant of a time when the past tense was produced not by adding the suffix '-ed' onto words, but by modifying a vowel in the stem. In a Semitic language like Hebrew, this is the rule, rather than the exception.

To complicate matters further, different kinds of affix do very different things. Some affixes are called *inflectional*; these include the plurals ('-s'), and the various ways of inflecting verbs (e.g. for 'govern': 'governs', 'governing', 'governed'). Inflectional affixes do not change the meaning of the word, but convey additional information relevant to it. *Derivational* affixes, on the other hand, do change the meaning; they are used to derive new words, so from 'govern' we can get 'governor', 'government', 'governance', 'governable', 'ungovernable', 'govern-ability', and so on. Although related in meaning, each of these words means something different, and in the case of 'governable' and 'ungovernable', they mean exactly the opposite. But not all derived words are related; 'casual' and 'casualty' are unrelated in meaning, as are 'depress' and 'express' (although a glance at the *OED* will reveal their common historical ancestry). Another complication (there are several more) is that although the majority of stems can be free-standing, there are some inflected words which do not contain a free-standing stem, such as the verbs 'permit' and 'submit'. And whereas the meaning of 'ungovernable' can be deduced by stripping away the affixes and recovering the meaning of the stem 'govern', the meaning of 'permit' and 'submit' cannot be deduced from the meaning of 'mit'.

So words are complicated things. And knowing whether it should be called a word or a morpheme, an affix or a stem, a prefix or a suffix, an inflection or a derivation, matters far less than knowing that words have an internal structure. Somehow we have to strip off the excess (but important) baggage, and reveal the word's core. And sometimes it looks as if we ought to do this, but in fact we should not (as in 'permit', 'report', and so on). Linguistics has told us an enormous amount about how words are structured and how the meaning of a word is dependent on the meanings of the different morphemes it is composed of; it tells us which kinds of morpheme can be combined with which other kinds, and in which order. But that is just the periodic table again—it tells us what the result is, but it does not really tell us how the result comes about. It does not explain how the brain comes to acquire the conventions that tell us that 'un-' on the front of a word results in a meaning that is the contrary of whatever the word meant in the first place. It does not tell us where this knowledge is stored, or how it is stored, or how the brain takes a complex word like 'unspeakable' and breaks it down into its components, or even whether it does break it down at all. All these questions fall under the remit of psycholinguistics. And sadly, there are few definite answers, only hints. But of one thing we can be certain: at the root of each word is a meaning, and recovering this meaning is precisely what a dictionary is for.

Of course, we knew all along that words convey meaning, and that the mental lexicon is a store of word meanings. But so is the *OED*, and yet physically they could hardly be more different. But what, if any, are the consequences of the physical differences? The fact that they evidently are different does not mean that they are necessarily used any differently—for instance, the *OED* in book form could hardly be more different from the *OED* on CD-ROM, and yet there are aspects of their use which are common to both of them. Apart from the fact that the *OED* and the mental lexicon are physically different, what else is different about them?

Accessing our dictionary

We already know that not all dictionaries are the same, and that depending on which dictionary we use, we can access the words (and narrow down the search) on the basis of how they are spelled, how they are pronounced, what they rhyme with, what they look like, how long they are (as in a crossword dictionary), or even how frequently they occur in the language at large (as in some specialized dictionaries used by psycholinguists). But crucially, however we do it (see Chapter 5 for some discussion of this), it is an inevitable consequence of accessing the dictionary that we will encounter, during the search, other words that share certain features with the word we are ultimately interested in finding, whether they share their spelling, pronunciation, rhyme, shape, length, or frequency. It is in this respect that our intuitions about what we do with a written dictionary are quite at odds with what we actually do with our own mental lexicon. For instance, although we do not burden our minds with the definitions of the other words that we pass as we scan down the page of a written dictionary, the same is not true of the process by which we access the mental lexicon. We do burden our minds with the contents of the neighbouring words we encounter as we

narrow down the search. Our intuition that we do not is wrong, and
our expectation on the basis of what appears to be a similar process
(using the *OED*) is also wrong. The challenge, of course, is to prove that
these intuitions are wrong.

It seems somewhat unreasonable to access the meanings of the words
'ram' and 'ramp' simply because they are encountered during the search
for 'rampart'. It would be equally unreasonable for an Australian
listening to the word 'acoustic' to access the entry for 'acubra' (a
traditional Australian hat) just because they start off sounding the same,
or for a naturalist to access the meaning of the word 'pichiciago' (a kind
of armadillo) just because it starts off like 'pitch'. It would surely make
sense only to look up the definition of the word being looked for, as we
do with written dictionaries, and not to look up the definitions of all the
other words that just happen to overlap in their first few sounds. So
why, when searching the mental lexicon, do we access the meanings of
neighbouring words? And how can we, as psycholinguists, be so sure
that this happens? As we shall see, it is unclear how things could possibly
happen any other way.

During the 1980s, William Marslen-Wilson demonstrated that we can
recognize a word even while it is still being heard (before, even, the
speaker has finished saying it). We therefore access the lexical entry of a

word well before the corresponding physical stimulation has ceased
(that is, before its *acoustic offset*). In one of the first demonstrations of
this, people were asked to repeat aloud as quickly as they could what they
heard over headphones (to *shadow* what they were listening to). Marslen-
Wilson found that often they would start to vocalize a word before
it had finished playing on the tape. This was not simply some blind
repetition of the sounds they heard, because if the words were jumbled
up so that they made no sense ('up words jumbled he they so no sense the
made'), people could no longer shadow as fast—so they were clearly
interpreting what they were listening to, and were therefore recognizing
the individual words before repeating them. In other experiments, he
asked people to press a button as soon as they heard a particular word on
a tape (*word-monitoring*, similar in spirit to the syllable-monitoring task
mentioned in Chapter 5). He found that once you took into account
the time it takes to decide to press a button, and the time it takes to press
it, people were responding so fast that they must have been initiating
their response well before the end of the word.

Marslen-Wilson found that the time it takes to recognize a word
correlates very well with how much of the word has to be heard before
it becomes uniquely distinguishable from all the other words in the
language that share the same beginning. So 'slander' becomes uniquely
distinguishable only when the /d/ is encountered. Before then, the
input would be compatible with 'slant'.

An important component of the account of lexical access developed
by Marslen-Wilson is that the entries in the mental lexicon are not
simply accessed, they are *activated*. The idea that information is activated
has a long established history in psychology, although its application to
word recognition became more widespread in the late 1960s following
the work of John Morton, now Director of the Medical Research
Council's Child Development Unit in London. One way to think
about this is to remember that ultimately, all the information in the
mental lexicon is stored within the neural structures of the brain. When
a pattern of light enters the eyes, or a sequence of sounds enters the ears,
those stimuli do not access anything within the brain, even if they result
in the recognition of, for instance, a politician speaking or a baby
babbling (or both, if they are indistinguishable). Instead, the stimulation
passes through the neural circuitry of the brain, being modified by, and
in turn, stimulating (or activating) different parts of the circuit. Only
certain kinds of stimulus will provide the right kind of stimulation for
some particular part of the neural circuit—the stimulus is a key that can

activate a part of the circuit, and depending on which part is activated, we experience 'seeing a politician' or 'hearing a baby'. There will be more of this later, but for now, the important point is that nothing is accessed; it is activated. And although we might just as well continue to refer to lexical entries, we shall return later to the idea that the mental lexicon is in fact a collection of highly complex neural circuits.

So what has this to do with why we access/activate the meaning of anything but the intended word? Why does this suddenly make it reasonable to suppose that we start to activate words and their meanings even before they become uniquely distinguishable from their neighbours? The answer has to do with the quite reasonable assumption that sounds entering the auditory system (i.e. the ear and beyond) stimulate the neural circuitry as they enter the system—a sequence of sounds is much like the combination to a safe; the tumblers in a combination lock fall into place as the correct sequence of rotations is performed, without waiting until the sequence is complete. Similarly, those neural circuits which require a particular sequence of sounds (before a particular word is 'experienced') will become activated as that sequence enters the system. So the neural circuits that encode what we think of as lexical entries could quite reasonably become activated on the basis of a developing (but not yet completely developed) sequence of sounds—/slan/ would activate the neural circuits associated with (and hence would activate the meanings of) both 'slander' and 'slant'. But so much for what is possible in principle. What actually happens? Where is the proof?

What we need is a way of establishing which meanings of a word have been activated, and when. The priming task (first mentioned in Chapter 1) does just this. The task here is to decide whether a word that has just appeared on a computer screen is a real word in their language (e.g. 'broom'), or a nonword (e.g. 'broam'). How long it takes people to make a response (a *lexical decision response*) depends on all sorts of things. Nonwords that are similar to real words take longer to say 'no' to than nonwords that are very different, and real words that are used infrequently take longer to say 'yes' to than words that are used frequently. But the recognition of a real word can also be faster if a related word has been seen beforehand—lexical decision times to 'broom' are faster following 'witch' than following the unrelated *control* word 'pitch'. This effect is called priming; 'witch' (the prime) can prime 'broom' (the target), 'doctor' can prime 'nurse', 'bug' can prime 'ant', and so on. Activating the prime causes the target to be activated faster.

Conversely, if a target word is activated faster (primed), you can be sure that the priming word must have been activated.

In the mid-1980s, a student of William Marslen-Wilson's, Pienie Zwitserlood, used a version of the priming task called *cross-modal priming* to explore when, during the sound sequence, words are activated. In cross-modal priming, the priming word is presented in the auditory modality, and the target is presented visually. Zwitserlood and Marslen-Wilson reasoned that if lexical entries are activated before the end of a word, and if this activation is all it takes to get priming to related words, it should be possible to find cross-modal priming effects when the visual target word is presented on the screen part way through the auditory presentation of the priming word. So people would hear only the first part of a word, and at the end of that part, a related word (or unrelated control word) would be flashed up on the screen. The actual experiment was performed in Dutch in The Netherlands, but it translates very easily into English.

Zwitserlood used the Dutch equivalent of 'captain', and played people a recording of this word up to and including the /t/. At this point, the sound stopped, and a related word (e.g. 'ship') appeared on the screen. Sure enough, she found priming—the word 'ship' was responded to faster than the corresponding control word. Of course, this simply shows that the lexical entry for 'captain' can be activated before the entire word has been heard. But the clever thing about this experiment was that 'captain' was not the only word compatible with the fragment played to people; 'captive' is just as good a continuation (the words can only be discriminated between on the basis of the final phoneme). And crucially, Zwitserlood also found priming to words related to these alternative continuations. In other words, the two alternatives that were compatible with the auditory input were both activated. And just to really prove the point, Zwitserlood demonstrated that if the visual targets were flashed up on the screen at the end of (and not part way through) 'captain' or 'captive', then only the related target words were primed—there would be no priming to words related to 'captive' when presented at the end of 'captain'.

So it looks pretty cut-and-dry; as the acoustic input enters the system, we activate all the lexical entries compatible with the input that we have heard so far. This is exactly what Marslen-Wilson's theory had predicted. And as the input becomes incompatible with certain alternatives, so those alternative entries begin to de-activate. But there was a further aspect to Zwitserlood's experiments that was important.

Recall that one of the determinants of response times in lexical decision experiments is the frequency of occurrence of that word in the language at large; the more common words are responded to faster than the less common words. And although the more common words tend also to be the shorter words, it has been shown that this is not simply a length effect—once length is held constant, it is still the case that more frequent words appear to be recognized faster than less frequent words. The priming words used by Zwitserlood ('captain' and 'captive' being just one pair) did not have the same frequencies; one member of the pair was always more frequent. And what Zwitserlood observed was that there was generally more priming from the more frequent word than from the less frequent word. It is as if the lexical entries corresponding to the more frequent words become more strongly activated on the basis of similar acoustic input than their less frequent neighbours. Again, this had been predicted by the theory.

So the cross-modal priming studies show that we activate the entries for all possible words compatible with the acoustic input. But does this not mean that there is a real danger of system overload? How do we prevent an explosion of lexical possibilities? How do we choose which possibilities are the right ones? And how is it possible that we can activate the meanings of all these words without recognizing that we have done so? Apparently, activation does not imply recognition. But if it does not, what exactly is recognition? What does it mean to say that we recognize (or even hear) a word? And when does this recognition happen? To return to the *OED* metaphor: it looks as if access is what goes on when we activate the possibilities, and recognition is what happens when we (somehow) determine which of these possibilities is the right one. But how do we do that?

The effects of acoustic mismatch

According to Marslen-Wilson's theory, lexical access is a kind of race; different lexical entries compete in the race, but there can be only one winner—we recognize a word when it has been identified as the winner. But for there to be a winner, there have to be losers. So what determines whether, and when, a competitor falls by the wayside?

The most obvious factor is compatibility with the acoustic input. There is extensive evidence showing that *acoustic mismatch* leads to a rapid decline in the activation of a lexical entry. Whereas a word like 'book' might prime 'page', the nonword 'boog' (pronounced to rhyme with 'book') would not—changing the voice onset time (see Chapter 3) of the final phoneme from a /k/ to a /g/ would be enough to cause rapid deactivation of the lexical entry for 'book'. But if the smallest deviation can lead to a decline in activation (and see Chapter 5 for further examples), what is going to happen each time we hear a word pronounced slightly differently, or each time a bit (or worse still, a lot) of background noise changes the acoustic signal? There has to be some *tolerance* in the system.

In fact, it turns out that there is; a slight deviation does not cause a lexical entry to self-destruct, it merely causes a decline in the activation, which means that the activation can pick up again if subsequent input is still compatible with that entry. Of course, if that deviation occurs at the start of a word, it may prevent the intended word from being activated in the first place. But it is not just any small deviation that leads to this; it is the smallest acoustic deviation that could in principle distinguish between one word in the language and another—in other words, the smallest detail that would cause one phoneme to be perceived as another. Indeed, the categorical perception of phonemes discussed in Chapter 3 is an example of how variation in the acoustic signal associated with a particular phoneme is tolerated up to a certain degree, beyond which any further variation causes the sound to be perceived quite differently.

In general, then, a word can be recognized when there has been sufficient mismatch between the acoustic input and that word's competitors. Often this will be before the word's acoustic offset, but sometimes it may be after. 'Ram' could continue as 'ramp' or 'rampart'. But if the sequence being heard was something like 'The ram roamed around', the lexical entries for 'ramp' and 'rampart' would become deactivated when 'roamed' was encountered, resulting in the eventual recognition of 'ram'.

So far so good. But there is one further detail that needs to be considered. Words are rarely spoken in isolation, but are spoken in the (seamless) context of other words coming before and after. And this is important for a number of reasons, not least because people are generally quite lazy in their articulation, and the position and shape of the articulators at any one moment reflects not simply the sound to be produced at that moment, but also the sound that will be produced next. We encountered a version of this phenomenon in Chapter 5 under the guise of co-articulation. Generally, the term is used to describe how a vowel, for instance, can be 'coloured' by the consonants that precede and follow it. The fact that vowels are not perceived categorically allows this colouring to be used in anticipating the identity of the following segment. But something very similar can occur when one consonant is followed by another. And this is where the problems start: if the consonant were to actually change as a result of this process, a mismatch would occur. And this would mean that we would then fail to activate the intended meaning. Just how bad is the problem?

The answer is that it is as bad as having to recognize 'Hameethathimboo' as meaning 'Hand me that thin book'. Word-final consonants such as the /d/ in 'hand', the /t/ in 'that' and the /k/ in 'book' are often dropped completely. And instead of articulating the /n/ in 'thin' by closing off the mouth with the tip of the tongue against the back of the upper teeth (and allowing air through the nasal passage), the speaker might anticipate the following /b/ and instead close off the mouth at the lips (still allowing air through the nasal passage). This would result in 'thin book' being articulated as 'thim book'. And because the /d/ had been dropped from 'hand me', the preceding /n/ may combine with the /m/ to produce 'hamee'. These kinds of changes, generally at the ends of words, are surprisingly common, although the extent to which they occur, and how they occur, can depend on the language being spoken. But if acoustic mismatch leads to the deactivation of lexical candidates, what hope is there of recognizing the intended words after these changes have occurred? If these kinds of effects are more common than not, how could we ever recognize a sentence in its entirety?

The answer, once again, is tolerance. In this case, the tolerance is *context-sensitive*. The nonword 'thim' will activate the meaning associated with 'thin', but only in the context of a following word. But it cannot be just any old word, it has to be a word in the context of which it would have made sense for what was originally an /n/ to become an /m/. Whereas the 'thim' in 'thim book' would activate the lexical entry for 'thin', the 'thim' in 'thim slice' would not. This was demonstrated by another student of William Marslen-Wilson's, Gareth Gaskell, in a series of experiments using variations on the priming theme. This naturally begs the question of how the system 'knows' to do this.

Linguists have produced a whole range of rules which describe the range of circumstances in which these different kinds of word-final changes can occur. The rules are complex—the *Cambridge encyclopedia of language* writes one such rule as: 'an alveolar nasal becomes bilabial before a following bilabial consonant'. Yet despite their complexity, there has been a temptation to believe that (or at least to talk as if) the human mind runs these rules in reverse in order to recover what was originally meant. Do we really do this?

The simplest answer is 'not necessarily'. And one way to imagine what we might do instead is to recall that the task of the infant is to associate sounds with meaning. The infant must therefore associate not just /thin/ with the meaning of 'thin', but also /thim/ with 'thin', and even /thing/ with 'thin' (as in 'The thin carpet was worn through', where 'thin' would be pronounced as /thing/). But what is actually being associated with the meaning of 'thin' is not just the sound that has been heard, but rather the sound that has been heard within a particular context. This context necessarily includes the surrounding sounds. The infant might therefore associate with the meaning of 'thin' all the following: /thin/ in combination with a following /t/ (e.g. 'thin tree'), /thim/ in combination with a following /b/ ('thin book'), or /thing/ in combination with a following /k/ ('thin carpet', where /k/ is the first phoneme of 'carpet'). As an adult, it is then just a matter of recovering whatever meaning was associated with a particular combination of sounds.

Not surprisingly, many linguists have objected to this last possibility—it would require the infant/adult to store all possible pronunciations of each word in all possible contexts. There would be enormous numbers of combinations possible, and it would surely be much easier to simply acquire a very much smaller number of rules to do the same job, each rule applying across a whole range of words (for instance, one rule could apply to all words ending in /n/ when followed by a /b/, /p/, or /m/). Of course, in order to learn the rule, the infant would still have to be exposed to all the different pronunciations in all the different contexts, but at least it would not have to remember each combination of pronunciation and context. And if it did remember each such combination, how much context would be required? The following phoneme? The following word? The entire utterance?

On what basis can anyone reasonably claim that rules are not run in reverse, but that the infant/adult has knowledge of all possible pronunciations in all possible contexts? Surely this would require the most enormous memory space. The fact that the entire OED, which we would also expect to take up a lot of space, fits into something that is less than a millimetre thick and just a few centimetres across does suggest that unimaginably huge volumes of information are none the less manageable. But so what? The brain is hardly a CD-ROM, and its own memory capacity may well be limited, especially given the huge amounts of memory that would be required to store information about all the different pronunciations of all the different words in all their different contexts. But even if all this information could be stored, could it feasibly be learned and feasibly be deployed? And is acquiring, storing, and deploying this information more feasible than acquiring, storing, and deploying what by comparison would be a very small number of rules?

Currently, there is no empirical way to establish conclusively which of these two possibilities we actually use. A rule-based approach appears to have all the advantages stacked up in its favour—it is low on memory, and easily deployed. The alternative approach, based on some representation of the individual pronunciations and their associated contexts, would place an excessive burden on memory, and for all sorts of reasons it has a somewhat implausible ring to it. But then again, so did the idea that we activate the meanings of all the neighbouring words we encounter during the search for the actual word that was spoken. So plausibility is not necessarily a good criterion by which to choose between the possibilities. A more useful criterion concerns the feasibility of the alternatives. This is where, in the absence of data on what we actually do, computational modelling can shed some light on the puzzle. Unfortunately, this means waiting until Chapter 13, and in the meantime we must accept that, one way or another, we can overcome the problems associated with the mispronunciation of words uttered in the context of continuous speech.

Getting at the meaning

We know something about how, and when, lexical entries are activated, and how, and when, they may become deactivated. But what information is contained within a lexical entry? How do we square a question like this with the idea that a lexical entry is simply a kind of neural circuit? Returning to the analogy of a combination lock, we can ask the same kind of question: given the arrangement of its tumblers, what information does a combination lock contain? On the one hand, there is a sense in which a combination lock itself contains no information at all. It is simply a physical arrangement of potentially moveable objects. On the other hand, the precise arrangement of the tumblers determines which

exact sequence will open the lock—the appropriate sequence has meaning by virtue of causing an effect to occur that is specific to that sequence,
and to no other. In this sense, the combination lock does contain information, and a skilled locksmith would be able to examine the arrangement of the tumblers, and figure out, on the basis of this information, the
sequence required to open the lock. Similarly, even if a lexical entry is
nothing more than the neural equivalent of a combination lock, it contains information by virtue of the effect that an input sequence can have
(and in Chapter 9 we shall discuss further the nature of meaning, and the
nature of the effects that a word may cause). And just as we can still refer
to lexical entries when what we are really talking about is some complex
neural circuitry, so we can refer to meaning when what we are really
talking about is the result of this circuitry becoming activated.

So lexical entries are where the meaning of a word resides. But one of
the first things one notices when opening up a large written dictionary is
that most words have more than one meaning. The word 'pitch', for
example, was introduced in Chapter 1 without any explicit definition.
And yet it would be almost impossible to look up the word and not
discover that it has several distinct senses or meanings: to pitch a ball; to
pitch a tent; the pitch of a roof; the pitch of a musical sound; the pitch
you get from distilling tar; the sales pitch; the football pitch, and so on.
Presumably the mental lexicon must also reflect this multiplicity of
meaning. But what are the implications for how we retrieve a single
meaning? Do we activate all possible meanings of a word that is
ambiguous and has more than one meaning? Do we somehow scan all
the meanings (to return, momentarily, to the dictionary metaphor) until
we get to the first one that is appropriate given the context in which the
word occurs, ignoring any others that we have yet to get reach? Or do
we somehow activate only the contextually appropriate meaning, so
avoiding a cluttering of our minds with all those other, inappropriate,
meanings?

In the late 1970s, David Swinney, then at Tufts University, published
a paper that was to prove extremely influential. Not only did it demonstrate (after many years of bitter argument and counter-argument) that
the alternative meanings of ambiguous words are activated, but it was
also the first demonstration of cross-modal priming, which we
encountered earlier. The specific question that Swinney considered was
whether or not we activate the alternative meanings of words even
when those words are heard in the context of sentences which are
compatible with only one of the meanings of the word. For instance, in

'He swam across to the far side of the river and scrambled up the bank before running off', it would hardly be appropriate to interpret 'bank' as a financial institution. Similarly in 'He walked across to the far side of the street and held up the bank before running off', it would hardly be appropriate to interpret 'bank' as a river bank (or to interpret 'hold up' as 'support'). In order to explore what actually happens when we hear sentences such as these, Swinney played people sentences similar in principle to these ones and immediately after they heard the word 'bank', he flashed up on a screen either 'money' or 'river'. The people knew to make a lexical decision as soon as they saw a word appear on the screen. Swinney found that, irrespective of which of the two sentences had been used, both 'money' and 'river' were primed. This showed that both meanings of 'bank' must have been activated.

Of course, at some stage, the inappropriate meaning of 'bank' must be suppressed, and, sure enough, Swinney found that if he presented the target words two or three syllables later (that is, *downstream* from the ambiguous word), only the target related to the contextually appropriate sense of the word was primed.

These findings aroused an enormous amount of interest, not least because some subsequent studies failed to show the same results. These studies found that in context, only the appropriate meaning was activated. Of course, certain meanings of a word will be produced more (or less) often than certain others, and the evidence suggests that the more frequent the meaning, the greater its activation. This is entirely consistent with the idea, discussed earlier in connection with Zwitserlood's experiment, that the more frequent a word, the greater the activation of its lexical entry. If the institution meaning of 'bank' is more frequent than the river meaning of 'bank', the institution meaning will be the more active. And if, in these studies, the inappropriate meaning is sufficiently infrequent, it might look as if the contextually inappropriate meaning has not been activated, but what has in fact happened is that its activation was so low that it was very quickly deactivated by the context. So despite some initial controversy surrounding Swinney's results, the general consensus is that they are right—we do activate all meanings of an ambiguous word.

At around the same time that Swinney performed his cross-modal priming experiments, Michael Tanenhaus and colleagues at Wayne State University in Detroit performed a similar experiment, using words that were ambiguous between a noun (e.g. 'watch' as a time-piece) and a verb (e.g. 'watch' as a kind of looking). In a sentence like 'John began to watch the game', only a verb can follow the fragment 'John began to . . .'. Armed with this information, we could scan a written dictionary and look only at the entry for 'watch'-as-verb, ignoring the entry for 'watch'-as-noun, and hence ignoring the time-piece meaning of 'watch'. But does the same thing happen when we search the mental lexicon? Can we eliminate from the lexical search all the words whose syntactic categories are inappropriate given the preceding words in the sentence? Apparently not. Tanenhaus found that the alternative meanings of 'watch', related to time-piece and looking, were activated when people listened to sequences such as 'John began to'. So knowledge of the type of word that must follow (that is, knowledge of its syntactic category) is not used to help constrain the possibilities. But why not? Is this some arbitrary property of the workings of the mental lexicon? Or is there some reason behind this?

Once again, perhaps we are too used to the convenient abbreviations that our written dictionaries provide us with; just because written dictionaries include the syntactic categories corresponding to the alternative meanings of each word does not mean that the mental lexicon does likewise. After all, the *OED* also includes the approximate date at which each word entered the language—but just because the *OED* includes this information, and can search for words on the basis of this information, does not mean that the mental lexicon does likewise. So perhaps the simplest interpretation of Tanenhaus's 'watch' experiment is to suppose that syntactic categories are not listed separately as in a dictionary. Why should they be? If the syntactic category of a word is nothing more than a reflection of its meaning (and there will be more about this in Chapters 9 and 13), they will not be listed separately. The meaning would have to be activated before the syntactic inappropriateness could be judged. And when we hear an ambiguous word like 'bank', how could we judge which meanings were inappropriate if we did not activate them all?

It looks, again, as if all that psycholinguists have done is come up with the obvious (although it is probably true to say that hindsight makes the results of any scientific endeavour seem obvious). But, however obvious it may be, the view that has developed of how we access the mental lexicon is substantially different from the view we might originally have had on the basis of how we access a dictionary like the *OED*. Accessing the mental lexicon is far less restrained. We activate all the lexical entries compatible with the developing sequence of sounds entering the ear. If the same sequence of sounds has more than one meaning, we activate all the meanings compatible with that sequence and only subsequently are the contextually inappropriate meanings suppressed. Of course, an inevitable by-product of all this is that we must activate all manner of spurious, unintended, meanings. But given that the mental lexicon must reside within the neural circuitry of the brain, this is in fact a natural (if initially counter-intuitive) way for the system to work—the neural circuits are like so many combination locks, and as the speech input unfolds through time, so do the tumblers of the different combination locks move around, until eventually, just those combination locks whose sequences are completed spring open.

Unlocking the combination

How far should the combination lock analogy be pushed? To return to the opening theme of this chapter, might this not be just another example of an analogy that is simply inappropriate, simply wrong, or simply confusing? Maybe. But the continued use of the analogy helps explain one further fact concerning the manner in which we access the mental lexicon. The fact itself concerns a prediction that can be made on the basis of the way a combination lock operates, although when the prediction was originally tested, combination locks were probably the furthest things from the mind of the tester. The prediction, quite simply, is that wherever in the speech input a sequence is found that could correspond to a word, the lexical entry for that word should be activated. After all, rotate the dial of an old-fashioned mechanical combination lock and so long as the sequence of rotations contains, somewhere within it, the correct sequence for that lock, the lock will open.

In the late 1980s, Richard Shillcock carried out an experiment to determine whether, for example, listeners activate the lexical entry corresponding to 'bone' if they hear the sequence 'He carefully placed the trombone on the table'. He used the cross-modal priming paradigm described earlier in which a word related to 'bone' (e.g. 'rib') would be flashed up on a screen at the offset of 'trombone'. Crucially, he also included sentences like 'He carefully placed the bone on the table'. Shillcock found that the amount of priming he got from 'trombone' to 'rib' was the same as that from 'bone' to 'rib'. In other words, the lexical entry corresponding to the word 'bone' is activated even when 'bone' is heard simply as part of the word 'trombone'.

Subsequent studies (in Italian) have shown similar effects with sentences equivalent to 'He broke all records for the new distance'. Here, the lexical entry corresponding to the word 'nudist' is activated (embedded in the sequence 'new distance'). And although no one has tested for which lexical entries are activated on hearing 'rampart', it would be surprising if the lexical entries for 'ram', 'am', 'amp', 'ramp', 'part', and 'art' were not activated in addition to that for 'rampart'.

So it looks increasingly as if the process of lexical access is in fact rather simple: we consider all possible hypotheses about what could be present at any point in the incoming speech signal. But with this simplicity comes an obvious worry; surely there would be an explosion of possibilities? How do we determine which are the right ones? How do we know that we should be reading about 'a new discovery' and that nudists have nothing to do with it (even though the meaning of 'nudist' is activated)? Presumably, the answers are to be found in the manner by which we string the meanings of words together to give a coherent meaning to the entire sentence. Why we are not even conscious of all these spurious words is another matter. But, perhaps unfortunately, consciousness is beyond the remit of our ascent of Babel.

Psycholinguists have only brushed the tip of a theoretical iceberg. Many questions remain, and controversies abound. For instance, we are still unsure as to the nature of the bilingual lexicon. Only now are we developing theories concerning the processing of morphologically complex words—recall that many of the questions asked in that section of this chapter were never answered. And only now are we developing a better understanding of the tools we use, and the effects that the tools themselves can have on the phenomena we try to observe. But one thing is for certain: whatever the limits of our understanding, we now know not to trust whatever intuitions we may have had on the basis of the dictionaries on our bookshelves.

Time flies like an arrow

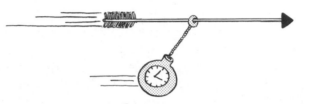

Without words there could be no language. Finding them, hidden away within the neural structures of our brains, is half the battle, but only half. Words are more than simple gestures, like pointing, or raising the eyebrows, or shaking the head. We use sequences of words to convey ideas, and by combining the words in different ways we change the idea being conveyed. Gestures and other signs do not have this property. Although they too convey ideas, the idea they convey is not altered simply by altering the sequence of signs. So the words themselves are only one ingredient—recognizing the way in which they are combined is another. Discovering that 'Sue would like to marry you' may be the most important thing in the world to you, but only if it can be distinguished from 'You would like to marry Sue'. Although this might also be true, it would say nothing about what Sue felt about it. So which way the words are combined is important. But it is important, and has meaning, only insofar as both the speaker and the hearer (or the writer and the reader) share some common knowledge regarding the significance of one combination or another. This shared knowledge is *grammar*.

But what has this to do with the title of this chapter? In fact, the title illustrates one of the most remarkable things about the way we interpret words and their combination. 'Time flies like an arrow' is a classic example used in textbooks on psycholinguistics. It is an important example because, time and time again, the textbooks get it wrong. They remark how, in principle, 'Time flies like an arrow' could be interpreted not as a proverb concerning the passage of time and the flight of an arrow, but as something similar to the sentence 'Fruit flies like a banana'. Well, that is certainly true, but hardly riveting. Presumably our lack of experience of any insect called a 'time fly' means that the only sensible interpretation we can come up with is the one in which time is doing the flying (not that you have ever seen it fly). But what really makes this sentence interesting is the way in which the textbooks get it wrong. There are not just two possible interpretations of the sentence, but at least 50. And if, instead of reading this sentence, we heard it, there would be well over 100.[3] And this is the puzzle—our knowledge of the meanings of the different words, and our knowledge about what is allowed by the grammar of the English language, permits each and every one of these different interpretations. So why are we not aware of them? Why are we not aware of the problems involved in eating pizza with a friend, or with a nice bottle of wine, or with extra anchovies, or even with a knife and fork? What prevents our brains from clogging up with the multitude of possibilities? Why do ambiguities pass us by without even the merest flicker of recognition?

The answer is not as straightforward as one would hope, and has to do, in part, with the way we use our knowledge of grammar.

The conventional aspects of language

The grammar of a language is in fact nothing more than a set of conventions, passed on from generation to generation. If we think of a sentence as conveying information about who-did-what-to-whom (or

[3] The first word could be 'time', as measured by a watch, or 'time' as in 'time that athlete', or 'thyme' (the herb) if spoken. 'Flies' could be what a plane does, or it could be an insect, or the zipper on a trouser (in British English). A native of Japan, who would not distinguish between /l/ and /r/ (see Chapter 3) could interpret the spoken form of 'flies' as 'fries' (which are either potato chips or the way you cook chips). 'Time flies' could be a kind of fly, a command, a new kind of zipper (similar in principle to a 'time lock'), or a subject and its verb. 'Like' could be what fruit flies think of bananas, or it could mean 'in the same way as' ('watch him like a hawk'). 'Arrow' could be the thing that is shot from a bow, or the thing that directs you in one direction or another. And there must be at least one person called Ann Arrow somewhere in the world. And should you 'watch him like a hawk would' or 'watch him like you'd watch a hawk'? Combine these possibilities together in all the different ways that the grammar of English permits, and you end up with more than 50 different interpretations (more than 80 if you are Japanese). It does not stop there — anything following 'a' or 'an' could refer to a specific thing, or any example of that thing ('he's looking for a book' could mean any book would do, or that he is looking for a specific one). Finally, the spoken version could even be understood as 'time flies like a narrow . . .' and 'time flies liken arrow(s to . . .)', giving a total of around *180* different interpretations.

what), then there is a convention, in English, for the subject to come
before the verb (who before did–what), and for the verb to come before
the object (did–what before whom). But this is not true of all languages.
It is simply a convention; it is true of languages like English and Italian,
but it is not true of Turkish or Japanese (subject-object-verb), or either
classical Hebrew or Welsh (verb-subject-object). Similarly, there is a
convention in English for adjectives to precede the nouns they modify
('the green spaghetti'), but in Italian and Spanish (and other languages
too), they tend to follow the nouns they modify ('la pasta verde').

   These conventions are no different really from the convention we
have adopted to interpret '512' as 'five hundred and twelve' and not
'two hundred and fifteen', or from the convention to drive in one
country on the left and in another country on the right. If you fail to
observe the convention, you do so with potentially disastrous consequences. And just as which side of the road you drive on determines on
which side of the car the foot pedals are found, so linguists have found
that certain grammatical conventions also tend to go together—if you
have one, you also have the other. For instance, if the prepositions in
the language come at the beginning of each prepositional phrase ('the
man *with* the freckles'), then the verbs will generally come before their
objects ('she *liked* the man'). But if the verbs come after their objects, as
happens in Japanese for example, then the prepositions generally come
at the end of each prepositional phrase. In contemporary linguistic

theory, the preposition/verb case arises because prepositions are assumed to have a grammatical function that is very similar to verbs— they both specify relationships between things: between 'the man' and 'the freckles' and between 'she' and 'the man'.

Whatever the conventions in any one language, their purpose is to signal specific patterns of meaning. The following two sentences, like the example given in the first paragraph, contain exactly the same words, and yet their meanings could not be more different:

   Politicians think that the public don't know.
      The public know that politicians don't think.

But so what? The same cooking ingredients, mixed and cooked in a different order, can lead to radically different dishes. What is so special about grammar? The words 'lips' and 'slip' contain exactly the same letters but in a different order, and they too mean different things—so why can we not simply say that each word in a sentence functions in exactly the same way as each phoneme or letter in a word?

One reason is that whereas we know the meanings of only a finite number of words, we have the potential to understand an infinite variety of sentences. We can store in the mental lexicon the meanings of each word we know, but we cannot store in some kind of super-lexicon all the meanings of all the possible sentences that we could ever understand. Instead, we have to create the meaning out of the parts. But what is it, exactly, that we create?

Within an individual word, each phoneme fulfils the same function: to narrow down the search through the mental lexicon. In this respect, the role of any one phoneme (or letter, if written) is the same as that of any other. But the same is not true of the words in a sentence. To return to an example used in Chapter 4: the function of 'the girl' in 'The girl thinks the language is beautiful' is different from the function of 'the language'; 'the girl' is the subject of the verb 'thinks'—she is the one doing the thinking while the language is, according to her, the thing that is being beautiful. So part of the process of creating, or more properly deriving, the meaning of a sentence involves figuring out the roles that each of the participants in the sentence plays. The term *participant* here refers simply to the different things that are themselves referred to in the sentence. So the thought 'the language is beautiful' participates in the sentence, and has a role to play as whatever was being thought. A verb like 'thinks' signals two roles: one for whoever is doing the thinking, and one for whatever is being thought. A verb like 'put' signals three roles: one for whoever is doing the putting, one for what is being put, and another for where it is being put. The grammar is simply the knowledge that tells us where in the sentence to find the things that fill these different roles. If we cannot find those things, we cannot understand the sentence.

This brings us back to an earlier theme—different languages employ different conventions for telling us where, within the sentence, to look for the recipients of the various roles that need to be assigned. In a language like English, we rely predominantly on word order. There is nothing to distinguish the different participants in 'The boy gave the letter to the teacher' except for their relative ordering within the sentence; the boy gave, the teacher received, and the letter was given. But languages like German, for instance, do not rely solely on word order:

▴─   *der Junge gab den Brief dem Lehrer*
     (the boy gave the letter (to) the teacher)

Here, different versions of the word 'the' (in this case, 'der', 'den', and 'dem') are used to reflect the role that the following noun plays in the sentence, and notice that as a result, the German version requires no preposition corresponding to the English 'to'. 'Der', 'den', and 'dem' are the same word, just *inflected* differently (see Chapter 6 for more on inflection and morphology). This kind of explicit marking of roles is called *case-marking*. And languages which explicitly mark their roles in this way do not require such a rigid ordering of the words as a language like English. Indeed, some languages allow almost (but not quite) un-restricted word order, relying instead on case-marking. So the German sentence given above could also appear as:

▴─   *den Brief gab der Junge dem Lehrer*
     dem Lehrer gab der Junge den Brief
     der Junge gab dem Lehrer den Brief

So different languages employ different conventions for marking the roles of the different participants in a sentence (or, more correctly, in the event described by the sentence). It all sounds quite simple, really. The grammar of the language is like a recipe; follow the recipe, mix the ingredients in the right order, and you end up creating exactly what the author of the recipe intended you to end up with. In language, you end up reconstructing the idea that the speaker or writer intended to convey. So what is the problem?

Coping with ambiguity

Often, the grammar-as-recipe provides alternative ways to mix the ingredients, and this is why 'time flies' could be a term to describe zippers that operate like a time lock on a safe, only opening at certain times. One of the jobs of the reader/listener is to work out which is the right mixture—that is, to work out which grammatical convention is intended by the writer/speaker. It is true that some of the blame for having to do this rests with the fact that the individual words within a sentence can often have more than one interpretation ('flies' as a noun or as a verb, for instance). But there are many cases where the words can be totally unambiguous, and yet we still have to figure out which of several grammatical interpretations is the right one. Eating pizza, with one's family or with one's fingers, is a case in point. The grammar of English permits whatever is in the position after 'with' to be assigned a variety of roles, but which role is actually assigned appears to depend on the meaning of whatever will fill the role. But does this mean that we recognize the meaning of something, and try and fit to it all possible roles that are permitted by the grammar? In effect, do we access all possible interpretations before picking the most plausible? And if not, how else could it possibly work?

Figuring out what to do with whatever, or whoever, you happen to be eating your pizza with is relatively easy—as long as you can figure out the alternatives, you can settle on the most plausible one. But if someone left the book they were reading on the bus, was it the leaving or the reading that happened on the bus? And if someone was supposed to remind you that you were going to read to them tomorrow, was it the reading or the reminding that would happen tomorrow? Yet again, unless explicitly alerted to the ambiguity, we probably would not notice it. But unlike the pizza case, these cases cannot be resolved on the basis that, of all the alternatives, some are plausible and some are not. One can just as plausibly leave something on the bus as read it on the bus, or read to someone tomorrow as be reminded tomorrow. So it is not just a matter of rejecting implausible alternatives. Something else is going on. But what?

All the examples discussed so far have involved ambiguities that go unnoticed. Unless our attention is explicitly drawn to them, we tend not to notice the ambiguities we encounter in our everyday language. Sometimes, however, an ambiguity is noticed, or rather, the consequence of not noticing the ambiguity is noticed, and with surprising effect. A photograph in the *Sunday Times* of Sam Shepard, the actor, and Chuck Yeager, the first pilot to fly faster than the speed of sound, was accompanied by the following caption:

 Sam Shepard, who plays the legendary test pilot Chuck Yeager, with the man himself (now a retired brigadier-general) and a replica of 'Glamorous Glennis', the X-1 named after his wife that crashed the sound barrier.

Some wife . . . And the following were headlines in US newspapers:

 Retired priest may marry Springsteen
Crowds rushing to see Pope trample six to death
Sisters reunited after 18 years in checkout line at supermarket

And of course, these kinds of example are restricted neither to newspapers nor to the USA; church bulletins in Britain are also a rich source of grammatical innovation:

The ladies of the church have cast off clothing of every kind. They can be seen in the church basement Saturday.
For those of you who have children and don't know it, we have a nursery downstairs.

Finally, a particularly innovative offer:

 Don't let worry kill you—let the church help.

As each of these examples shows, not noticing an ambiguity can have interesting consequences. With the exception of that last case, little harm is done—the consequence is that we simply interpret the sentence the wrong way. But there are other cases where the consequence is that we fail to make sense of the sentence, and we think either that it is ungrammatical, or that a word is missing:

 If someone read this sentence thought it was ungrammatical because it missed an 'and' between 'sentence' and 'thought' they would be wrong. The same person might tell the writer that he or she could not understand to get help.

These two sentences are perfectly grammatical, even if on first reading they did not seem to be. You probably interpreted the first as meaning that the person was doing the reading. But 'someone read this sentence' can also be used to mean 'a person who was read this sentence'—the word 'read' is ambiguous between a main verb and a passive verb; a verb like 'give' does not suffer this problem, and 'The person given this sentence' is easily interpreted as a passive form. The reason readers consistently misinterpret that first sentence in the last paragraph is because they consistently interpret 'read' as a main verb when it should be interpreted as a passive. But why?

In the second problematic sentence, the sequence 'The same person might tell the writer that' is ambiguous because the word 'that' can either introduce whatever it was that was told, or it can introduce some further information about the writer (e.g. 'The writer that wrote this book')—'that' can signal two different roles for the following material. If the sentence had started 'The same person might want the writer that', there would be no confusion, because the verb 'want' is incompatible with one of the interpretations of 'that', forcing it to be ruled out.

What appears to be going on in these problematic cases is that there is a consistent preference, consistent across all people, to interpret 'read' or 'that' in a way that is in fact inconsistent with the rest of the sentence. Again, why?

One further piece in the puzzle is that these kinds of effects can occur even in the absence of words such as 'that' and 'read', which have more than one meaning. Earlier, we considered the example of being reminded to read something tomorrow. Here is a similar, but now much more problematic version:

≜   *I was lent a book that I shall avidly read yesterday.*

Most readers will have tried to interpret 'I shall avidly read yesterday' as a single grammatical unit, and this turns out to be the wrong decision because the *future tense* of 'I shall read' is incompatible with 'yesterday'. The only way to make sense of the sentence (that is, to interpret it grammatically) is to assume instead that yesterday is when the lending must have happened. Once again, we must ask why there is such a consistent preference for one attempted reading rather than for another.

Why we cope the way we do

The reason we all show such consistent preferences in the face of ambiguity has been the source of considerable controversy since the early 1970s. This is not simply because there are different theories regarding the explanation for these phenomena (each theory having important, and different, implications for the way language understanding occurs), but because researchers have often disagreed about how to interpret the experimental tools they employ in their search for an answer (the dip-stick problem outlined in Chapter 5).

The ambiguities we have considered so far arise because at some point in the sentence, it is unclear which grammatical convention is being signalled. One school of thought maintains that there exist preferences to assume certain kinds of convention rather than certain others. In fact, the descriptions that linguists come up with for describing sentences and their meanings suggest that the less preferred interpretations in all the cases described earlier (and there are many others) all require more complex descriptions, and perhaps more complex mental processes. So perhaps ambiguities are resolved in favour of whichever grammatical convention leads to the simplest interpretation.

Another school of thought maintains that when faced with a choice of conventions, we assume that the most frequently used of those conventions is the one that is intended. Of course, it may turn out that the most frequently used conventions (or *grammatical structures*) are also the least complex, but the basis on which the choice is made would not be in terms of complexity itself.

The choice could even be made on the basis of which structure is most frequently associated with the individual words in the ambiguous part of the sentence. For example, 'She told' can be followed by all sorts of things:

≜   *She told . . .*
          . . . Sam.
          . . . a story.
          . . . Sam off.
          . . . Sam a story.
          . . . Sam about the Princess.
          . . . Sam that it was bedtime.

Each one of these corresponds to a different structure associated with 'told', and they are all used with different frequencies. When we read 'She told Sam . . . ', perhaps we anticipate whichever grammatical structure is most frequently associated with the word 'told'. Similarly, 'read' as a main verb occurs more commonly than 'read' as a passive, so perhaps we assume the main verb form just because it is the most frequently occurring.

What makes these schools of thought so interesting is the counterintuitive claim they make about the way language understanding proceeds. They both agree that ambiguities involving grammatical structure (that is, involving a decision with respect to which grammatical convention is intended) are resolved without taking into account the meaning of the words involved.

This last idea sounds absurd. Surely we do take into account meaning?

Putting things in context

Until the mid–1980s, the majority of work on these ambiguous sentences involved looking at the problems people have with these sentences in isolation—that is, without the usual context that might accompany these sentences in normal conversation. (We shall come to how this was done in a short while.) Similarly, many researchers interested in how children learn the significance of different kinds of grammatical structure studied children's understanding of different kinds of sentence, without taking into account the sorts of context that would be appropriate for those sentences. But in the early 1980s, Stephen Crain discovered at the University of California that children's abilities changed quite remarkably as soon as they were given the sentences in a context that 'made sense'. For instance, it was well established that young children have problems with certain kinds of *relative clause*—the underlined sequence in the following example:

≡   *The elephant that a giraffe bumped against lay down and went to sleep.*

(Elephants and giraffes are apparently more interesting to children than many other things.) Researchers can investigate children's ability by asking them to act out whatever the sentence means using toy models. And often, children would act out the elephant sentence assuming that it was the elephant that bumped against the giraffe, and not the other way around—they would not distinguish between that last sentence and this:

≡   *The elephant that bumped against a giraffe lay down and went to sleep.*

But what Crain took into account was that, generally, relative clauses are used so that the listener or reader can figure out which elephant is being referred to, on the assumption that there is more than one. In a variety of studies, he and his colleague Henry Hamburger found that children *could* act out the event described by each sentence, but only if there was more than one elephant. Children could even *produce* the appropriate relative clauses when shown these events. So whereas research into how children interpret isolated sentences concluded that children of a certain age could not distinguish between certain kinds of grammatical structure, research which embedded these same sentences in an appropriate context showed that children could distinguish between the different structures. The moral for research into adult sentence processing was clear: sentences should be studied in the contexts in which they might normally occur.

There followed, as a result of this research, a number of experiments into adult sentence processing that tried to find out whether some of the preferences we encountered earlier would go away if the sentences were embedded in suitable contexts. One common technique for finding this out involves seating people in front of a computer screen and measuring the movements of their eyes as they read a sentence. There are different ways of keeping track of eye movements, but perhaps the simplest involves shining an infra-red beam into the eye. Some of this is reflected back from the white of the eye (the *sclera*), and the more the eyes turn, the more white shows, and the greater the reflection. This can be measured using a photo-cell, which puts out a voltage in proportion to the amount of reflection. By having the person look at different parts of the screen, one can equate the voltage with position, and so figure out where the eyes are looking at each moment.

Consider the following sentence (which is a slightly modified version of one of the earlier problematic ones):

 Sam told the writer that he couldn't understand to get some help from a decent editor.

Because of the preference to interpret 'that' as introducing a message (and not as introducing a relative clause), the segment 'to get' will be particularly difficult to interpret. Generally, a number of things can happen when reading a problematic region: either the eyes spend more time on it, or they move back to earlier parts of the sentence, or they do both, and generally this is all quite unconscious (see Chapter 11 for more about eye movements). By keeping track of what the eyes do when they get to 'to get', we can figure out whether that region is problematic or not. Of course, we need some sort of baseline against which to compare our patterns so that we can be sure that, when there is a problem, the pattern is readily distinguishable from when there is no problem. This can be done by replacing the verb 'told' with the verb 'asked', which does not allow the word 'that' to be interpreted as introducing a message:

Sam asked the writer that he couldn't understand to get some help from a decent editor.

In this case, we would not expect any problem reading 'to get', as there is now only one possible interpretation for the sentence (and so there is no chance that there could be a preference to choose the wrong one).

The pattern of eye movements in the 'told' case is indeed different from the pattern in the 'asked' case, reflecting the difference between when there is, and when there is not, a problem with 'to get'. We can now ask what will happen if the 'told' case is embedded in a context which mentions that there are several writers (a bit like the several elephants in Stephen Crain's studies), and which also mentions that Sam did not understand one of them.

If Crain's work with children generalizes to adults, we should find that people have no problem reading these sentences, and that the pattern of eye movements is the same irrespective of whether, for instance, the verb 'told' is used or the verb 'asked' is used. In fact, when the appropriate experiments were run, this is exactly what was found—the difficulties experienced when these sentences were read in isolation completely disappeared when they were instead embedded in a natural context.

As a result of experiments such as these, it began to look as if at least certain kinds of ambiguity could be resolved by taking into account the way in which the alternative interpretations (that is, their meanings) fitted in with the context. The general consensus now is that in fact a whole variety of factors influence the decisions that have to be made when an ambiguity is found. The fit with context is one of these factors, but so it seems is the frequency of occurrence of the different structures associated with the ambiguous words. Accounts based on frequency originated in the early 1980s, but it was only in the early to mid-1990s, when a sufficient number of different experiments had been run, all using different sentences, that it was possible to analyse all the data together and see what factors could possibly explain the overall pattern across the different studies. A number of subsequent studies then manipulated these factors, by using, for instance, different verbs that were associated with the same alternative structures but with different frequencies. They showed that there were occasions when interpretations were chosen according to their frequency of occurrence with that particular verb.

Of course, what may be important may not be the frequency of occurrence of the grammatical structures associated with each word, but rather the frequency of occurrence of the different meanings associated with each word. One might well ask how one could tell the two apart, and this is a big problem, because the meaning of a word determines the grammatical structures in which that word can be found. This is one of those cases where two opposing theories have gradually inched closer and closer until they have become, in effect, the same. It is rather like arguing about whether a bottle of wine is half full or half empty.

Where does this leave us? One consequence of different kinds of information being taken into account when resolving ambiguities, is that if one kind of information is missing—for instance, if there is no contextual information available on which basis to interpret what is being read or heard—other kinds of information will be used instead. Many of those cases where preferences were observed when sentences were read in isolation can probably now be explained by frequency of occurrence. But there is still much controversy over exactly what kinds of information are used, and whether certain kinds of information take precedence over certain other kinds. Is the plausibility of the alternative role assignments more important than the frequency with which the alternative grammatical structures occur? And what about the fit with context? Does that take precedence over the relative frequencies? Or is precedence the wrong way to think about the interaction between the different kinds of knowledge? Do they instead each narrow down (or *constrain*) the range of possible interpretations, with no one kind of information more or less influential than any other kind? There are, currently, no hard and fast answers to these questions, but we shall return to them in Chapter 13, and will discuss a possible resolution of some of them.

A role for prosody

Many kinds of information may influence the decisions that must be made when ambiguities are encountered. But until now, we have ignored one potentially important source of information. We have ignored it because we have also ignored the distinction between written and spoken language. What the spoken form contains that the written lacks is, of course, *prosody* (intonation, rhythm, pausing, and so on—see Chapter 2 for a more complete definition). For instance, the sequence 'Sam told the writer that he couldn't understand . . .' would be uttered very differently depending on whether everything after the word 'that' was supposed to be something about the writer or something about the message. And this information could probably be used to disambiguate the sequence. But does this mean that it is a waste of time studying these kinds of sentence in their written form? Fortunately (for those people who study them), the answer is 'no'. Many of the ambiguities we have encountered are as ambiguous in the spoken form as in the written form. Whether the waiter picks up the pizza with the extra anchovies, or whether he picks up the pizza with the oven gloves, cannot be resolved on the basis of prosodic differences alone—linguists do not always find any in these cases. Instead, this example would be resolved with reference to whether there was just one pizza on the kitchen table, or more than one. So the principles we derive by studying sentences which might be resolved by prosodic information still apply to other sentences which cannot be resolved (or are not resolved) prosodically.

But the presence of prosodic variation in the spoken form is important in other ways, and not just in terms of being yet another source of information for disambiguating the kinds of ambiguity we have encountered so far. The extent to which the different words may be emphasized, or stressed, conveys important additional information that is not conveyed by the words themselves. In the following dialogue, the word that receives the main stress (in the spoken form) is written in capitals:

Joe: Hey—did you hear? Sam took Mary out and bought her a
         pizza!
Mike: You're wrong—Sam didn't buy Mary a PIZZA
         [he bought her something else]

The sequence in parentheses indicates the additional meaning conveyed by the stress. Each of the following could also have been uttered in response to that first 'Did you hear?' sentence:

You're wrong—Sam didn't buy MARY a pizza
    [he bought it for someone else]
You're wrong—Sam didn't BUY Mary a pizza
    [he made her one]
You're wrong—Sam DIDN'T buy Mary a pizza
    [he did something else, or nothing at all]
You're wrong—SAM didn't buy Mary a pizza
    [someone else did]

In each one of these cases, the speaker can use *emphatic stress* to convey some extra meaning in addition to the literal meaning of the sentence itself. But whether we would say that the sentence 'Sam didn't buy Mary a pizza', in its written form, is ambiguous, because we cannot figure out which of the many alternative meanings is intended, is unclear. Does the stress disambiguate the alternative meanings, or add alternative meanings? Probably, in some cases it does one, and in other cases it does the other. Either way, there is a lot more to figure out when listening to sentences than one might expect on the basis of our experience of reading them.

So the role of prosody in all of this is still unclear. Although there are extremely good accounts of what kinds of thing prosody can and cannot signal, there is still considerable controversy about when the signals are used. Are they used after all the other things are worked out, like ambiguity, or literal meaning? Or can they influence the ways in which these other things are worked out in the first place? Even though these issues have been around for a long time, it is only very recently that researchers have begun to explore these issues. At present, they are far from being resolved.

On minds, meanings, and grammar

There is no doubt that in order to recognize meaning, we have to recognize the grammatical conventions (including the prosodic ones) that signal that meaning. But although we must construct *mental representations* which capture the meanings conveyed by the sentences we hear and read, do we also construct mental representations that do nothing more than characterize the grammatical conventions themselves? Do we construct mental representations that capture the prosodic characteristics of the spoken sentence without capturing the meaning that these characteristics convey?

The descriptions that linguists use to characterize the grammatical conventions employed in a language are expressed in terms of syntactic categories such as noun and verb. These descriptions encompass the fact that 'The girl likes the language' and 'The boy ate the pizza' share certain common properties; the language is the object of the liking just as the pizza is the object of the eating, and the boy is the eater just as the girl is the liker. A description of this similarity requires no appreciation, in fact, of what the individual words in the two sentences actually mean. We could just as well say of each sentence that 'There is an X being Y'd, and a Z that is doing the Y'ing'. But although this description makes no reference to the meanings of X, Y, and Z, it does nonetheless capture an important element of that meaning. To understand these sentences, it is not enough to simply know the meanings of the words 'girl', 'language', 'likes', and so on. We need also to know that other element. But does this mean that some aspect of our own mental representation of these sentences corresponds to that element? Is there some aspect of our own mental representation of these sentences which is *also* independent of, and expressed without reference to, the meanings of these sentences?

Another way of asking the same question is to ask whether the kinds of mental representations that are constructed when listening to, or reading, a sentence somehow mirror the descriptions and linguistic representations that linguists use. The question is an important one, because of the claim we encountered earlier that certain kinds of ambiguity may be resolved on the basis of which grammatical conventions (which linguistic representations) are least complex, or are most frequently encountered in the language at large. To resolve ambiguities on such bases would presumably require some mental version of those conventions—a version of those conventions that was divorced from the individual meanings they would normally convey.

Whether or not such mental representations are in fact derived as we hear and read is at the heart of many a psycholinguistic debate—what could a psycholinguist possibly want except to discover the nature of the internal representations that are constructed to depict the who-did-what-to-whom of sentence understanding? It is unlikely that we shall ever discover the nature of these representations. We cannot open up the brain and have a look. We must instead look to our theories of what meaning and understanding are, and how they may be contained within the neural structures of the brain. In Chapters 9 and 13 we shall do just this.

To a certain extent, the kinds of ambiguity we have encountered in this chapter have been the battleground on which opposing theories have been paraded and fought over. But ambiguities are just a part of the problem that faces us each time we have to understand a sentence. Sentence processing is not simply a matter of resolving the multitude of ambiguities that can occur in the language. It is about figuring out who or what the individual participants are in the real-world situation being described. It is about figuring out what roles are being played out, and consequently which roles should be assigned to which participants. The kinds of ambiguity we have dealt with so far complicate this whole process because they make it hard to figure these things out. But they do need to be figured out, and it is to how we might do this that we now turn.

Who did what, and to whom?

As children, we work hard to learn about words and the different ways of combining them. As adults, we rarely stop to think about the meanings of the individual words and about how we unscramble their combination. We do not notice that, despite a lifetime spent learning about meaning and grammar, we often ignore both. We use words with no meaning and we ignore grammatical convention.

Words have meanings in much the same way that objects have meanings. We use the objects around us in different ways according to how they work and what they are for. A car, for example, has various things that enable us to use it in a particular way; things like its accelerator, clutch, brakes, gears, and so on. These things contribute to whatever it is that makes a car a car—they contribute to its meaning.

But when we drive that car, we need more than just its accelerator, clutch, brakes and gears. We need also a set of conventions to tell us which side of the road to drive on, what to do at a red light, where not to park, and so on. These conventions are the equivalent of a grammar. So to now say, returning to language, that we ignore meaning and we ignore grammar is to say that we do the linguistic equivalent of driving on the wrong side of the road, through red, with no brakes!

Perhaps that is a slight exaggeration. We do not use words that have no meaning. We just use words whose meanings can change—as if the car had pedals, but what the pedals did could change. And we do not ignore grammar. We just anticipate grammatical conventions before knowing for sure which ones are actually being used—we go through the lights without checking they are green. It all sounds rather dangerous. How do we manage? Which are these words that can take on different meanings? And why the grammatical recklessness?

What we do when we interpret a sentence can be described very simply: we establish who is doing what to whom. If the sentence is a theatre stage, the who and the whom are the actors, and the what determines their roles. If we identify the actors, and identify which particular one is doing what to which other, then we have established the who-did-what-to-whom. Within the sentence, the nouns describe the actors, and the verb conveys the roles being acted out. The grammar, of course, tells us which roles should be assigned to which actors. The problems start to arise when we use words which, on their own, do not describe anything.

In the previous chapter we encountered the ambiguity introduced by the word 'that'. But if ambiguity means that something has more than one meaning, what are the different meanings of 'that'? Its meanings are, in fact, pretty hard to tie down. As we saw in Chapter 7, it is a word whose function, sometimes, is to signal how to interpret subsequent words, either as a relative clause ('the car that he drove'), or as part of a message ('he told her that it was superb'). In these cases, it really has no meaning of its own. But what about when it is used as an alternative to 'this'? Although it still has no really tangible meaning here, what it signals is very different from what it signals in the earlier cases.

Words like 'this' and 'that' are used to direct attention to somewhere, and they are sometimes referred to as *pointing* words. As such, they highlight one of the most important aspects of language—the fact that many of the words in the language refer to things. Pointing is one way to convey what thing is being referred to, but when we speak, we rarely point (except when giving directions), and when we write, pointing is out of the question. Generally, this is not a problem, because words have meaning and the meaning of a word determines what it refers to. In fact, using words can be a lot better than pointing—saying 'Sam bit his tongue' is a lot more specific than saying 'Sam bit' and pointing in the vague direction of his head. So words like 'tongue' are great for referring to things out there in the world. If there happens to be more than one thing out there that has that name, then we can use additional descriptions, like relative clauses, to indicate which specific thing we intend. So we could say 'The baby who's wearing the pretty frock' to indicate which baby ('who', unlike 'that', unambiguously signals a relative clause). But sometimes we need to be able to refer to someone or something that we have just been talking about. In these cases, what could we possibly point at even if we wanted to point? Instead, we use *pronouns* such as 'he', 'she', 'it', 'they', and so on. Sounds simple enough. But, as usual, it is not.

Why 'he' is not 'himself'

In a language like American Sign Language, and other sign languages of the world, the equivalent to using a pronoun is to do something that really is very much like pointing. When one introduces someone into the topic of conversation, the sign for them is made in a particular location of the space in front of the signer. This individual can then be referred to by pointing to that location. But another way of referring to them, for instance as having done something to someone else, is to start the sign for the appropriate verb in the location at which that first individual was introduced, and to finish the sign for that verb in the location at which the second individual (to whom the something was done) was introduced. In this respect, sign languages have the advantage over spoken and written languages. And a part of this advantage is the ability to explicitly represent in space the individuals being referred to. This avoids the kinds of ambiguity that we encounter in sentences like 'The president discussed his resignation with him'. Who did the resigning?

But so what? Surely we normally speak and write in such a way as to avoid these kinds of ambiguity? How often do we really say things like 'The president discussed his resignation with him' without first being absolutely clear about who had resigned and who the president was having his discussion with? How often do parents give each of their children the same name? Not often, because no matter how much they like a name, they probably have an inkling of the confusion they would cause. But does this reflect some startling insight into human nature? Probably not. But the way in which we use pronouns does offer some interesting insights into, if not human nature, human language.

A pronoun like 'him' can be used either to refer to someone physically present, or to refer to someone already mentioned in the conversation. Why a pronoun like 'him', or even 'he', is used instead of an expression like 'the president' (if that is who the pronoun is referring to) will be discussed in more detail in the next chapter. Here, we shall be concerned more with what pronouns cannot refer to. A pronoun cannot refer to just anyone already mentioned. In 'The president wrote him a letter', the pronoun 'him' *cannot* refer to the president. They have to be different people. In a sentence like 'The president wrote himself a letter', the *reflexive* pronoun 'himself' *must* refer to the president. But in 'A friend of the president wrote himself a letter', the reflexive pronoun *must not* refer to the president. The facts surrounding what a reflexive pronoun can and cannot refer to are not too surprising given what it means to use such a pronoun. Generally, it indicates that an action was *self-oriented*—done to oneself—which means that the pronoun should only refer to whoever did the doing. And in a sentence like 'The attorney-general said the president's letter to himself was a fake', the pronoun refers to the president simply because what has been done is a letter, and who *did* the letter is the president.

So much for reflexive pronouns. On the face of it, they look quite easy. Nonreflexive pronouns like 'him' or 'her' can refer to just about anything, but are *other-oriented*; 'him' cannot refer to the president in 'The president wrote him a letter'. It turns out that if you replace a reflexive pronoun ('himself') by an ordinary nonreflexive one ('him'), the 'him' version can never refer to the same person that the 'himself' version would have referred to. This is not just a fact about English. It is apparently true of every language that has both kinds of pronouns.

Intermission: innateness revisited

For years, linguists have searched for properties of language that were universal to all languages. If such properties existed, they would most likely reflect something that was common to the minds of the speakers of all those different languages. The argument has been taken further. Many linguists (and psycholinguists) believe that these universal properties of language must reflect universal and *innate* knowledge about language. Only in this way could each different language have some piece of itself that was the same as an equivalent piece in every other language. The him/himself facts are a good example of this kind of reasoning. Many linguists believe that these facts have to be explained in terms of the child having innate knowledge that reflexive pronouns (like 'himself') must do something different from what nonreflexive pronouns (like 'him') do. Many go further and believe that the child has innate knowledge of what each kind of pronoun does. That is, of what each kind of pronoun can and cannot refer to (the child does not know that 'him' is nonreflexive, or 'himself' reflexive, but has innate knowledge of these types and of what these types should or should not refer to). Some linguists go so far as to suggest that even though children get the facts wrong for quite a while, they still 'know' the facts—there just happen to be various good reasons why they might ignore them.

Children take a long time to learn the correct facts about what pronouns can and cannot refer to. Errors on both kinds of pronoun can be found up until around 10 years of age, although children tend to get pretty good at them by between four and six years (and they learn about what the reflexive 'himself'-like pronouns can refer to sooner than they learn about what the nonreflexive 'him'-like pronouns cannot refer to). When children do make mistakes, they might interpret 'The monkey is tickling him' to mean the monkey is tickling himself.

We shall come back to children in a moment. For now, what counts is that, although pronouns may seem like things of little consequence, they present to linguists and psycholinguists alike an enduring puzzle whose solution is the source of considerable controversy and debate.

Ambiguity, pronouns, and children's instincts

So 'him' and 'himself' cannot refer to the same things if they are in the same position within the sentence. In all likelihood there *is* an innate cause for this, as we shall see.

For every rule there is an exception. In Frisian, a language from the North Netherlands, the equivalent of 'him' can, on occasion, be used like 'himself'. However, Frisian allows this kind of thing to happen only in those cases where no ambiguity would ensue. Might this be a hint as to why 'him' and 'himself' cannot be swapped around with impunity?

Nonreflexive pronouns like 'him', as we have seen, can refer to just about anything, and it is often unclear which person or thing they are supposed to refer to. Languages tolerate this kind of uncertainty (that is, their users do). But if we tolerate the ambiguity in 'The president says he voted for him', why do we not also tolerate the ambiguity, and let 'him' refer to the president, in 'The president voted for him'? That is the real puzzle—we tolerate all kinds of ambiguity except this one. And what is surprising is that 'The president says he voted for him' contains many more possibilities regarding who the 'he' and 'him' could refer to than the sentence 'The president voted for him' would contain if 'him' could refer to the president. So by excluding this kind of ambiguity from the language we save absolutely nothing. We are still left with having to figure out where this constraint on what these pronouns can and cannot refer to comes from. Again, why does it appear to operate across different languages?

We can really only speculate at this point. Perhaps the linguists who claim that it is all innate are right. But perhaps children are the key to a slightly different solution. Perhaps the facts concerning these pronouns stem from the instinct described in Chapter 4 which generally prevents children from associating two different words with the same thing. When learning new words, children assume that if they already have a word for something, a new word should not refer to that same something. Pronouns are just the same. 'Him' cannot refer to the same thing as 'himself'. Perhaps children already suspect this. In this sense, perhaps the him/himself facts do after all stem from innate factors, whose origins can be traced, perhaps, to properties of associative learning. And perhaps children take a long time to get the facts straight because the meaning of a pronoun, what it can refer to, is changing the whole time. They are chasing a moving target.

Basically, we can only speculate about why the him/himself constraint exists. Most people agree that it has its roots in abilities that are innate. But as suggested in Chapter 4, what is contentious is not that such abilities might exist, but that they might be specific to language.

Role assignment: faster than the speed of grammar

'Him' and 'himself' are just one kind of pronoun. There are others which have completely different properties, and are interesting because they tell us something fundamental about how roles are assigned during sentence processing. About how, in effect, we ignore grammar. The pronouns in question are, in fact, the pronouns in questions.

If Bertie tickled Cecily, one can ask 'Who did Bertie tickle?'. 'Who' is a pronoun whose function (in effect, its meaning) is to get you to recall, from your knowledge about Bertie (if you have any), whoever he tickled. Questions of the 'who' kind are clearly and systematically related to the statements that answer them—a single statement could answer many different who- or what- questions:

Cecily hoped her second cousin would propose marriage to her.

Who did Cecily hope her second cousin would propose marriage to?
What did Cecily hope her second cousin would propose to her?
Who did Cecily hope would propose marriage to her?
What did Cecily hope?
. . . And so on.

Each question is related to its answer systematically. In 'What did Cecily hope her second cousin would propose to her?', the 'what' refers to whatever would ordinarily occur (in the active statement version) after 'propose' and before 'to'. It is as if, in the question, something is missing in this position—as if there is a gap between the two. We can represent this by marking the questions as follows:

Who did Cecily hope her second cousin would propose marriage to _?
What did Cecily hope her second cousin would propose _ to her?
Who did Cecily hope _ would propose marriage to her?
What did Cecily hope _?
. . . And so on.

The idea that each question contains a gap helps explain how we interpret these kinds of questions. The point of asking a question is to find out who fulfilled some particular role. And to figure this out, we can look for where the gap is. We do that by finding the position in the sentence where something is missing. In 'Who did she propose marriage to?' there is something missing after 'to' and before '?'. After identifying the location of this gap, we can then figure out what role the thing that should be in this position would have (in this last example, the person whom the marriage was proposed to). We can then, finally, retrieve from our memory the information about who fulfilled that role.

There are other kinds of sentences that also have these gaps. Sentences with relative clauses:

≜   *The person who Cecily eventually proposed marriage to _ was her second cousin*

They are interpreted in a similar way—in order to know which person is being referred to, you need to identify the gap, identify the role that would normally be associated with something in that position, and so figure out, in this case, that Cecily proposed marriage to this person. Hopefully you then know who this person is.

The fact that relative clauses and questions starting with 'who' or 'what' or 'which' are very similar probably explains why 'who' and 'which' can start both questions and relative clauses ('The boy who . . .', 'The car which . . .'). And despite the fact that it is considered bad grammar to say 'The book what I bought', people do say it!

So far, nothing has been said that is too surprising. Locating the gap is obviously an important thing to do. We do it every day, whenever someone asks a question or uses a relative clause. Sometimes, we have to wait quite a while before getting to the gap, as the second of these examples shows:

≜   *Which woman did Bertie present a wedding ring to _ before falling over?*
    Which woman did Bertie present the wedding ring to his fiancée in front of _?

(Probably, this second question was a little difficult to process, and we shall come to why shortly.) In each case, identifying where the gap is is crucial. It tells us which woman is being referred to—whether it is the woman doing the receiving, or the woman in front of whom the whole thing took place.

But here, now, is the surprising thing. We do not wait to find out where the gap is. But if not, how else could we work out which woman was being referred to?

The verb 'present' allows two kinds of object: the thing being presented (the wedding ring) and the thing, or person, it is being presented to (the woman or the fiancée). The roles associated with these two kinds of object are defined by the meaning of the verb 'present'. As soon as we hear (or read) the sequence 'Which woman did Bertie present . . .', we can infer, from the meaning of 'present' that there are two possible roles up for grabs—the thing-that-was-presented role, and the person-that-it-was-presented-to role. In principle, therefore, we could simply take our pick. How? By selecting whichever role could most plausibly fit the woman.

But how do we know that this is what happens, and that we do not wait around until we have worked out where the gap is?

This question was addressed in a series of elegant experiments run in the late 1980s and early 1990s by a research group in Rochester, USA, headed by Michael Tanenhaus. He and his colleagues reasoned that there was a very simple way to distinguish between the two possibilities, by using two sentences that were almost identical:

> *Which <u>woman</u> did Bertie present a wedding ring to _?*
> *Which <u>horse</u> did Bertie present a wedding ring to _?*

If we start figuring out what role the woman or horse is supposed to be playing as soon as we get to the verb 'present' (and without waiting to find that gap), we should realize that the woman or horse is either the thing being presented, or the recipient of whatever it was that was presented. When we get to 'wedding ring', we realize this wedding ring is the thing being presented, and that the woman or the horse must therefore be the recipient. However, a wedding ring is a plausible thing to present to a woman, but not to a horse. And in principle, we ought to notice the implausibility of this (in the horse question) as soon as we get to the wedding ring.

If we did wait until finding the gap before figuring out that the woman or the horse is the recipient of the wedding ring, we would not notice the implausibility of the horse-as-recipient until the gap itself. So all we need is a way of figuring out, as psycholinguists, when the implausibility is noticed. To cut the methodological story short, Tanenhaus and colleagues found that the implausibility is noticed when the wedding ring is found, not when the gap is found. Here is how they found it out (if you prefer, you can skip this paragraph).

There are several ways of figuring out when an implausibility is noticed. One of them is relatively simple—you sit a person in front of a computer screen and arrange things so that each time they press a button, the next word in a sentence appears on the screen in front of them. By recording how long it takes each person to press the buttons, you can get an idea of how long it took them to read each word in the sentence. Experiments such as this show consistently that if a word is

implausible it takes longer to read. Another technique is technologically more exciting, and involves measuring the electrical activity produced in the upper layers of the brain. This requires the use of an electroencephalogram (EEG), a device that is routinely used in hospitals to monitor brain activity, and which is now used in a number of psycholinguistics labs. In the early 1980s, Marta Kutas and her colleagues at the University of California in San Diego demonstrated that precise and identifiable patterns of brain activity could be found in response to words which were contextually implausible. Such a pattern would be found after the word 'horse' in 'Bertie presented a wedding ring to his horse before falling off'. But this same pattern would not be found in 'Bertie presented a sugar-lump to his horse before falling off'.

In the sentences used by Tanenhaus and his colleagues ('Which woman/horse did Bertie present a wedding ring to _?'), waiting until the gap would unambiguously tell us which role should be given to the woman or to the horse. But we do not wait—what we do instead is take a gamble, and assign a role to the woman or horse as soon as we have one to assign. In fact, the available evidence suggests that when we have heard or read the fragment 'Which woman did Bertie present . . .', we first assume that the woman is the thing being presented (as in 'Which woman did Bertie present _ to his mother?'). Only subsequently do we revise this assignment when we see that the fragment continues 'Which woman did Bertie present the wedding ring . . .'. This explains why one of the earlier examples may have seemed a little awkward:

≜   *Which woman did Bertie present the wedding ring to his fiancée in front of _?*

The reason it may seem awkward is that on encountering 'the wedding ring' we immediately assume that the woman was the person that the wedding ring was presented to. But when we then find 'to his fiancée', this assumption turns out to be wrong, and we have to 'unassume' that the woman received the wedding ring—we have to undo that particular role assignment, leaving the woman role-less, until the end of the sentence. Of course, if we bothered to wait until finding the gap, we would not have to revise the initial assignments.

In general, what seems to happen is that as soon as we know which roles are being played out, and as soon as we know which participants are involved, we try and fit the two together. We do not wait, necessarily, until the point in the sentence at which the grammar confirms that we have made the right fit. In this sense, we ignore the grammar. But why are we so impatient?

Sentence processing is something that happens in time. And in that time, we need to integrate the information we come across with all the information we have built up so far. In the examples about Bertie, his horse, the wedding ring, and his fiancée, we could in principle wait around until our knowledge of the grammar (and hence our identification of the gaps) unambiguously told us which were the correct role assignments to make. But this would mean that certain participants would be role-less, at least for a while. Could it be that we assign roles early, without waiting around, simply to avoid a role-less vacuum? Why might we do this? Why do we want to avoid such a vacuum? And what about all the languages like Japanese and Turkish in which the verb comes at the end of the sentence? In these languages, the identity of the roles is only revealed after all the participants in the sentence have already been encountered.

In fact, these last languages are a little like German, which uses different versions of the word for 'the' to indicate certain aspects of the role that the subsequent noun plays in the sentence (this was discussed in more detail in the last chapter). There is an important difference in German between 'der Junge' ('the boy') and 'den Junge' (also 'the boy')—'der' indicates that the boy is the subject of the verb, whereas 'den' indicates that it is the object of the verb (and there are finer distinctions also, regarding what kind of object). These *case-marked* languages therefore provide clues to the listener or reader about which participants did something, and which had something done to them, without the listener knowing what that actual something was. Even in these languages, then, the participants do not remain absolutely role-less. Perhaps there really is some underlying need to allocate each participant, as it is encountered, at least some kind of role. But this still leaves unclear why we should be in such a hurry to do this, and why we are even prepared to make preliminary role assignments which must subsequently be revised. For now, we shall just have to accept that this is the case. We shall return to this issue in Chapter 13, armed with some insights borrowed from computational models of learning.

Obeying the conventions

Much of what we now know about when specific roles are assigned during sentence processing has come from the study of sentences with gaps. But aside from their use as a kind of tool with which to study the nature and timing of role assignment, they are also interesting in their own right. We have already seen how from a single statement, many different questions can be formed, each with their gaps in a different location. But there are constraints on where the gaps can go. In the following examples, the questions marked with an asterisk are ungrammatical:

She thought Bertie's offer of marriage was long overdue.

> *What did she think __ was long overdue?*
> * *What did she think Bertie's offer of __ was long overdue?*
> * *What did she think Bertie's __ of marriage was long overdue?*
> * *Who did she think __'s offer of marriage was long overdue?*
> * *What was Bertie's offer of marriage long __?*

If, from that first statement, we can create that first question, why can we not also create the others? In each case, it is actually quite easy to figure out what the intended interpretation is. But why are they so definitely ungrammatical? Nothing appears to be gained by preventing these questions, and yet something prevents us from interpreting them as grammatical. Similar constraints on where the gaps can go exist for the relative clause equivalents:

The marriage that she thought __ was long overdue took place last week.
* *The marriage that she thought Bertie's offer of __ was long overdue took place last week.*

Unlike the him/himself facts that we encountered earlier, and which apparently apply to all languages, the facts about where gaps can and cannot appear change according to which language is spoken. In English we can easily ask 'Who did Bertie's mother sit next to __ at the wedding?'. In a language like German one has to ask instead (translated literally) 'Next to whom did Bertie's mother at the wedding sit?'. The problem in German is that one cannot have a gap after a preposition, and to avoid this, one has to move the entire prepositional phrase to the front of the sentence.

So what does all of this mean? Languages contain constraints on what can and cannot be said. Some of these constraints apply across all languages, and some do not. In some respects many of these constraints appear quite arbitrary—that is, in principle we could understand some sentences that violated the constraints. So why bother with them?

There is a tension between, on the one hand, those facts which show a rigid obedience to what the conventions of the language dictate (no matter how arbitrary the conventions appear) and, on the other, those facts showing a blatant disregard for these conventions when we ignore what they have to offer and instead second-guess the correct assignment of roles to the different participants in a sentence.

The tension is, in fact, easily resolved, because we do not actually disregard the conventions when assigning roles. When we second-guess which roles to assign to which participants, we use the actual location of the gap (that is, we use the conventions within the language which tell us where that gap is) to *confirm* or *disconfirm* the original assignments. And if those assignments are disconfirmed, new assignments are made on the basis of where the gap was found. And in sentences without gaps ('Bertie loves Cecily'), we still need those conventions to tell us which participants in which locations should receive which roles. The only puzzle that needs to be explained from all this is the reason why there exist conventions which apparently serve no purpose whatsoever.

One possible solution is to assume that the seemingly arbitrary constraints on what can and cannot be done arise because in fact they reflect underlying, nonarbitrary, conventions. Here is one example of how this might work for English: the convention for interpreting questions like 'Which woman did Bertie marry _?' says, in effect, 'If you are trying to identify which participant is intended, you need to establish first what role it played. You can do that by looking at the verb, and seeing which roles are going, and you can then work out which role is most suitable for the participant you are interested in. Later on, you will encounter a gap in the position that will unambiguously signal which role should have been assigned to that participant, and this will either confirm or disconfirm your earlier assignment'. The important thing here is that the role that is played by the thing you are trying to identify is a role that is indicated by the verb. But not everything in a sentence can be assigned a role handed out by the verb. Here is that earlier example again:

> *She thought Bertie's offer of marriage was long overdue.*

The two verbs are 'thought' and 'was'. The verb 'thought' signals two roles—one for the person doing the thinking (the subject of the verb), and one for the thing that was thought (the object). In this case, the subject is 'She', and the object is 'Bertie's offer of marriage was long overdue'. The verb 'was' also signals two roles—one for a subject ('Bertie's offer of marriage') and one for an adjectival phrase ('long overdue'). But this means that 'Bertie', 'offer', 'marriage' and 'overdue' do not receive roles from the verbs. So the convention which allows us to interpret a question (or a relative clause, come to that) will not quite work if we try and ask something like 'What did she think Bertie's offer of _ was long overdue?', because the gap is in a position (corresponding to 'marriage') that does not receive a role from the verb. A similar problem arises in the relative clause construction 'The marriage that she thought Bertie's offer of _ was long overdue took place last week'. Once again, the gap is in a position that does not correspond to one of the roles assigned by the verb. So things are not as arbitrary as they may at first have seemed.

We are still a long way off from being able to explain away all the constraints, let alone the fact that different languages have markedly different kinds of constraints. Some of these differences may be due to whether a language is case-marked, as German is (this was explained earlier). Other differences might be due to whether the verb appears early in the sentence, or late. Characterizing these differences, and identifying the commonalities (a prerequisite for ultimately under-standing the reasons underlying the various constraints on the different sentence forms) is the remit of linguistics. And even if the goals of psycholinguistics and linguistics differ (see Chapter 1), the two are not easily separated, and nor should they be. None the less, since the early days of contemporary linguistics (as started by Noam Chomsky), there has been a tension between the two. Partly it has to do with the distinction between what is grammatical and what is processable. A sentence like 'What did you throw the tray that you brought the book that I didn't want to be read to out of up on away for?' is grammatical, but pretty hard to process. Similarly a sentence like 'The wedding ring the woman the man the cousin loved loved loved tarnished' is gram-matical, but is also, to all intents and purposes, pure gibberish. Why it is gibberish is still a matter of speculation. Our ability to keep track of who did what to whom just cannot keep up with what grammatical convention allows. And whereas in these cases, the human limitations do not appear to have constrained the evolution of those grammatical conventions, only future research will determine the extent to which such limitations may nonetheless have influenced aspects of the grammars that we each use every day.

Neither this chapter nor the previous one have really addressed the most fundamental issue of all—what does a sentence *mean*? How is this meaning integrated into the meaning of the surrounding sentences? And what, exactly, is meaning? What these last two chapters have done is move us some little way closer towards understanding how a meaning is arrived at. And there is no magic behind this, only the seemingly mundane task of identifying who or what is being referred to, and what roles they should have. Along the way, we have encountered some enduring puzzles, such as, on the one hand, the surprising degree of ambiguity that languages tolerate, and on the other, the surprising con-straints on what kinds of ambiguity are not tolerated (these were the him/himself facts). But none of this tells us what meaning really is. In principle, we could write a computer program that could do much of what has been described here, and such programs do exist. But would such a computer really understand? In the next chapter, we take a closer look at what meaning might be.

9

On the meaning of meaning

Within the Babel metaphor, the tower's summit touches the very essence of language—the ability to convey meaning. Language itself is merely a tool, a tool of the trade in meaning. But like any trade, there is a difference between the trade itself—how it should be conducted, the conventions used, and so on—and the thing that is traded. Knowing something about how we convey meaning is quite far-removed from knowing what this thing is that we are conveying. Getting to the summit is quite different from being able to look around once we have got there.

The distinction between the meaning conveyed and the conventions used to convey it is perhaps most famously captured in Lewis Carroll's poem *Jabberwocky*.

> 'Twas brillig, and the slithy toves
> Did gyre and gimble in the wabe:
> All mimsy were the borogoves,
> And the mome raths outgrabe.

Anyone reading this verse would have an idea of what it ought to mean if only they knew the meaning of all the words. It is as if the grammatical conventions have been kept, and the individual meanings thrown out. Fortunately, a translation was provided, through the looking-glass, by Humpty Dumpty, who knew a thing or two about meaning:

> "When I use a word", Humpty Dumpty said, in a rather scornful tone, "it means just what I choose it to mean—neither more nor less."

He then went on to discuss the temper that some words have, and the extra wages he would pay them if he made them mean a great deal. Sadly, on our side of the looking-glass, words do not quite work in this way. On the other hand, Humpty Dumpty's assertion, about his choosing what a word should mean, is not as absurd as Lewis Carroll might have thought—we do use words to mean just what we choose them to mean. The challenge is to understand why everyone appears to have made the same choices.

This challenge is all the more intriguing given that speakers can invent new meanings for words, or use words in new ways, and still be understood. An example from British English makes use of the fact that the 'anorak', a kind of coat, is the much favoured garment of the 'nerd' and the train-spotter. A novel use of the word is slowly entering some circles: 'to anorak' as in 'You're not still anoraking away at your computer, are you?'. Many readers will recognize the intended meaning, even if they have never heard 'anorak' used in this way before.

So what exactly is meaning, and what does it take to understand an utterance? What do we need other than a few dictionary definitions and a knowledge of the language's grammatical conventions? After all, many a child has suffered too many years at school learning another language in exactly this way, using a grammar book and a dictionary—hardly an enjoyable way to learn a language, and, by all accounts, hardly a successful way either. But the trouble with the dictionary approach to meaning is that we do need more; definitions are not enough. If each dictionary definition were expressed simply in terms of other words in the same dictionary, it would be impossible to know what any single word meant. The word 'speech', for instance, is defined in the *OED* (second edition), using the term 'word', whilst 'word' is defined using the word 'speech'. It is because of this inherent circularity that a dictionary is not a repository of meaning. Those English children would not get very far if they were given a dictionary written entirely in French, or German, or whatever other language they were learning. And never mind about learning a second language, what about learning the first? Children could not possibly learn the meanings of new words in terms of words they had already learned, because in the early stages of word learning, they quite simply would not know enough words to put together the definition of a new one. And yet from the ages of 18 months to around six years, they none the less manage to learn upwards of nine new words each day. That is a lot of words. According to the *OED*, which also defines 'speech' as 'the natural exercise of the vocal organs', it is also a lot of exercise!

Trying to understand the nature of meaning is complicated by the fact that, just like the tower at Babel, there are different levels of meaning, each supporting, and supported by, the other levels. For instance, the gist of a conversation is a kind of meaning that differs considerably from the meaning of an individual utterance that may have been a part of that conversation. In turn, the meaning of that utterance will be quite different from the meaning of any one of its individual words. And what about the meaning conveyed by the inflections -ing, ed, s, able, re , un , and so on? Aspects of the meaning of an utterance may not even be conveyed using words at all; the same words uttered with a different intonation can signify quite different things (see Chapter 7).

Evidently, meaning is a complex concept—intonation, words, utterances, and whole conversations all convey meaning, but different kinds of meaning. Meaning can even be conveyed without any sound at all; gestures, such as a shake of the head, or a shrug, can augment an utterance, or even replace it. Meaning can even be conveyed without words or gestures—by a well-placed silence, for instance. And to complicate matters further, the intended meaning of an utterance might not be its actual meaning; it could be the exact opposite. Someone eating an ice cream with particular enthusiasm might respond to 'You like that, do you?' with 'No, I can't stand it, but I'm on a strict diet'. Irony and sarcasm are not the only times that the literal and intended meanings may differ: 'Could you pass the relish?', asked during a meal, is rarely responded to with a simple 'Yes'.

There is no one thing that we can call 'meaning'. Instead, there are many different kinds. If ever there was a whole that was greater than the sum of its parts, meaning is it. But although there is no one thing called 'meaning', the different kinds can be divided into two broad varieties: the meanings of individual words and the meanings of combinations of words.

On the meaning of words

At its simplest, the meaning of a word is the knowledge that one has of the situations or contexts in which it would be appropriate to use that word. But this is a far cry from practical reality, which is that meaning is what happens when some particular neural circuitry somewhere in the brain is stimulated into activation. That is hardly a helpful description, but it does have its uses. Imagine that we could picture the activation of the individual neurons in someone's brain, and that by chance, we happened to picture the neurons whose pattern of activity corresponded to the meaning of, for instance, the word 'linguist'. How would the brain itself know that the activation of these cells corresponded to 'linguist' and not to 'fish', or to the sensation of an itch on the arm? It sounds like an impossible question to answer. But there is an answer. And the answer requires us to imagine that we can also picture the activation of the neurons in someone else's brain whose activation is also equated with the meaning of 'linguist'. The chances are that these neurons will not be exactly the same as the ones in the first person's brain. They might have slightly different connections with other neighbouring neurons, they might be bigger or smaller, there might be more of them, they might be in a slightly different part of the brain, and so on. But if the two sets of neurons (one in each brain) are so different, how come their activation can nonetheless be equated with the same thing—the meaning of 'linguist'?

The answer to this last question is simple: it does not matter that the neurons differ from person to person, so long as they would become activated in just the same situations. All that really matters is that one pattern of neural activity arises whenever the word 'linguist' is heard, and another pattern arises whenever 'fish' is heard. So long as the two sets of neurons only become active on those respective occasions, the brain will distinguish between the two words on the basis of the distinct patterns of activity they evoke. And if the brain responds differently, the brain's owner (for want of a better description) will also respond differently.

But something is missing. It is all very well to say that the brain can distinguish between the words 'linguist' and 'fish', but is that enough? Anyone could distinguish between two unknown words without knowing what they meant, or between two mystery objects without understanding what they were. Once again, what *is* understanding? What gives it its essence?

There has been a long (and to some people, odd) tradition of scientists and philosophers who believe that the essence of meaning, and indeed the essence of 'thought', does not reside in the physical stuff of the brain at all. For instance, in the seventeenth century, René Descartes (of 'I think, therefore I am' fame) believed that the mind is quite separate from the brain, with some kind of spiritual link between the two. Even in the twentieth century, various philosophers have believed that there is something magical in the brain, that we can neither see nor measure, but which makes the brain more than just a machine. But as we move into the twenty-first century, let us assume that there is no magic, and that meaning and understanding are somehow related to whatever is going on in the brain. Let us also assume, as we did at the start of this section, that the meaning of a word is really just the knowledge—which in turn is just the accumulated experience—of the situations in which it would be appropriate to produce that word. The next question is what is experience to a bunch of nerve cells?

Experience as the essence of meaning

There is considerable evidence to support the idea that the pattern of activity across the neurons associated, for instance, with the concept of fish gradually changes each time a fish is encountered, becoming each time more specific to just those contexts in which fish are encountered. This gradual change has much in common with the way Pavlov's dogs learned the relationship between the bell and their dinner. The association between the two progressively strengthened with each pairing of the bell and dinner—in effect, the neural activity associated with the bell progressively changed to reflect the context in which the bell occurred (i.e. dinner). In the fish case, the association between 'fish' and the contexts in which fish can occur would also strengthen, with the neural activity associated with 'fish' gradually changing to reflect these contexts (we return later to why these changes come about).

So patterns of neural activity change as a result of the accumulated experience of things, including both their physical characteristics and the contexts in which they have occurred. In effect, these patterns are a reflection of those experiences. And naturally, objects that are similar to one another will tend to occur in similar contexts, to behave in similar ways, and to lead to similar experiences. Consequently, the neural activity associated with them will also be similar. Although the pattern of activity that is evoked in response to a shark will be different from the pattern evoked in response to a goldfish, components of those patterns will be similar, because the two fish share certain attributes. It is this similarity in their patterns of neural activity that corresponds to the concept of fish.

Of course, the neural activity that is evoked when we see a fish may not be the same as the activity that is evoked when we think about a fish, or when we hear the word 'fish', or when we eat a fish. In all likelihood, these patterns do differ. But because they may each occur in similar contexts (we might hear the word 'fish' when we see one, or eat one), there will be elements of the corresponding patterns which are similar. Whether we call one pattern a concept, and another pattern a meaning is unimportant. What is important is that the meaning of 'fish' is simply a pattern that has become associated with the contexts appropriate to the things that 'fish' refers to—and it is this that is the essence of its meaning.

But what about all those words that do not refer to objects? In fact, they could all work on pretty much the same principle—the concept associated with something is the accumulated experience of that something, whether it is an object, an event (e.g. running, flying), a property (e.g. yellow, fast, high), or whatever. And in each case, the meaning of the word is simply a pattern of neural activity that reflects that accumulated experience.

Intermission: if neural activity is just complicated chemistry, could we not fill a test-tube with meaning?

The last few pages have been based mainly on conjecture. We cannot observe the patterns of neural activity that we have been talking about, or watch those neural structures change as they accumulate experience. But much work in neurobiology *has* directly observed how neural systems react and change as a function of experience. Admittedly, much of this work has been carried out, for both ethical and practical reasons, on slugs and the like. But if slugs can do it, then presumably we can too—only better.

One feature of this approach which may make some people uncomfortable is that meaning has been reduced, in effect, to just some very complicated chemistry.

No—we could not fill a test-tube with meaning. But imagine that a computer could do something that was exactly equivalent to what we suppose to be happening in the brain. Would such a computer, through its own (perhaps limited) experience, accumulate meaning? Would it understand? Would it, by virtue of any such understanding, have ethical and moral rights? Would we dare switch it off?

As we delve deeper into the brain's workings, such questions necessarily come closer to the surface of our understanding. Fortunately, questions like these, and their answers, are beyond the remit of our current ascent of Babel. But that will not make the questions go away, or the answers any easier to accept, whatever those answers happen to be.

Beyond the meaning of individual words

The meaning of a multi-word sentence is a very different beast from the meaning of an individual word—whether in terms of neural activity or in the terms that we are probably more used to. So it is as well to take a step back from the brain, and to just stick for the moment with our everyday vocabulary.

To understand a sentence generally requires knowledge not just of the meanings of the words making up that sentence, but also, and amongst other things, knowledge of the world within which specific things, and events, occur. For instance, imagine a non-fluent speaker of English having trouble with something they were reading and asking 'What does the man she saw last night mean?' It is unclear how one might best go about answering this question. But now imagine a slightly different version of this same question, whispered in the context of two people gossiping: 'Whom did she mean by the man she saw last night ?' In this case, it is extremely clear what would need to be known in order to answer the question.[4] Here, the sequence 'the man she saw last night' is used to refer to someone quite specific who inhabits the world that the speaker and hearer, or writer and reader, share. To know who was being referred to requires knowledge about this world; who was in it, what they were doing, and who they were doing it with (not to mention how often and for how long).

The meanings of individual words are the building blocks which allow the hearer or reader to (re)construct some aspect of the speaker or writer's world. But what is it that is constructed? In what form can one person's world exist in another person's mind? Indeed, in another person's brain?

The language of the mind

The fact that we can use language to describe the world around us suggested to philosophers and logicians that we translate what we hear or read into little more than a mental description of the things being talked about—the mental equivalent of a language, in fact. Logicians were keen on this approach because they found that they could think about the meaning of an utterance in terms of the mathematical languages that they worked with. Meaning could be talked about by analogy to mathematics and logic, and all that was required was a procedure for translating the sentences of, say, English, into the 'sentences' of the mathematical language.

To say that what we hear or read is translated into another, albeit mental, language is simply passing the buck, however. If we had access to the mental language, we would still have to explain what any

---

[4] This example is borrowed, with thanks, from Alan Garnham, a psycholinguist working on aspects of text understanding.

sentence expressed in that language meant. And we would still have to say how it came to have that meaning.

In the late 1970s and early 1980s, Phil Johnson-Laird, at the University of Sussex, proposed instead that what happens when we hear or listen to language (in effect, its meaning) has much in common with what would happen if we directly observed the situation that the language described. Alan Garnham, a student of his at the time, devised an ingeniously simple experiment to establish whether this was right. His aim was to distinguish between meaning as the mental equivalent of the language used to describe something, or as the mental equivalent of what happens when one observes that something directly. He gave people some short stories to read, one of which, for instance, contained the following information:

> 🔺 *By the window was a man with a martini.*

Subsequently, they read that this person waved at the hostess of the party he was at (recall that this experiment was devised in the late 1970s, when parties, martinis, and hostesses were still an important part of the social calendar). But in a memory test carried out later, people could not remember which of the following two sentences they had in fact read:

> 🔺 *The man with the martini waved at the hostess.*
> *The man by the window waved at the hostess.*

The fact that people confused these two sentences suggested that the information that had originally been used to describe the man who did the waving was lost. If the meaning of the text (used to narrate the story) had been stored in terms of the mental equivalent of the sentences that made up that text, one would not expect this kind of information to disappear from memory. But if the meaning of the text had been stored in terms of the mental equivalent of something like a film of what had happened, it would not be at all surprising. If, in such a film, the man who waved at the hostess had been holding a drink, and had been standing by a window, it would be impossible to tell whether the script for the film (i.e. the text itself) had said that the man with the martini had done the waving, or that the man by the window had done the waving.

Of course, it is all well and fine to talk about a text as a film script, and as the meaning of that text as the film itself. But what does it mean to say that we store the meaning of something as the equivalent of a film in our head? Where is the cinema screen?

Wor(l)ds in the mind

Films are basically just memories on celluloid. They allow images to be projected in the absence of the original source of the image. Language is similar in some respects—it allows us to communicate ideas that relate to things which are not around us. In these cases, the language we use refers really to some kind of memory of the things we are talking about. But although 'Whom did she mean by the man she saw last night?' can only be *answered* with reference to a memory of the individuals concerned, it can be *understood* without any such memory—it is enough to know what kind of memory would be required.

Of course, 'memory' is not quite the right word. In the absence of a specific memory about the man she met last night, what is really evoked in response to this phrase is a kind of mental picture of the world, and the way that world would have to be for that sentence to be true. In effect, it is a model of the world, much like a model of a plane, or a medieval castle. The fact that these things are built of balsa wood, or Lego bricks, is immaterial if what we want to do is represent how many wings the plane has, or rooms the castle has. The beauty of these models is that they do not have to represent anything real:

    ≜   *The winged unicorn flew high across the fiery skies.*

Despite the fact that there are no winged unicorns, we can construct a (mental) model of what the world would be like if unicorns did exist and if the sky was fiery. So one way to think about what we do when we hear a sentence is to imagine that we build a kind of *mental model* of whatever is being described. But if the information we need to represent in our minds is the mental equivalent of a Lego model (with moving parts), out of what mental material do we build the model?

The Lego model has the property that if an arch supports a rampart in the real castle, then an arch supports a rampart in the model castle. But whereas in the Lego model, an arch can physically support a rampart, in the brain, physical support of this kind is just not possible. There are no little arches in there busily supporting little ramparts. So should we abandon the idea that there is a mental equivalent of Legoland? No: seeing an arch has an effect on the neural circuitry of the brain. So does thinking an arch. The two effects will not be quite the same, but we can suppose that the neural activity that happens when we think the arch somehow reflects what is common to all the different patterns of neural activity that have been evoked when we have experienced arches (whether by walking under them, seeing them, reading about them, whatever). We supposed something very similar when thinking earlier about the meanings of single words. The difference, then, between mental models and Lego models is that in the Lego model, there is a one-to-one correspondence between things in the model and the things in the world that are being modelled. But in the mental model, there is instead a one-to-one correspondence between the neural activity that corresponds to the mental model and the neural activity that corresponds to actually experiencing (by whatever means) the things being represented. So the mental equivalent of a Lego model is not too far-fetched.

Building a mental world

How does a sentence cause the mental model to be added to and updated? How does it cause the appropriate patterns of neural activity?

These questions can best be answered by considering some real examples. First, a simple case:

≜   *A balding linguist ate a very large fish.*

This sentence is relatively straightforward. Grammatical convention tells us to add two entities into the model—one representing the linguist and another representing the fish. We also add that the linguist is balding, because the grammatical conventions of English tell us that the word immediately before 'linguist' describes a property of the linguist (and similarly for 'very large' and 'fish'). The conventions also tell us the roles that the characters each play, the roles themselves being defined by the verb 'ate'. In this case, the fish has the role of being eaten, while the linguist has the role of doing the eating. Of course, this is just metaphor-speak—mental models are just patterns of neural activity. So for anyone who prefers to read about these patterns, the following points ought to do the trick (and anyone who wants to stick to metaphor-speak should just skip them).

≜   The pattern of neural activity associated with 'a balding linguist' will have something in common, we can suppose, with the pattern that would be evoked when a balding linguist (as opposed to any other kind of linguist) was actually seen.

≜   The sequence of patterns that would be evoked by the entire sentence would, likewise, have something in common with the sequence that would be evoked if a balding linguist were actually seen to eat a very large fish.

≜   The pattern of activity evoked by the example sentence would differ from that elicited by 'A very large fish ate a balding linguist', even though the two sentences share the same words—paralleling the fact that seeing the corresponding events would also elicit different patterns. And although the patterns of neural activity in response to 'a balding linguist ate' and 'a very large fish ate' would differ, they would also reflect a feature that is common to both, namely that the characters mentioned are the ones doing the eating. This commonality, combined with the different individual patterns evoked by 'a balding linguist' and 'a very large fish', would ensure that the difference in the overall sequence of neural activity reflected the difference in who did the eating and who was eaten. To put it crudely, the changing pattern of neural activity directly encodes who did what to whom, and it is this changing pattern that corresponds, in our model metaphor, to building the model.

Whether we use metaphor-speak, or neuro-speak, the final result is the same; a mental representation is built of what the example sentence describes. But there is one further point that is fundamental to the entire notion of mental models and their neural equivalents; the mental model must exist for more than just the lifetime of an individual sentence, otherwise the information conveyed by a new sentence could not be integrated within that model. The model is not simply what happens when one reads a sentence, but rather it is a memory of what happened, and it is this memory that gets updated as other sentences are read (or heard). Fortunately, the nature of human memory is outside the remit of this book, so we shall just take it for granted.

What should be clear by now is that an individual sentence, or an individual utterance, is really just a specification of what should be done to the mental model. In Lego terms, it is like the instruction leaflet that details which things to add into the model, in what order, and next to which other things. It sounds easy but, as with real Lego, figuring out which pieces the instruction leaflet is referring to is quite another matter.

Keeping track of all the pieces

Linguists eating fish are hardly inspiring, and a more extended example will give a better flavour of the range of operations that mental modelling normally requires.

A stonemason and his apprentice set down a block of stone by the side of the road. They were hungry. The stonemason had left their lunch under a nearby olive tree. It was a hot day but fortunately the beer was still cold. There was a large piece of nougat too, but when the apprentice tried to cut through it, the knife broke. They decided to eat it later. After lunch, the stonemason picked up his tools, and headed towards the tower. Another few weeks and it would be finished.

The one redeeming feature of this otherwise somewhat boring text is
that it illustrates a range of model-building processes, including the most
important of all—the ability to keep track of the things that are added to
the model. This is reflected in the relationship between phrases such as
'*a* stonemason', '*the* stonemason', and '*he*'. The difference between these
is fundamental, as the following adaptation shows (one of the sentences
is omitted as it is not relevant to this point):

> *A stonemason and an apprentice set down a slab of stone by a side of a
> road. A stonemason and an apprentice were hungry. A stonemason had
> left a stonemason and an apprentice's lunch under a nearby olive tree.
> There was a large piece of nougat, but when an apprentice tried to cut
> through a large piece of nougat, a knife broke. A stonemason and an
> apprentice decided to eat a large piece of nougat later. After lunch, a
> stonemason picked up a stonemason's tools, and headed towards a tower.
> Another few weeks and a tower would be finished.*

Perhaps the first thing that comes to mind when reading this rather
odd passage is that it is quite unclear whether or not the same people, or
the same things, are being referred to at different points in the text. It is
a little like a film in which, from one scene to the next, the same role is
being assumed by different actors—keeping track of whether a new
actor is playing the part of someone already established within the plot,
or is playing the part of someone new, would be impossible. The reason
this text gives rise to a similar problem is that, ordinarily, an expression
like 'a stonemason' introduces a new actor playing a new part. If what is
needed is an actor to play an established part (i.e. one that has been
introduced earlier), then either 'he' or 'the stonemason' would be used.
Not surprisingly, there is an important distinction between these two as
well. Words like 'he' or 'it' tend to refer to characters or things that are,
in metaphor-speak, centre-stage. But if more than one character, or
thing, is centre-stage, then a way is needed to distinguish between
them, which is where 'the' comes in ('They were hungry. The stonemason . . .'). Occasionally, one needs also to distinguish between
characters or things that are no longer centre-stage, perhaps because
they have not been mentioned for a while. Here again, 'the' comes in
handy; the sentence 'It didn't fill him up' is probably harder to make
sense of at this point than the sentence 'The lunch which the
stonemason had left under the olive tree didn't fill him up'.

So the differences between 'a', 'the', and 'he/she/it' allow us to keep track of which pieces are being referred to at any one time. The reason we need to do this is because we tend to talk or write about things— the earlier part of each sentence tends to establish what is being talked about, and the later part tends to introduce new information about it.

It all sounds simple enough, really. But as usual, things are more complex than they may at first appear. Although the grammatical conventions we use do, for the most part, successfully dictate who or what is being referred to, it is a sad fact that often they do not go nearly far enough. For instance, what did 'it' refer to each time it was used in the stonemason's story?

≜   *They were hungry. The stonemason had left their lunch under a nearby olive tree. **It** was a hot day but fortunately the beer was still cold. There was a large piece of nougat too, but when the apprentice tried to cut through **it**, the knife broke. They decided to eat **it** later.*

Needless to say, 'it' does not always refer to the same thing, and much hinges on being able to work out, each time we come across it, what it means. For instance the first 'it' does not refer to anything already mentioned, but instead refers to the time at which this episode took place. But we can only work this out once we get to the word 'day', as the sentence could just as easily have started 'It [the lunch] was a hot pastrami sandwich'. The second occurrence of 'it' is easier, because the last-mentioned thing was the nougat. But when we get to the third 'it', the last-mentioned thing was the knife. In this case, we need to use general knowledge about what is eatable in order to rule out the possibility that the thing being referred to is the knife.

So figuring out which pieces in the mental model are being referred to is not always straightforward. Another complication is that sometimes pieces are referred to which do not actually exist within the model— instead, their existence is assumed:

≜   *The stonemason had left their lunch under a nearby olive tree. It was a hot day but fortunately the beer was still cold.*

Whereas the stonemason had already been mentioned, the beer had not. It can only be inferred on the basis of the likelihood that lunch might include beer. If 'beer' were to be replaced by 'bear', the sentence would seem very odd indeed, because no bears could be inferred to exist in the model on the basis of what had been read so far—it would be impossible to establish a coherent link between the bear and anything else.

What makes a text or a conversation understandable is that there is continuity between the different sentences regarding who or what is being talked about (the equivalent is true for films also). This continuity often relies, as we have just seen, on being able to infer links between the different things being talked about, as when the beer's relationship to the previously mentioned lunch had to be inferred. Another kind of inference happened in the following case:

> *When the apprentice tried to cut through the nougat, the knife broke.*

In this case, the knife could be inferred because the meaning of the verb 'cut' implies the use of something to do the cutting with. This is a different kind of inference from the lunch-beer one. That case was based on general knowledge, while this one is based on knowledge about the meaning of one of the items in the sentence.

But why not just accept, at face value, the introduction of the beer, or the knife? Why not simply add the new piece into the model? Why bother with these inferences? The fact that the following adaptation of the stonemason text is so bizarre demonstrates that we care very much about linking things together.

> *A stonemason and his apprentice set down a block of stone by the side of the road. They were hungry. The stonemason had left their batteries under a nearby olive tree. It was a hot day but fortunately the bear was still cold. There was a large piece of nougat too, but when the juggler tried to cut through it, the ball broke . . .*

What is so special about trying to link everything to everything else?

The role of prediction in language understanding

It is not difficult to imagine a film in which no character remains on-screen for long, or in which the actors keep changing, or in which the storyline is fragmented and incomprehensible. If you want to make a decent film, the key ingredient, in the right dose, is predictability. Of course, if things are too predictable, nothing can happen in the film that is new or interesting. But if things are too unpredictable, then the film ends up being a series of unconnected and random events—perhaps a great artform, but not much else.

Reading the stonemason text, there were many different levels at which what you were really doing was trying to predict, subconsciously, and from one moment to the next, what was going on. In effect, these predictions constitute a kind of expectation (although as we shall see in Chapter 13, they probably *are* predictions). For instance, you may have conjured up an image of a sunny day, with clear-blue skies and Mediterranean scenery. None of these was explicitly mentioned, but they were each predictable, or expected, from the text. Some of these expectations may even have arisen against your better judgement:

> *Envied by his colleagues, the stonemason had picked his apprentice carefully. A more skilled pair of hands he had never seen. They were the colour of light marble, as was her face.*

Most people reading this passage might have expected the apprentice to be male—indeed, might have predicted the apprentice to be male.

The image that is left behind in the mind's eye after reading the stonemason's story is far richer than the literal content of the story. But expectation and prediction do more than just influence what is left after a text has been read, or a conversation listened to.

When the apprentice and the stonemason decided 'to eat it later', the 'it' referred not to the knife that had been used unsuccessfully to cut the nougat, but to the nougat itself. Figuring this out involved nothing more than the making of a prediction: of all the things mentioned—the block of stone, the olive tree, the lunch, the beer, the nougat, the knife—which could one predict would be eaten? It has to be either the lunch or the nougat, with the nougat being more likely (it was the more recently mentioned of the two). And when 'the knife' was mentioned, its existence could be predicted from the meaning of 'cut'. Similarly, the beer could be predicted (perhaps not with any great certainty, but we shall come to that in a moment) on the basis of the lunch. And the fact that the beer was cold could be predicted on the basis of both the hot day and the sequence 'but fortunately the beer was . . .' (what else could plausibly be predicted at this point?). The lunch itself could have been predicted, from 'they were hungry'. Even the block of stone could be predicted, given the stonemason's trade. It is surprising, really, just how little in the text could not be anticipated.

Experiments confirm the extent to which predictions are continuously being made, by showing that the time it takes to recognize a word is determined by how predictable that word is from the context in which it appears. The word 'stone' in 'A stonemason and his apprentice set down a block of stone . . .' would be recognized faster than the equivalent word in 'A stonemason and his apprentice set down a block of wood . . .'. But does this mean that at each word we evaluate how predictable that word is from the context and from general knowledge about the ways of the world? That would surely be too much effort. What would the advantage be?

Prediction and meaning

The neural activity evoked in response to something, whether it is a word, a thing, an event, or whatever, comes to reflect not just the thing itself, but also the contexts in which the thing tends to occur. But it does not come to reflect just any aspect of those contexts. Instead, it reflects just those bits that could be predicted by the occurrence of that something. Why? Because that is the way this kind of learning works. Imagine being taught Mandarin Chinese and being shown a glass of beer that you are told is an example of 'bōli'. Imagine that you are then shown a bottle of beer and told the same thing. Presumably 'bōli' means 'beer'. Now you are shown a glass of lager (a light-coloured beer, for readers who do not distinguish one beer from another), and you are again told that it is 'bōli'. You probably assume, now, that the Chinese, like Americans, do not distinguish between beer and lager. But now imagine that you are shown a glass of water, a bottle of Coke, a windowpane, and that each time you are told it is 'bōli'. The chances are that you do not assume that the word 'bōli' has several meanings, one for each of the things you were shown. Instead, you assume that 'bōli' means the one thing that was common to, and could be predicted by, the occurrence of 'bōli'—glass. This same principle will be revisited in Chapter 13 on artificial brains and what they can learn.

In effect, then, the neural activity that is evoked after many experiences of 'glass' will constitute a prediction of what will correlate, in the environment, with the occurrence of that word. Generally, it is that transparent hard stuff around your beer, or in your window. But not always. It could be molten glass. In the case of 'lunch', things are more complicated, because the neural activity associated with 'lunch' will reflect the myriad of possibilities (or predictions) associated with lunch. And because repeated experience leads to the progressive strengthening of associations (as in the case of the bell–dinner pairing for Pavlov's dogs), the more commonly associated things (e.g. glasses, beer) will be reflected more strongly in the pattern of neural activity than the less commonly associated things (e.g. roast boar).

So the predictions that are made at each point in a text or conversation are really nothing more than the patterns of neural activity that have been evoked by the sequence of words up to that point. And all that business of wanting things to be coherent, and wanting to link everything to everything else, to the point of inferring links where necessary, is nothing to do with 'wanting' at all. It is just an inevitable consequence of the way we acquire meaning. It is just an inevitable consequence of what meaning is.

Taking care of the loose ends

So is that it? Basically, yes. The same principles that apply to the meanings of individual words in fact apply to the meanings of combinations of words. And just as 'linguist' and 'fish' evoke different patterns of neural activity that reflect different experiences (and consequently different predictions), so do 'a balding linguist ate' and 'a very large fish ate'. In this case, the different patterns reflect not just our experiences of fish, linguists, and eating, but also our experiences of the common linguistic context: 'an X ate', reflecting the fact that something, X, was doing the eating.

Eating fish, or just eating, or just fish, are things we can experience directly, and we can suppose that the neural activity evoked by hearing these words does have something in common with the activity that would be evoked by experiencing the corresponding things directly. But not all words share this property.

> In the mid-1990s, it was believed that a change of government would do the country some good.

Not a single word in this sentence refers to anything that can be seen, or even, come to that, experienced. So how do we learn their meaning? In fact, no differently from any other word. With sufficient experience of the circumstances in which people use a word like 'government', for instance, the neural activity evoked in response to this word will come to reflect whatever it is about those circumstances that is predictive of, and can be predicted by, the word 'government'. In effect, this is just knowledge of the circumstances in which it is appropriate to use the word. And that, basically, is nothing more than what the word means. Of course, its meaning could also be learned by definition: the body of persons charged, collectively, with the duty of ruling and administration. But that is just another circumstance, which soon blends in with all the others we experience—which is why we rarely remember the definitions we have been told. Once again, it just boils down to patterns of neural activity that reflect our experience of which aspects of the contexts we have encountered, which words we have encountered, and which are predictive of which other.

But what about all that earlier talk of mental models, pieces in the model, being centre-stage, and so on? It all seems so far removed from where we have ended up (and indeed, from where we started off when thinking about the meanings of individual words). But that was all just metaphor-speak. The neural equivalent of the mental model reflects what would be common to all the experiences of all the situations in which, for instance, things get eaten, things do the eating, linguists do things, and fish have things done to them. The pieces in the model—the linguist and the fish—are again just patterns of neural activity reflecting our common experiences of the things they are associated with. And whether they are centre-stage or not is really a reflection of their predictability given the accumulated experience of the ways in which texts and conversations develop.

But if mental models seemed far removed from patterns of neural activity, what about that earlier talk of different kinds of meaning—of gists, of word inflections, of intonation, of shrugs? The quick-and-easy answer is that the same principles apply to them too. The neural consequences of seeing a shrug or hearing a particular intonation may simply reflect what is common across each experience of that kind of shrug or that kind of intonation.

It all sounds too good to be true. After all, a video tape is also a record of accumulated experience—instead of neural patterns, it has magnetic patterns, and these also change in response to experience. So does this mean that the video tape can also understand? No. Because the magnetic patterns, once laid down on the tape, are never changed; new patterns do not modify earlier patterns; they replace them. But imagine an alien life-form. It may be intelligent, or it may be the alien equivalent of a vegetable. How would you decide? One way would be to see how it reacted to its environment. Imagine that it started off by making random noises, but that after a while, it tailored those noises so that it only made a particular noise in the presence of something specific in its environment (perhaps an object, perhaps something happening to that object). The noises might even sound a little like the ones it heard from the humans around it. And imagine further that whenever it made something a bit like a crying noise, you gave it a banana, which it then ate. Finally, imagine that one day, instead of crying, it made the noise for banana even though there were none around. What would you deduce? That it was hungry? That it wanted a banana? That it had understood enough of our world to be able to ask for something?

What might actually have happened, in this last example, is that the associations between the noises and the things the alien encountered in its environment gradually strengthened so that each noise it heard, and subsequently produced, became more specifically 'tuned to' a particular thing. When it got hungry (just another kind of neural activity), it made a noise, was given a banana, and gradually associated that hunger signal with bananas. And one day, this association had become so strong that when it got hungry, it produced the noise associated with the thing that was in turn associated with that hunger. So where is the understanding? And that is the point—what we call understanding need be nothing more than complex neural associations.

Whether all that talk of neural activity has seemed far-fetched or incomprehensible to you does not really matter, so long as the difference between the video tape and the alien banana-eater is clear—there is nothing about the video that could be mistaken for understanding, but there is something very compelling about the behaviour of the alien that allows us to talk of it as if it understood. That is the most we can ever do. We cannot see into the brains of our loved ones and point to something and say 'Look: there's the understanding'. All we can say is that they behave as if they understand.

⣀⣀⣀

This has, by necessity, been a rather simplified account of the nature of meaning, and things are not quite as simple as they have been made out to be. Much has been skipped in order to make the ascent as smooth as possible. Sadly, the summit we have arrived at is not the true summit—recall that the Tower of Babel was never completed, and the true summit never reached. But at least the view from where we have got to is a little like the view from the actual summit (were it to exist).

There is still some way to go. We have said nothing yet about how we produce language, or how we learn the correspondence between the spoken language and the written language. A plateau may have been reached, but our ascent is not over yet.

Exercising the vocal organs

Our ability to use language at all is remarkable enough. Even more remarkable is the fact that we make sense of what we hear so effortlessly. Indeed, so effortless and automatic is it that we cannot help but make sense of what we hear—we cannot choose not to extract the meanings of the words we encounter; only if our attention wanders, or the words are from a language that we do not know, do we not automatically extract their meaning. In this respect, our ability to understand language is very different from our ability to produce it—we can exercise control over what we say and how we say it. Just as we can choose to wiggle one finger or another, or shut one eye or the other, so we can choose to open our mouth, or keep it shut.

So production is voluntary, but what is it that we voluntarily do when we speak? Basically, it seems as if we just get on with it, without much awareness of what we shall say until we actually say it. Yet, for all this lack of awareness, there is an awful lot that goes on whilst we speak. At any one moment we seem to be articulating one word, selecting the next, thinking more broadly about what we are about to say, working out the grammatical conventions we shall need, and so on. If there is any feat of language processing that seems to require the mental equivalent of juggling, this is it.

It is hard enough learning how to juggle when you can watch what a juggler is doing, see what the things being juggled are doing, and see how the two depend on one another. Imagine trying to figure it all out when all you can do is *hear* the juggling. Yet that is exactly what it is like to try and work out what happens during speech production. We can hear the result of the production process, but no more. We cannot see the mental input to that process.

Presumably, that input must have something in common with the end result of language understanding: in one case, meanings are generated from sounds, and in the other, sounds are generated from meanings. Of course, the route from meaning to sound cannot simply be the reverse of that from sound to meaning—after all, we hear with our ears but we do not talk with them as well. Still, one way or another, it is a well-travelled route. But what makes us take that route? What causes us to speak?

The will to speak

Asking why anyone should suddenly, out of the blue, start speaking is a little like asking why anyone should, again out of the blue, offer to help someone cross the road, or offer to carry a heavy load for an expectant mother. In each case, one of the people has a need, and the other can fulfil that need. Language is no different—the person doing the talking will generally believe that the person doing the listening either lacks the information being communicated, or has the information that is desired. The crucial element here is that the speaker must have an idea of what is (or is not) in someone else's mind. What drives the production process is the difference between what speakers have in their own minds, and what they believe to be in their listeners' minds.

Having an idea of the contents of someone else's mind is a little like having a model of whatever it is one thinks is in there—in fact, a mental model of the kind discussed in the previous chapter. The patterns of neural activity that correspond to this model may simply be based on the accumulated experience of the ways in which people (including the experiencer) have acted in many different situations. These patterns, which in effect reflect what might be in someone else's mind, may then be triggered by particular properties of the current situation. For present purposes, however, we need simply think of these models as information regarding what is presumed to be in someone else's mind. We are still a long way from really understanding those neural events and the manner in which they come about. It is enough to know that, somehow, we do generally manage to anticipate what is in someone else's mind. Exactly how we manage this extends far beyond psycholinguistic theory.

So, somehow, speakers have a model of what is in their listeners' minds. But what drives the production process is not just the discrepancy between what the speaker has in mind and what the speaker believes the listener has in mind. If it were, we would be forever shooting our mouths off with no regard for whether anyone was at all interested. Something else needs to be added to the equation. And just as the person we offer help to has to both need and want that help, so the listener must also want to listen. So speaker and listener cooperate, and signal their willingness to do so when they initiate, and maintain, their spoken interaction.

In many ways, conversation is just like a game of chess—we anticipate the other's intentions, combine this with our own intentions, and then make our move. After we have done that, it becomes the other player's turn. But unlike chess, it is less obvious in conversation when it is time to take that turn, and make that move. How do we know that it is our turn? Perhaps surprisingly, the clearest signal that it is time for the listener to become the speaker has almost nothing at all to do with the content of what is said, even though it is the content that determines when the speaker is ready to give up his or her turn. In chess, the change of play occurs as soon as one player sees the other physically move his or her piece, irrespective of what that move is. Similarly, in spoken conversation what determines when the speaker has finished is, more often than not, a physical signal. Sometimes that signal is given by a shift in where the speaker is looking, towards the listener. Other times, it is a property of the speech itself—its prosody.

In English at least, there are quite distinct cues to the end of turn. Speakers tend to slow down, lengthen their syllables, and drop both pitch and loudness. Sometimes, though, the listener might think that the speaker has reached the end of their turn, even when the speaker believes otherwise. The 1982 Christmas issue of the scientific journal *Nature* carried an article which analysed the end-of-turn cues used by the then UK prime minister, Margaret Thatcher. She was renowned for her irritation at being frequently interrupted during interviews—her interviewers were evidently insensitive to the I-have-not-finished-yet cues she believed she was providing. Unlike Mrs Thatcher, many speakers often speed up at the ends of their sentences if they have not reached the end of their turn, to prevent the listener from trying to butt in at an otherwise inopportune moment.

So (at least) two things drive a conversation: the turn-taking cues, which signal when to say something; and the discrepancies between what the speaker knows and what the speaker presumes the listener to know, which signal what to say. Sometimes the two work independently, as when the speaker comes to an end and there is an awkward silence whilst the listener, sensitive to the change of turn, desperately tries to think of something pertinent to say. At the opposite extreme, the discrepancy between the participants in a conversation can be so great that turn-taking is abandoned and each participant is driven simply by the discrepancy between their own thoughts and the thoughts they attribute to the other. Over-heated arguments are a good example of this. They often consist of little more than one interruption after another, with much simultaneous speaking, and both speakers raising their voices, and pitch, to signal that neither is ready, or willing, to relinquish their turn.

This all points to the obvious fact that the desire to say something, the will to speak, is a function of having something to say, having someone to say it to, and having an opportunity to say it. But what about the content of what is said? What drives that?

Why we say what we say

In some cases, it is pretty clear what drives the content of an utterance. Ask someone the time, or the way to the cathedral, and they will say something in answer to whatever you have asked. Invite them to give a lecture or tell a story or say what they think about the government and they will say something that is a reflection of their knowledge, or their views. Put someone in a situation where they require help and the chances are they will say something intended to elicit your cooperation. Informal conversation can be a mixture of all of these. Often though, things are said in conversation for no apparent reason—things like 'uh-huh', 'I know', 'mmm', and 'yes', which are said simply to show a kind of solidarity with the speaker. Another complication is that once a topic has been sufficiently covered, and the discrepancy between speaker and hearer minimized, one of the participants in the conversation may decide to switch to a new topic. Sometimes this happens for no other reason than boredom with the earlier one. But what determines the chosen topic is harder to explain, and psycholinguistics has relatively little to say about this.

Once a topic has been chosen, it is a little easier to see what drives the content of the individual utterances that make up the conversation. Listeners, like all model builders, need more than just a list of mental pieces. They need to know what to do with the pieces. This means they need to know where, within the model, these pieces should go, and to which pre-existing pieces they should be attached. So before identifying what specific modifications need to be made to the model, the speaker has to identify which parts of the model need modifying. Paradoxically, therefore, much of the information that a speaker provides is already known to the listener, referring to information that is already in the listener's model. We tend to structure what we say (and write) to reflect this two-step process—we present what is mutually known first, and what is new second:

 The prime minister who was renowned for consistently giving out misleading signals about when she had finished speaking <u>had even been coached on how to speak</u>.

Only the underlined text provides information that is not already known (except to those readers who are already acquainted with the story behind Margaret Thatcher's distinctive speaking style).

Occasionally, and most often in response to questions, the speaker does not have to provide any information that is already in the listener's model. When someone asks a question, they often do so because they know what to do within the model, but not to which pieces, or because they know some of the pieces which are involved, but not what to do with them. These different situations give rise to different kinds of question, and consequently, different kinds of answer:

 Who was always interrupted when interviewed on TV?
Margaret Thatcher.

 Why was Mrs Thatcher always so irritated when interviewed on TV?
Because she was always interrupted.

Depending on the question, the speaker answering it does not need to identify all of the mental pieces, or all of what to do with them. Sometimes, the speaker does not need to identify anything at all:

 Is it true that Mrs Thatcher was always interrupted by her interviewers?
Uh-huh.

How much information the speaker provides that is already known to the listener is one factor that determines the form of the utterance. But actually providing that information, in a way that is recognizable to the listener, is another.

The speaker has to ensure, when referring to something or someone, that the listener will be able to work out, from their own perspective, who or what is being referred to. It is no good saying 'she' if the listener will not know who this refers to, or 'the politician' if the listener will not know which politician. The speaker must therefore choose appropriate ways for referring to things, where 'appropriate' is defined in terms of what the speaker believes the listener knows. Often, this is based on what has gone on in the conversation so far. For instance, if 'The politician who was so often interrupted' had been uttered in a recent conversational turn, the speaker could use the expression 'she', but only if the listener could be assumed to know who 'she' was. And if the politician had last been mentioned some while back, then the speaker would need to use a different kind of referring expression, one that would enable the listener to bring the politician in question back into the attentional spotlight (such as 'that politician', 'the politician who . . .', 'Margaret Thatcher'). Some of this was discussed in Chapter 9.

Much of what a speaker says is determined, therefore, by what the listener needs to know in order to add something new to his or her body of knowledge, and what the listener is presumed to know. Of course, for the listener to be able to do anything at all with the information supplied by the speaker, the words used to convey that information must be organized in the right way given the grammatical conventions of the language. Without these conventions, speaker and hearer might just as well give up. But then again, without any words, there would be no use for any conventions. At what stage in the whole process do words, and the way they are organized, get chosen?

Paradoxically, the best way to address these questions is to consider what happens when the speaker chooses the wrong words.

Goings-on and goings-wrong in speech production

Some of the most famous, and most often quoted speech errors were made by the Reverend William Spooner (1844–1930). He once told his congregation, for instance, that 'The Lord is a shoving leopard', and his students that they had 'tasted the whole worm'. Whether these were genuine errors or not is unclear—he is rumoured to have intentionally produced at least some of his errors in order to amuse his students at New College, Oxford. But these kinds of error do occur in spontaneous everyday speech. The mistakes are interesting because they say some quite surprising things about the production process. For instance, some errors tell us that, contrary to intuition, we do not first choose the words we shall utter, and then choose what order to put them in. We do it the other way around—we choose the order we will put the words in *before* choosing the words themselves.

The following were all genuine errors, and are borrowed from various collections of such errors that have been published in the psycholinguistic literature. In each case, the speakers blended two words with similar meanings:

> *It's a lot of brothel* [from *bother/trouble*]
> *The competition is a little stougher* [from *stiffer/tougher*]
> *It's difficult to valify* [from *validate/verify*]

When it came to saying the critical word, each speaker obviously had more than one word in mind, and ended up saying a mixture of the two. But the speaker put this mixture in the right place given the grammatical conventions that the sentence required. The speaker must have selected the appropriate grammatical conventions before was selecting the specific words to which those conventions applied. But why does it work this way, and how?

On the application of grammatical convention

The answer to this quite paradoxical state of affairs lies in the nature of the grammatical conventions we employ during speech production. Chapter 9 suggested that our knowledge of grammar is not stored as a large list of rules nestling somewhere within the folds of our brains. Instead, it suggested that 'a balding linguist ate' and 'a very large fish ate' would evoke patterns of neural activity which, although different, would reflect the accumulated experience of things doing eating. These patterns would reflect the convention in English for placing the *subject* (the thing doing the eating) before the verb. If sequences of the form *thing-action-thing* were associated instead with the second thing doing the action to the first thing, then the neural activity associated with these sequences would reflect a grammatical convention which placed the *object* of the verb (the thing being eaten, in this case) before the verb. So grammatical conventions are embodied in the neural response to language input. But if these conventions are embodied in the response to language, how can they be applied during the production of language?

There is, currently, no complete theory that links language understanding with language production. Similarly, there is as yet no complete single theory of how the embodiment of grammatical conventions used to *decode* language is tied to the embodiment of those conventions when used to *encode* language. But there are hints. What follows should give a feel for what such a theory might look like.

During language learning, similar input sequences become associated with similar patterns of neural activity. A particular sentence structure, and hence a particular grammatical convention, becomes associated with a particular pattern of neural activity. In effect, it becomes associated with a particular kind of meaning. This process of association involves a gradual changing of the connections between the different neurons (that is how the patterns of neural activity come to change). So those conventions are actually embodied in the connections between the neurons. This means that the associations could in principle work both ways—sequences of certain kinds would become associated (that is, would give rise to) meanings of certain kinds, and working the other way, those kinds of meaning could give rise to those kinds of sequences. Given that the appropriate associations develop when we learn to extract meaning from what we hear, it is possible that the same associations (but effectively in reverse) ensure that the appropriate sequencing happens when we, in turn, wish to convey meaning with what we speak.

This is necessarily an oversimplification. In Chapter 12, on language disorders, we shall discover that the decoding of grammatical knowledge during understanding, and the encoding of grammatical knowledge during production, rely on associations that, although a little like mirror-images of one another, are actually separate. How two distinct sets of associations can, in effect, do the opposite of one another will be discussed in that chapter. For present purposes, though, whether there is one set of associations that can work in both directions, or two sets of associations that happen to work in opposite directions, is immaterial.

If it is true that decoding and encoding grammatical structure are linked in this way, why should it look as if the ordering of the words is decided before there are any words to order?

In language understanding, sequences of certain kinds evoke meanings of certain kinds. But these sequences are more than just sequences of words—they are actually sequences of concepts. Each word we hear evokes a neural response corresponding to the concept to which that word refers, and it is the changing pattern of these neural responses that corresponds to the meaning of the sequence as a whole. In production, when the associations are run in reverse, particular kinds of meaning are associated with particular orderings of the concepts that make up those meanings. In effect, you have order—grammatical convention—before you select the words that will express those concepts.

Of course, much depends on what you call 'a word'. If a word is its physical form then, yes, those conventions are chosen beforehand. But if a word is its meaning (that is, is the concept to which it refers) then, no, those conventions are not really chosen before the words to which they will apply. In fact, and as we shall shortly see, words are both of these things—each word can be described in terms of a conceptual component and a physical component.

One way or another, words do eventually get uttered. How? Once again, it is informative to look at what happens when things go wrong.

Getting it wrong, again . . . and again . . . and again

Perhaps the most basic thing that speech errors tell us is that when uttering one word, we already have in mind words that are waiting to be uttered, as in the following examples:

> Hey, _joke_, have you heard the _Mike_ about . . .?
> I got into _this guy_ with _a discussion_ . . .

In each case, the words affected by the error must have been simultaneously available for the exchange to have happened. It should not be too surprising that words (and other things) are available simultaneously—after all, we can have in mind a word like 'lips', but we cannot physically say the individual phonemes /l/, /i/, /p/, and /s/ simultaneously. They have to be placed in the mental equivalent of a queue, or buffer. Similarly, when we want to convey information about who–did–what–to–whom, we necessarily have in mind the who, what, and whom. But again, it is impossible to express them simultaneously—

they also must be stored in a queue. And each one of these may need to be expressed with more than one word ('each one of these' corresponds to a single 'who'), and because they also cannot all be articulated simultaneously, they too have to be put in a queue (more of which later).

But not all accidental exchanges involve whole words:

≜   *I'd <u>hear</u> one if I <u>knew</u> it . . .*
But she <u>writes</u> her <u>slanting</u> . . .

Again, two words have exchanged position. But it is a little different in these cases, because if it were a strict exchange (that is, of the whole word, including its physical form), the errors would have ended up as 'I'd heard one if I know it' and 'But she writing her slants'. What actually happened is that the information regarding the intended *tense* of each verb stayed in the right position (as did the affix '-ing'), but the vocabulary items to which this information should have applied exchanged position. Although the tense information was applied to the wrong word in these cases, it was applied correctly given the peculiarities of each word (the error created 'knew', not 'knowed').

These errors suggest that it was not actual (physical) words that changed position, rather it was some more abstract representation of those words which changed position—something similar perhaps to the concept corresponding to the words' meanings. In effect, then, there is a conceptual version of the word that appears to be separable from the physical version. Of course, if the conceptual equivalent of a word can move to the wrong place, leaving the affix in the right place, we should also find the converse error, in which the conceptual equivalents of affixes move, leaving behind the words to which they should have applied. And we do:

≜   *I <u>dis</u>regard this as _precise* [from *I regard this as imprecise*]

What appears to have happened is that the affix meaning 'not' attached itself to the wrong word—to 'regard' instead of 'precise'. But, interestingly, it was not the actual affix that moved, as otherwise the sentence would have been 'I imregard this . . .'. Instead, what moved was the conceptual affix—information that an affix meaning 'not' was required. Although this information was applied to the wrong word, it was applied correctly, as in the previous examples, given the peculiarities of the affected word—when the physical form of the word + affix combination was chosen, the right form was chosen for that particular word.

The idiosyncratic properties of individual words are not always respected when things get out of order:

≜   I *randomed* some *samply* . . .
     I hate *raining* on a *hitchy* day . . .

These exchanges are quite unlike the 'I'd hear one if I knew it' and 'disregard' cases. One cannot create a verb by attaching a verb-like inflection ('-ed') to 'random', or an adverb by attaching an adverbial inflection ('-ly') to 'sample', or an adjective by attaching an adjectival inflection ('-y') to 'hitch'. It is as if the *stems* of each word ('random' in 'randomly', 'sample' in 'sampled', 'rain' in 'rainy', and 'hitch' in 'hitching') have exchanged position, leaving their affixes behind. But whereas the previous errors showed due regard for the properties of the words that were affected by the error, these errors showed no such regard. Why not? Perhaps because these errors happened at a different stage from the others. That is, they happened once the actual stems, affixes, and inflections had been chosen.

So the production of an utterance can be thought of as taking place in stages, with certain things happening before certain others. Further evidence for these distinct stages comes not from errors involving words or inflections, but from errors involving individual phonemes (these are the most frequently made errors):

≜   *heft lemisphere* [from *left hemisphere*]
     He dealt a blushing crow [from *He dealt a crushing blow*]
     a kice ream cone [from *an ice cream cone*]
     Serp is souved [from *Soup is served*]
     Ouch! I have a stick neff [from *Ouch! I have a stiff neck*]

These cases are straightforward exchanges of phonemes. And although Spooner was most famous for those of his errors which led to real words being produced (the 'blushing crow' example is one of his), phoneme exchange errors often lead to the production of anomalous nonwords. Interestingly, when 'an ice cream cone' became 'a kice ream cone', the word that should have been 'an' became 'a', reflecting the fact that the following word now started with a consonant. So the process responsible for changing 'a' into 'an' must happen at a stage in the processing that takes place after the specific words have been selected, and after their phonemes have been selected.

Finally, here is an error which illustrates one last thing that can go wrong once everything else, including the phonemes, has been correctly selected:

⏺   _glear plue_ sky [from _clear blue sky_]
    pig and _vat_ [from _big and fat_]

Here, information about whether or not a phoneme should be _voiced_ has exchanged (see Chapter 3). The phonemes /g/, /b/, and /v/ are produced with the vocal folds vibrating, and are voiced, whereas /k/, /p/, and /f/ are not, and are unvoiced. The first phoneme of 'clear' should have been unvoiced, and the first phoneme of 'blue' voiced. But the relevant information switched around, so that 'clear' became 'glear' and 'blue' became 'plue'. What has exchanged here is one of the component properties of each phoneme. Other properties also can exchange.

All of these errors involved either an exchange of elements, or (in the case of the 'I disregard this as precise' error) the movement of a single element. But there are other errors too. Sometimes, the exchange is never completed, so that something from later on in the utterance can replace something earlier on, but without the corresponding movement of that earlier thing to later on (e.g. 'the pirst part' for 'the first part'). And sometimes the earlier thing can replace a later thing, without that later thing moving to the earlier position (e.g. 'beef needle' for 'beef noodle').

There are a number of fundamental things that all these errors, taken together, tell us about the production process. They provide evidence both of the nature of the elements that are queued, or buffered (anything that can move from later in an utterance to earlier is one such queuing element), and of the ordering of the different stages in the production process, with different kinds of error occurring at each different stage.

There is one further piece of evidence that is fundamental in terms of shaping an account of how production proceeds: these errors are not just random events. If they were, then anything ought to be able to move to anywhere else. But there is one element which, surprisingly, is never involved in these kinds of error—the syllable. The sentence 'He plays the trombone' could never give rise to an error like 'He troms the playbone' because 'trom' is neither a word nor an affix. It is a syllable, and syllables never migrate. Parts of syllables do, but never whole syllables, unless they are also a word, or an affix. We shall come to this a little later on, because syllables do none the less have a vital role to play in the production process. But there is another, non-random feature of these errors which is even more important: there are no errors in which an entire word swaps with just a phoneme, or where the first phoneme of a syllable swaps with the last phoneme of a syllable, or where an affix at the beginning of a word (a prefix) moves to the end of another word. In all cases, an element can only exchange with an element of the same kind, or can only replace an element of the same kind, or can only move to a position normally occupied by an element of the same kind. Where does this like-for-like constraint come from?

Sketching out the utterance

When we speak, we provide our listeners with a specification (a builder's plan) of what to construct within their mental models.

And like all specifications and plans, this one cannot come into being instantaneously. Instead, it must be created in stages, with something more being added to the plan at each stage. The fact that errors affect only one kind of element at a time suggests that the production of an utterance involves a sketching-out process in which one level of detail, involving just one kind of element, is sketched out before another. And as we have seen, different kinds of errors provide important clues regarding the sequence in which things are sketched out, and the nature of the elements that can be independently queued or buffered (that is, added to the sketch as an independent piece of information).

To begin with, the utterance is sketched out as an ordered sequence of concepts. These concepts may then be fleshed out some more, so that information about the actual words that will express those concepts is added to the sketch. But this information is again only in sketch form. For instance, the concept corresponding to a verb like 'slants' would be fleshed out to include the information that a word corresponding to the concept 'slant' is required, and the information that it must be inflected for third person singular. The part of the sketch corresponding to the concept 'slant' would be fleshed out to include information about the actual word that will be used to express it. Similarly for the inflection. This would include information about the onset of each syllable (the 'sl' of 'slants'), and the remainder ('ants'). And the remainder would be further sketched out in terms of its component phonemes: the vowel and the consonants following. Finally, these phonemes would be sketched out in terms of their component properties, including the ways in which they should be articulated, whether they should be voiced or not, and whether the mouth should close completely or not. These properties, or *features*, specify the *motor program* (the muscular movements) that causes the actual articulation.[5]

This sketching out process is nothing more than the operation of the neural circuitry. One way to think of it is in terms of different circuits corresponding to the different levels of the sketch, with the activation of one circuit causing the activation of the next, one after the other. Some circuits probably feed into several others which, operating in parallel, then together feed in to a single circuit further along the chain. But how could a single chain of circuits simultaneously encode the sketch for more than one concept? In other words, if this chain of circuits encodes

[5] This sketching-out framework owes much to Merrill Garrett, now at the University of Arizona, and subsequently Gary Dell, at the University of Illinois. Almost all contemporary models of speech production borrow something from their work.

the sketching out for what should become 'slants', how can this same circuit also encode the sketch for a later word in the sentence—for what will become 'writing'? How does the brain do queues?

There are no real queues in the brain, just connections between neurons, and patterns of neural activity that happen when some of those neurons become activated and in turn activate the neurons they are connected to. A mental queue is nothing more than different patterns of activity, corresponding to the different things in the queue, with one pattern (the first thing in the queue) more active than another (the second thing) which is more active than another (the third) and so on. The equivalent of things getting removed from the queue is when that first pattern rapidly decreases in activity (having first triggered some neural consequence—another neural circuit), leaving what had previously been the second most active pattern to become more active, to the point where it also triggers some neural consequence, before also decreasing in activity.[6] It is as if there is something pointing at each pattern in turn and telling it to become more active as a function of how near the top of the mental queue it is. Exactly what controls this changing profile of activation is unclear, although in Chapter 13, on artificial brains, we shall see how the activation of a single set of (artificial) neurons can lead to a sequence just like this. What matters for the moment is that the brain can do queues.

The basic idea, then, is that there is a chain of circuits in which each circuit encodes some particular level of the sketch. If a circuit at one end of the chain encodes concepts, say, and a circuit at the other end encodes phonemes, then the pattern of activity spreading across that entire chain will correspond to the sketching out of a particular concept in the manner outlined earlier. And there may be a second, less activated pattern also spreading across that entire chain, which corresponds to the sketching out of another concept in the queue. Within any one circuit, components of these two patterns will both exist, one more strongly than the other. In effect, each neural circuit encodes its own mini-queue.

These different neural circuits do not need to be physically separate. It is possible, in principle, for the same set of neurons to encode different circuits. It is also possible for the same set of neurons to encode a queue in which the same phoneme, word, or whatever, appears at different positions within that same queue. Saying 'bath the baby', for instance,

---

[6] William James described this same idea in 1890 in his two-volume work *Principles of Psychology*.

requires the /b/ phoneme to appear at different positions within the phoneme queue. Some of the artificial neural circuits described in Chapter 13 do just this. For the moment, whether the different neural circuits are encoded across different neurons, or the same ones, does not matter.

If each neural circuit encodes its own mini-queue, then it follows that if one pattern within that circuit gets a bit of a boost (we shall see why it might in a moment), it could swap positions with another pattern that is 'higher up' that circuit's queue. And because each circuit represents just one kind of element, any misordering errors within a queue will affect only one kind of element—the like-for-like constraint.

Why might a pattern of activity get an error-causing boost? In the first experimental study to elicit speech errors back in the early 1970s, Bernard Baars and colleagues at the University of California in Los Angeles asked people to read pairs of words as quickly as possible. They made errors, like 'barn door' instead of 'darn bore', as much as 15% of the time, but only when the pair was preceded by pairs such as 'born dart' which shared the initial phonemes of the error they hoped to induce. So if they saw 'born dart' then 'darn bore', they were likely to say 'born dart' correctly, then 'barn door'. Presumably, the errors occurred because the pattern corresponding to the queue for syllable-initial phonemes (/b/ at the top of the queue, then /d/) had existed previously (in response to 'born dart'), and some residual activity may still have been present. In support of this is the finding that errors are more likely the faster the speech rate, which gives even less time for those patterns of activity to reduce enough (tongue-twisters are no fun when said slowly). But not all errors involve overlaps with patterns that had existed previously, or with patterns later on in the queue, and no doubt some errors are simply due to random noise within the system.

But is it not a little contrived to suggest that there is a queue devoted only to *syllable-initial phonemes*? It would certainly explain why they can be subject to errors and can swap places with one another. But is it reasonable to suppose that there is one queue for syllable-initial phonemes, another for syllable-final phonemes, and another even for the vowel in the middle? The answer to this question lies in the manner by which the neural circuitry itself develops. In Chapter 9, which dealt with neural circuitry and meaning, we saw that patterns of neural activity change as a function of experience; they come to reflect those experiences. Things which can occur in similar contexts will give rise to patterns of activity that are similar, but with subtle differences reflecting the actual differences between the different things. To take a concrete example: phonemes can occur in fairly similar contexts, although each is subtly different from the others. So all phonemes will give rise to similar, but subtly different, patterns. In effect, our experience of phonemes causes the development of a neural circuit—a set of connections between neurons which gives rise to the patterns of activation corresponding to the different phonemes. But phonemes at the beginnings of syllables necessarily occur in contexts which are different from those in which phonemes at the ends of syllables occur. This difference will give rise to different components in the neural patterns that encode those phonemes—and these different components constitute different circuits.

Finally, where do syllables figure in all of this? Syllables are articulatory *gestures*. The movement of the articulators does not proceed phoneme-by-phoneme, but syllable-by-syllable. Try saying the phoneme /b/ on its own. You simply cannot. You *can* say /ba/, or /bi/, or /b some-other-vowel/. In other words, you can only say it in the context of a syllable. Vowels, unlike consonants, can be uttered as single phonemes, but then they can also be single syllables—the word 'a' is a single phoneme, a single syllable, and a single word. Syllables, therefore, are the last thing to be added to the sketch. Everything that comes before, including phonemes and their features, serves this final act. Unlike the other components in speech production, syllables specify actions. The neural circuitry associated with these specifications is similar, in some respects, to the circuitry responsible for other kinds of muscular movement. And that is what makes syllables different—they are connected to a different kind of circuitry, and this is reflected in the finding that they are not subject to the same kinds of misordering as the other elements implicated in speech production.

Beyond speech errors

Psycholinguistics owes much to the imperfect mechanism it studies—if we made no errors, there would be no basis for speculating about the kinds of mechanism that could give rise to them. But there are other ways of studying that mechanism, although the issues remain the same. For example, having established that there are different kinds of mental queue, we could try to determine how long each queue was by looking at how far apart different kinds of element need to be before they can no longer exchange (words exchange over far greater distances than phonemes, for example).

Much of the time when we speak we do nothing of the sort. We pause. But the pattern of pausing in normal spontaneous speech is quite different from the pattern when reading aloud. Reading aloud does not require any planning at the conceptual level (that is, at the level of the content of what is to be said); the words and their order are determined by the text. Basically, all the speaker need worry about is getting the sounds right for each word—putting the information about those sounds onto the appropriate queues in the right order. But when is that information put onto the queues? And how far ahead does that information stretch? If the answer to the first question is 'during the pauses', then the answer to the second would be 'as far ahead as the next pause'. A big 'if', but it leads to some interesting conclusions.

Marilyn Ford, an Australian psycholinguist working in the USA in the early 1980s, measured the brief pauses in a large sample of spontaneous speech. She found that the majority of the pauses divided each utterance into 'chunks', where each chunk was a *clause*, containing just one verb. In effect, each of these clauses was a single who–did–what-to-whom statement (see Chapter 7 for discussion of who–did–what-to-whom). This suggests, if queuing does indeed happen during pausing, that the concepts associated with each who–did–what-to-whom statement were put on the mental queue just before each such statement was to be uttered. Apparently, then, the concept queue is as long as necessary to convey the who, what, and whom.

Around the same time that Marilyn Ford was measuring the pauses in spontaneous speech, Paul Gee and François Grosjean in Boston were doing the equivalent with read speech. They found, to simplify somewhat, that the pause pattern most naturally divided each sentence into chunks containing a single content word and any function words that preceded it. In effect, each chunk was whatever was required to express a single concept and its grammatical role. This suggests that the information regarding the sounds of each word was being queued more or less one concept (one who, what, or whom) at a time.

In a sense this is quite counter-intuitive—surely we pause and hesitate far more in spontaneous speaking than during reading aloud? Yet it looks from these data as if there were more pauses (or at least, people paused after shorter intervals) in the reading case. In fact, during normal spontaneous speech, there are frequent pauses all over the place. But the major pauses, in Ford's measurements, occurred between clauses. In fact, pausing is not the only thing that divides speech up into chunks. The melody and rhythms of speech do too, and these also often reflect the conceptual and clausal structure. It is possible, even, that how far each queue extends is in part determined by those melodies and rhythms. This is the focus of much research.

Beyond the dysfluencies of speech

Until the late 1980s, most of what we knew about how we speak was based on the dysfluencies with which we speak. But since then, research into speech production has undergone a small revolution, much of which has been inspired by a group in The Netherlands headed by Willem Levelt. Experimental techniques have been developed there (and subsequently elsewhere) which allow the researcher to delve more deeply into the individual stages of the process, and monitor what is going on as it happens. And yet, despite the major advances that this offers, the basic model of speech production that is almost universally accepted within the psycholinguistic community is the same one as had been developed from the error data. What has changed is that we can now both confirm that model, and add to it.

Many of these experimental techniques involve a variation on the priming theme. In Chapter 6 we saw that the time it takes to recognize a target word can be shortened if a word is presented beforehand which is related in meaning (as 'brush' is to 'broom'). It turns out that the time to say a word can also be reduced if an appropriate prime is presented beforehand. How the target words are presented varies from study to study. In many of these studies, people simply have to name a picture of a common object. But whether or not the time to name that picture can be reduced, by presenting a prime beforehand, depends on a number of factors.

If utterances are sketched out in the way that was described earlier, there will be a stage during the production of a word when the physical form of a word (its sounds) will not yet have been chosen, but the concept associated with that word will have been. Only later will information about that word's physical form become available. This means that there will be an early stage during the preparation of the target's utterance when a priming word related in meaning could influence the time to produce the target, but a priming word with some of the same phonemes would not. Only at a later stage would the sound-related prime be effective. This is exactly what was found in a study conducted by Herbert Schriefers, Antje Meyer, and Willem Levelt. They asked people to name pictures of objects shown to them as quickly as possible, while playing over headphones a word that was related either in meaning or in sound to each object's name. And when they varied the delay between playing that word, and showing the picture, they found exactly the predicted pattern—to be effective, meaning-related words had to be played earlier (relative to when the picture appeared) than sound-related words.

For priming-by-sound to occur, as in this last study, the overlapping sounds must be presented at just the right time. Too soon and the activation they cause dies down completely before the target word is sketched out. Too late and the target word has been sketched out already and the relevant circuits activated. If the initial sounds of the target word are added to the sketch before the final sounds (as opposed to at the same time, which could in principle happen), something which will prime those initial sounds must be presented sooner than something that will prime those final sounds. And this was also found; primes sharing the initial sounds of the target had to be presented earlier than primes sharing the later sounds of the target.

The use of priming techniques to study the production process is still, at the time of writing, in its infancy. An even newer procedure for studying these same issues has been developed by Miranda van Turennout, also in The Netherlands, who has found that electrical activity within the brain can vary depending on when meaning-related or sound-related information is activated before naming a picture. Taken together, these new techniques mean we now no longer need to rely exclusively on detailed analyses of just the output of the language production process. We may not know much about what the input is to that process, but at least we can now tamper with it, and observe the effects of the tampering on the output. The study of language production is now an experimental science.

≜

To produce language, and to understand it, are the most natural of adult human activities. But words are transient things, lasting little more than the moment it takes to speak them, or the moment it takes to comprehend them. At any one moment, the majority of words exist not in spoken form, but in written form. Such words usually exist for as long as the paper exists on which they are written, and yet reading those words is a surprisingly unnatural human activity. It is the activity to which we turn next.

The written word

Many of the world's languages exist not just in spoken form but in written form too. The advent of the written word must surely rank, together with fire and the wheel, as one of mankind's greatest achievements. John Maynard Smith, an evolutionist, has described the invention of writing as one of the major evolutionary transitions to have taken place since the creation of life itself—the only other time that evolution came up with a system for storing and transmitting information was when it came up with the genetic code. The practical consequences of this development are innumerable. Science and technology would hardly have progressed beyond the Dark Ages were it not for the written word—science simply relies on too much information for it to be passed down through the generations by word of mouth alone. Even within a single generation, or for a single individual, there is too much to commit to memory. Where would Einstein have been without his notes? But paradoxically, the earliest writings were not devised so as to enable scientific or cultural progress. They were neither religious manuscripts nor philosophical treatises. Those earliest writings were devised instead for the purposes of trade—they were, in effect, ledgers.

The precursor of the modern book—pages of goat or sheep skin sewn together and bound between wooden boards—dates from about 200 BC, and was developed in Ancient Greece, although papyrus scrolls had existed in Egypt since around 2500 BC. But some of the earliest writing systems were hardly writing systems at all—they were based on small clay tokens whose different shapes and markings represented a variety of different things (animals, body parts, substances, and so on). These tokens were used between around 9000 BC and 3000 BC. Some of the same shapes and patterns can be found in written scripts which developed in southern Mesopotamia (now Iraq). These scripts (called *cuneiform*) were originally derived from a hieroglyphic writing system, although not from the better known Egyptian variety. Egyptian hieroglyphics date from about 3500 BC, and were amongst the earliest and longest lasting of the hieroglyphic systems. Hieroglyphics were not particularly suited to mass production, and so more convenient versions were developed. The first of these were the Mesopotamian cuneiform scripts and the Egyptian *demotic* script.

The evolution of writing systems

The earliest writers suffered from a dearth of readers. There was no alternative in pre-hieroglyphic times but to use signs that fairly directly represented whatever it was that was being conveyed. As these signs became more widely used, they gradually changed and became more stylized, until they hardly resembled any more the things that they stood for. This process can be seen in cave paintings from as early as 20 000 BC. Of course, as writers became more expressive and wanted to refer to things which could not be pictured directly, it was inevitable that symbols would be introduced which bore less and less resemblance to the things being referred to ('horse' is easy, 'summer' less so, and 'fresh' a real challenge). But such writing systems are necessarily limited, because the more things you want to refer to, the more symbols you need to devise, and the more symbols you, as either the writer or the reader, need to learn. Fortunately, two developments occurred which relieved readers and writers alike from an overdose of symbols.

First, symbols started to be used to refer not to things out there in the world, but to the spoken words that were themselves used to refer to those things. This meant, for instance, that two words that sounded the same could have the same symbol. Many words sound alike, but are not identical (e.g. 'peach' and 'speech'), and the second development was that *phonetic* symbols were introduced to represent individual sounds (a symbol for the /s/ sound could be tacked onto the symbol for 'peach'). The hieroglyphic and cuneiform scripts used combinations of symbols in exactly this way.

It is not hard to see how someone could have figured out that the next step should be the development of a fully sound-based writing system. The first such systems were in fact *syllabaries*—one symbol for each syllable. Japanese is an example of a language that uses a syllabary. In fact, it uses two—*hiragana* and *katakana*. Both these syllabaries, dating from around the ninth century, can represent all the syllables of the language, although katakana is more often used to represent words imported from other languages. Hiragana is the first script taught in school.

Modern *alphabets*—one symbol per phoneme in the language—owe their origins to the semitic alphabet developed in Syria and Palestine between 1500 BC and 2000 BC. It was itself based, probably, on a syllabary that had been developed from the Egyptian hieroglyphics. This semitic alphabet contained only consonants (and to this day, vowels are only optionally shown in Hebrew and Arabic scripts). It was not until around 1000 BC that the Ancient Greeks added the vowels to create a full alphabet. It was from the Greek alphabet that the Roman alphabet (used in English and other European languages) was derived.

Alphabetic systems are a great improvement on the earlier ones, because no more symbols are required than there are individual phonemes in the spoken language. Often, fewer symbols are required. In English, for instance, there are about 44 phonemes, but just 26 letters. Combinations of letters are used to represent some of the individual phonemes, for example in 'chatter', 'shout', 'thunder', 'sing'. The number of symbols can increase if different *pitch patterns* need to be marked—in the *pinyin* version of Mandarin Chinese (which transcribes spoken Chinese using the Roman alphabet), 'bōli' means 'glass', whilst 'bōlí' means 'to peel off (e.g. skin)' and 'bólì' means 'small profits'—but even so only a relatively small number of symbols are required. Syllabaries are a nice idea in principle, but in a language like English, with around 12 000 syllables, many of which are rarely used, a syllabary would be rather unwieldy. By comparison, Japanese uses fewer than 120 syllables, and like other languages with small numbers of syllables, it relies on having lots of syllables in each word. In English, by contrast, many words are just single syllables.

The development of the alphabet was a landmark in writing design— if you knew the mapping between the written symbols and the spoken sounds of your language, you could in principle read any printed word, even one that you had never seen before. Simple really—although the fact that the written version of the most spoken language in the world, Mandarin Chinese, does not use an alphabetic script is somewhat paradoxical. Chinese consists of *logograms*—a single character represents, in effect, a whole word. English has logograms too: $, £, @, and % are examples, as are many road signs, and the numerals 1, 2, 3, and so on. English can also combine some of its logograms with phonetic symbols, something which is common in Chinese and hieroglyphics: '1st', '2nd', and '3rd', for instance. But what have ancient history and modern Chinese got to do with how we read?

The characters you see on the page in front of you are just arbitrary shapes based on just one of the different kinds of writing system that have developed through the ages. Chinese has very much more in common with hieroglyphics than it does with the Roman alphabet. The Japanese syllabic scripts are different again, and have more in common with the written form of Cherokee (another syllabary) than they do with either English or Chinese. But does the existence of these different writing systems mean that their respective readers do profoundly different things when reading? Japanese writing commonly uses different writing systems in the space of a single line (*kanji* symbols, borrowed from the Chinese, and one or other or both of the syllabic scripts)—but does this mean that Japanese readers switch between one kind of reading and another in the space of a single line? The fact that some languages read top-to-bottom, some read right to left, and others left-to-right (although none, apparently, read bottom-to-top) seems like an almost trivial difference by comparison with the different kinds of script that are possible—alphabetic, syllabic, or logographic. What are the implications of these differences for the ways in which we read? Surprisingly, there are very few. And to see why, we need to look at not just how we, as adults, read, but also how children learn to read. For convenience, we shall start with how children learn just one of the many possible scripts in use today—*this* one.

Learning to read

How children learn to read, and how best to teach them to read, has been the subject of much controversy over the last 20 years or so. How children read, and what factors contribute to their reading skill, has often been overlooked. There is no doubt that the child's home environment plays an important part; even simplistic measures such as how many books there are in the household have been found to correlate with how well the child reads in later years. Of course, correlations do not imply causes—the sheer number of books in a household does not itself cause good reading. It probably means that parents who are keen readers are more likely to read with their children, and that this gives the children the advantage. Recently, it has even been claimed that children under one year of age who are given books to play with are likely to read better, later on, than children who have not been given books to play with at this age. But home environment is just one factor. A more complete picture of what influences the child's development of reading skills (which includes not just how well they read but how they read) would of course have to include the way in which the child is taught to read, not to mention the time spent learning to read, and the time spent practising what has been learned.

As adults, we forget how much we needed to be taught about reading. Some of it is so basic that we probably cannot imagine ever not knowing it. For instance, one consequence of an alphabetic system is that, generally, the more sounds in a spoken word, the more characters in the written version of that word. But this is something we need to learn. If you show pre-literate children the words TWO and TOOTH-BRUSH, and ask them to point to which one corresponds to the spoken word 'two', or to the spoken word 'toothbrush', they can do no better than guess—they do not naturally assume that the longer sounding word must go with the longer looking word.[7] Even children who are just starting to read, as well as adults who have never learned to read, will often make mistakes. So the printed word starts off as a meaningless jumble.

The first task for the young child is to realize that written words correspond to spoken words. But the child also needs to know the nature of that correspondence—whether the characters it sees correspond to phonemes, syllables, whole words, or some combination of these. To a certain extent, the way in which the child is explicitly taught to read determines the way in which the child approaches the correspondence problem. The *phonics* method of teaching introduces the child to the notion of *sounding out*. When the child encounters a new word, he or she can sound it out and in this way retrieve the spoken version. This method explicitly teaches the correspondence between letters and sounds, something which, in principle, should be ideal for an alphabetic system. In practice, though, it may not be. English is a very irregular language—the same sounds can be written using different letters (e.g. 'see'/'sea'/'ceiling'), and the same letters can stand for different sounds (e.g. 'gist'/'gift'). The English-speaking child has somehow to be able to cope with this irregularity. Speakers of Finnish or Arabic, for example, do not; these languages are almost totally regular.

An alternative to phonics is the *whole-word* (or look-and-say) method. Here, the aim is to get children to recognize written words without having to first break them down into letters and then figure out the sounds of those letters. Often, this method is taught by labelling objects around the classroom, or using pictures of objects with their labels underneath. There are two advantages to this approach: it avoids the problem, in English at least, of the vast irregularity of the written/spoken correspondence, and it also teaches children to concentrate not on how a word sounds, but on what it means. But is one method better than the other?

---

[7] Letters in upper case will be used here to transcribe written words. Words in quotes (e.g. 'dog') will generally refer, for the purposes of this chapter, to the spoken form of the word. Letters in slashes (e.g. /d/) refer to phonemes, as before.

It is this last question that has caused so much argument and controversy. The arguments are complex. On the one hand, alphabetic writing systems seem designed for a phonics-style approach. On the other hand, and as we shall see below, there is evidence suggesting that proficient adult readers do not break down each written word into the individual sounds that the different letters represent—instead they appear to access the meaning directly from the visual form in much the same way as the whole-word approach to teaching encourages. Moreover, they appear to do this even if they had been taught by the phonics method. But just because adults do not necessarily take advantage of letter-to-sound correspondences when reading, does not mean that children should not need to acquire knowledge of those correspondences when learning to read. The evidence suggests, in fact, that the phonics method leads to better reading by the time the child is nine or ten. We shall return to this shortly.

But which way children are taught to read fails to address the psycholinguistic issue of how these children actually read, and how they extract meaning from the characters on the page. Do they extract meaning directly? Or do they first translate the letters into sounds, and get at the meaning that way? In fact, it seems that they do a bit of both, but at different stages in the development of their reading skill, and only partly determined by the way they have been taught.

To begin with, children develop what is called a *sight vocabulary*. They associate, for instance, the sequence of letters D-O-G with the word 'dog' directly, and not by having associated the letter D with the phoneme /d/, O with /o/, and G with /g/. So at this stage, the written form of 'dog' could just as well be CAT. If you cannot imagine what it would be like not to use letter-to-sound correspondences when recognizing written words, it is a little like recognizing $5 as 'five dollars', or 204 as 'two hundred and four', or 'I ♥ New York' as 'I *love* New York', or, finally, YACHT as 'yacht'. This word is so irregular that only the letter-to-sound correspondences of the first and last letters are of much use.

There is some evidence that children taught by the phonics method never develop a pure sight vocabulary, but do use some information about letter-to-sound correspondences when reading certain words. But the information they use is very limited—in these earliest stages of reading development almost all children focus their attention on just parts of the written word (mainly the first letter, and to a certain extent, the last letter also). Children at this stage thus ignore much of the letter information contained within the written word. If they do have any letter-to-sound awareness, they might use this awareness as a clue regarding which word is intended. But without that awareness, the shape alone (of certain letters) would be the main clue.

As children become more proficient at reading, their knowledge about letter-to-sound correspondences becomes more developed. Even children taught by the whole-word method will become aware of the similarities in pronunciation that exist between words that are spelled similarly. They therefore develop, and use, two routes to accessing the meanings of written words—one of them via letter-to-sound correspondences, and the other directly. What changes as the child develops is how much each is relied on. Proficient adult readers rely more on the direct route, although individuals (and especially children) may differ quite markedly in how much reliance they place on each of those two routes. But is this the only difference between adult and child readers? It sounds somewhat counter-intuitive to suggest that what adult readers do is most similar to what beginning readers do (relying mainly on a sight vocabulary), and is most different from what intermediary readers do (placing increased reliance on letter-to-sound correspondences). And indeed, this is the subject of considerable controversy, as exemplified by this question: is the 'direct' route used by adults the same route that children employ when they recognize a word by sight alone? Some researchers believe it is, and others believe it is not.

The idea that adults, and children too, rely on two different routes to accessing the meanings of written words is not without its theoretical difficulties—how, for instance, do you decide which route to use? And why go to all that effort to establish letter-to-sound correspondences if, as an adult, you will apparently throw much of it away in favour of a more whole-word approach? Is it inevitable that things work this way, or is this just some psychological oddity? In fact, it is inevitable, and this inevitability explains why what children do in China, when they learn to read, is not much different from what children do anywhere else.

On learning that ink blots have meaning

The child's task, when learning to read, is to associate written words with their meanings. This, after all, is the purpose of the written word—to convey meaning. The meaning is provided, so to speak, by the teacher; either by saying the word, or by pointing to a picture, or by having attached a label with that word onto the thing that the word stands for, although to begin with it is nothing more than just a complicated ink blot. This does not present a problem, because this ink blot (or however much of it the child attends to) can still become associated with the meaning. The way this works is simple: things which tend to occur together gradually become associated with one another. Encountering one thing (e.g. the ink blot) will, after learning, evoke a pattern of neural activity that would be similar to that evoked by the other (e.g. the meaning).

This learning mechanism is driven by things occurring together, and more specifically, the occurrence of one thing predicting the occurrence of the other (see Chapters 9 and 13). But reading involves more than just ink blots and meanings. If each word is said out loud as part of the teaching method, the sounds of each word will also be present. The word-as-ink-blot can therefore become associated both with its meaning directly, and with its corresponding sounds, which are, in turn, associated with that meaning.

But the associations do not stop there, because certain sounds will tend to occur only when certain parts of the various ink blots are present. These parts (the individual letters) occur in different combinations in different words, so the word-as-ink-blot is soon replaced by the word-as-combinations-of-letters. And because these letters will tend to predict those different sounds, they will become associated with those sounds. These associations may form either with help, in the case of children explicitly taught the letter-to-sound correspondences, or without, in the case of children who have not yet been taught those correspondences but who none the less develop an awareness of them.

One complication, in English at least, is that letters which have tended to occur with only certain sounds may, on certain occasions, occur with different sounds—E, I, and G, for example, do not normally occur with the sound that corresponds to the sequence EIG in REIGN. In this case, the combination of letters (or, again, whichever letters the child attends to) will become associated with the actual sounds that are heard, because it is this combination that predicts the appropriate sounds. Things become more complex still when one considers that combinations of letters may become associated not just with the sounds that the child hears, but with the sounds that the child produces when pronouncing each word. Consequently, combinations of letters may become associated with the gestures of pronunciation—with syllables, for instance (see Chapter 10 for more about syllabic gestures).

So there are a lot of different associations, all happening, potentially, at the same time. It sounds terribly complex, with lots of things being associated with lots of other things. But with these complexities comes a very definite advantage—it does not matter whether the script is alphabetic, syllabic, or logographic; the manner in which we are able to learn associations will apply equally well to each one. This is why Japanese, Chinese, Arabic, and English children (in fact, all children) probably start off doing pretty much the same thing when learning to read. The result of their learning will look quite different, though, because the different written forms of these languages mean that different features of the ink blots predict different aspects of the spoken language (predicting either phonemes, syllables, whole words, or a combination of these, as is required in, for instance, Chinese).

This is all very well, but what about the fact that proficient readers of English appear to abandon the alphabetic principle—the letter-to-sound correspondences—when accessing the meanings of written words? On the assumption that individual letter-to-sound pairings are very much more common than individual word-to-meaning pairings, we should expect the letter-to-sound associations to be very much stronger, and very much more influential, than the word-to-meaning associations, because a basic property of associative learning is that the more common the pairings, the stronger the associations. Yet it is those word-to-meaning associations that are apparently favoured in adulthood, not the letter-to-sound ones. How can this be explained?

This is a controversial issue. In all likelihood, a number of factors contribute to the pattern. One of these may be that the direct associations between print and meaning (that is, bypassing sound) are simply more consistent than those from letters to sounds, because of the irregularities of languages like English. Another reason may be that as children get older, they stop reading aloud as part of their reading classes, and start to read for meaning—for themselves. This means that their task, as learners, is not to predict from the print on the page the correct pronunciation for that word, but to predict its correct meaning. The associations from letters to sounds allow such prediction only indirectly. And if we assume (as before) that associations form, and are strengthened, in order to allow such predictions to be made, it follows that the direct associations from print to meaning will be strengthened with each successive pairing of a word and its meaning. So for any given word, the child may progress from a stage when only the letter-to-sound and sound-to-meaning associations are strong enough to enable the word's meaning to be retrieved, through a stage when these associations work together with the direct

print-to-meaning associations to retrieve that word's meaning, to a stage
when the word's meaning is effectively retrieved on the basis of the
direct print-to-meaning associations alone.

An important aspect of this gradual shift is that although the print-to-
meaning associations predominate, both sets of associations will be
operating, so to speak; it is just that in certain cases (e.g. commonly
encountered words) the direct word-to-meaning associations will be
stronger, and in certain other cases (e.g. infrequently encountered
words) the word-to-sound-to-meaning associations will be stronger.
Even in the case of commonly encountered words, because both kinds of
association are operating, aspects of the sound structure of the spoken
version of each word (aspects of its pronunciation, perhaps) will be
retrieved, but not as a prerequisite to retrieving the word's meaning.
What this means, in answer to an earlier question, is that the direct route
used by adults to retrieve the meaning of a word is not quite the same
as the route used by children when they recognize words by sight
alone. The adult route is a rich, but delicately balanced, combination of
associations.

Even though, as adults, we do not generally retrieve meanings on the
basis of simple letter-to-sound correspondences, these correspondences
are not lost. If they were, we would not be able to read new words that
we had never encountered before, or words which we encountered so
rarely that the word-to-meaning associations had not formed strongly
enough to allow the meaning to be activated on the basis of the visual
information alone. This may also contribute, in part, to another paradox
we encountered earlier—that the phonics approach to the teaching of
reading, not the whole-word approach, apparently leads to better
reading later on. Children taught this way are able to read new words
they have not seen before, which in turn means that when practising
their new-found skill, they are likely to access the appropriate meanings
more successfully than children who, having been taught by the whole-
word method, cannot cope so well when left to their own devices. As
always, practice makes perfect, but only when the practice is successful.

The next step is to attempt to verify all this.

Getting it wrong, yet again

One of the most productive research tools for discovering how children
read is an analysis of the errors they produce. If beginning readers

recognized words according to letter-to-sound correspondences, we would expect errors to happen when the child applied a letter-to-sound correspondence that just happened, because of the irregularities of English, to be inappropriate (e.g. 'fatty' for FATE, 'fairy' for FARE, or perhaps 'ray-gun' for REIGN). We would also expect such children to be able to read new words that they had not seen before, but only when they had regular spellings. But if young readers recognize words by their visual shape, independently of the sounds associated with the individual letters, then we would expect the errors to be related by shape and not sound (e.g. perhaps 'dad', for BED). In addition, these readers should do badly with new words, whether regular or irregular. And if children focus more on certain letters in the word (e.g. the first letter) than certain others, then we would expect the errors to share either their sound, or their shape with those letters, but not necessarily with the others. Seeing how these patterns of errors change over time provides an important indication of what kinds of reading strategies the child adopts at different stages in his or her reading development.

Working out what adults do is harder, because they rarely make errors. There are circumstances, though, when even adults make large numbers of reading errors. Admittedly, these circumstances are confined in the most part to psycholinguistic laboratories. In the mid-1980s, Guy van Orden at the University of California in San Diego took advantage of the fact that when adults are asked to say, as fast as possible, whether a word like FEAT is a part of the body, they will often say 'yes', even though this response would only be appropriate for the like-sounding word FEET. Similarly for HARE and HAIR. A clever feature of this work was that van Orden ensured that such errors are not due to just the physical similarity of the words. If they were, adults should also mistakenly judge FELT, or PAIR, to be a part of the body. But they do not. (The actual examples used by van Orden differed from the ones shown here, although the principle is exactly the same.)

The fact that FEAT–FEET errors were made seems to contradict the view that the sound of a word does not influence the access of that word's meaning. It turns out, in fact, that these errors only occur for words which are infrequent in the language—they tend not to happen for very frequent words in pairs like SUN–SON.

The overall picture with proficient adult readers, then, is that the meanings of the most commonly encountered words are accessed directly, and not via sounds. Less frequently encountered words, and novel words that have never been encountered before, are accessed using letter-to-sound correspondences.

It is beginning to look as if there is not that much more to say about reading. For the printed word to become associated with meaning requires processes that are essentially the same, irrespective of which script, or which language, we read in. As usual, what we do as adults is very much a by-product of the way in which we learn, as children.

An interesting example of one such by-product is the strong feeling we often have that our reading is accompanied by some kind of inner speech (often referred to as *subvocalization*). Various studies have shown that there is some muscular involvement in this inner speech: we do not just imagine it. They also show that subvocalization happens to a far greater extent in earlier reading than in later reading—earlier reading tends to place greater emphasis on overt vocalization. So reading can be a quite active process, involving more than just the route (whichever route that is) from print to meaning. But the story is not over yet. There is still one more very active ingredient to reading which, although essential, is all too easily overlooked—the role of the eyes.

Moving eyes

Eye movements are a little like breathing—we can take conscious control of them, but we can also let go of that control and allow automatic processes that are unavailable to our consciousness to take over. Much of what happens when we move our eyes during reading is under such automatic control. It is for this reason that we are generally unaware, for instance, that the time we spend looking at any one word can depend on factors such as: its length (shorter times for shorter words); its frequency of occurrence in the language (shorter times for more frequent words, even once length is controlled for); its grammatical function (longer times, for instance, on verbs than on nouns); its predictability from the context (shorter times for more predictable words); and the complexity of what is being read (see Chapter 7 for an example of how this last effect can be used to study language processing).

The information that we receive from our eyes is complex. And whilst it is easy enough to say that the information on a page is associated with sounds, or with meaning, life is not quite that simple. For a start, the same letters can have different shapes (g, G, or **g**, for example), and different fonts (such as **bold** or *italic*) add to the range of different shapes that each letter can have. And yet, once we have learned the lower-to-uppercase correspondence, we have little difficulty interpreting all the different varieties of print, even varieties that we may never have seen before. So when talking about associations between letters and sounds or meanings, we do not mean associations with specific visual images of letters (in which case even s, *s*, and s would each be different). Instead, what must happen is that, with experience, these different versions of the letter 's' come to evoke the same pattern of neural activity. And it is this pattern, which in effect represents the concept of the letter 's', that is associated with sound or meaning. Exactly how these different images give rise to the same concept is unclear—in all likelihood it is a process that is very similar to the one described in Chapter 9. The idea there was that the patterns of neural activity that are evoked by something come to reflect the contexts in which that something can occur. If things occur in similar contexts, then they will evoke similar patterns of neural activity. The context may include the physical attributes of the things in question, but also other aspects of the context in which these things occur. So no matter what the 's' looks like, each version has something in common, physically, contextually, and predictively, and it is this commonality that is picked up on.

But different letter shapes is the least of the problems that the reader has to contend with. Far more serious is the fact that the print we read is constantly moving. Well, not quite. But whereas the page tends to stay still, our eyes do not. And because our eyes move across the page, the image of that page on our retinas also moves. On the face of it, the way in which the eyes move will necessarily influence the nature of the image that reaches the brain, and will therefore have important consequences for the way in which information can be 'lifted', so to speak, from the page.

Perhaps the most basic fact about eye movements in reading is that the eyes do not move smoothly across the text—the movement is instead quite jerky. Typically, for an alphabetic language like English, the eyes will move in jumps (called *saccades*) which are about eight characters long and last around 25–30 milliseconds. Most jumps are rightwards in a left-to-right language like English, but between 10% and 15% are leftwards. The size of each jump depends on the script being read—in Chinese it is about 2 characters; in Japanese it is about 3.5 characters; in Hebrew it is about 5.5 characters. What this pattern shows is that the more information you can extract from the characters, the shorter the jumps. Hebrew is informationally more dense than English, because the written words often lack vowels, and the grammatical function words often exist as *inflections* attached to the content words. So more information gets packed into the same space (as defined by the number of characters). Japanese is denser still, as it uses a combination of logographic and syllabic symbols. So you can pack even more into that same space. And Chinese is the densest, with each character (each logogram) corresponding to an entire word. Interestingly, the size of the script makes little difference to how far the eyes move.

A quite puzzling property of eye movements is that whilst the eye is moving, it is effectively 'switched off'—information seems to be taken up from the printed page (or whatever we happen to be looking at) only when the eyes are still. This is probably just as well, as little sense could be made of the rapidly moving and exceedingly blurred image that exists during the saccade. Dave Irwin, a vision scientist working in Illinois, has pointed out that we make around 100 000 saccadic movements in the typical day (whilst awake), and if each takes between 25 and 30 milliseconds, that adds up to a total of 50 minutes of 'down time' every day.

Fortunately, the eyes do stay still, at least some of the time. Between each saccade the eyes stay still for, on average, between 200 and 250 milliseconds. It is during this time (the *fixation*) that all the hard work gets done. Fixation times, like the length of the saccades, also depend on the script being read—the more information in the characters (with logograms at one extreme, and full alphabets at the other), the longer the fixation.

What the eyes see, and from where

Inevitably, each fixation provides a snapshot of the page from a slightly different view. In the following line, a letter near the centre of the line is underlined. If you stare at t̲h̲at underlined letter you will imagine that you can see the whole line. But how many words can you really make out? One very strong sensation is that you can see to either side of the underlined letter. But although the image on the retina is more or less symmetrical around the fixation point, it turns out that useful information (that is, useful with respect to the process of reading) is extracted from only a part of this image. During normal reading, this part corresponds, more or less, to about 15 characters to the right of the fixation point, and just a few characters to the left (generally, to the beginning of the word in which one is fixating). If, during the course of normal reading, your eyes had landed on the underlined letter in that earlier line, the extent of the text from which you would have extracted anything useful would have looked something like:

that underlined l

And on the next fixation, it may have been something like:

underlined letter yo

In effect, the information we extract from the printed page reaches our brain via a constantly shifting window through which we view that page. Information from within that window can aid in the identification of whatever is written there, whilst information from outside the window cannot.

George McConkie and Keith Rayner discovered this in the mid-1970s whilst working at the universities of Cornell and Rochester respectively. In a series of complex experiments they monitored the eye movements of people reading sentences on a computer display. They changed the display each time the people's eyes moved so that only certain letters were visible around the point at which the eyes were looking (a bit like the example shown above). They then measured the time it took to read each sentence as a function of how many letters were visible on each fixation, and where. In effect, McConkie and Rayner artificially manipulated the width of that viewing window. Anything more than 15 letters to the right, and anything further than the beginning of the currently fixated word, did nothing to improve reading times. Anything less, and it took much longer to read the sentence. So shrinking that window had a detrimental effect on reading, whilst expanding it provided no benefit.

The asymmetry of that window is easily explained. When reading left-to-right, the eyes have already seen whatever is to the left of the fixation point. So there is no need to attend to it anymore. Of course, this would predict that in languages which are read right-to-left (e.g. Hebrew), an asymmetry in the opposite direction should show up. Sure enough, this is exactly what is found. Comparisons with other languages have also shown that the size of the viewing window changes as a function of the kind of script being read—generally, it is about twice as wide, in numbers of characters, as the length of the typical saccade.

The fact that information can be extracted quite a way to the right of the fixation point does not mean that all the letters, and all the words, in that region can be made out. In general, it seems that only the currently fixated word is recognized. But this does not mean that information elsewhere in that extended region is not useful. Rayner asked people to read a sentence that contained a nonword (e.g. SPAACH) in place of one of the real words (e.g. SPEECH). The original sentence might have been something like THE POLITICIAN READ THE SPEECH TO HIS COLLEAGUES. Rayner set his system up so that when the eyes got to within some number of characters of SPAACH, it was changed back into SPEECH. He then measured how long the eyes spent on SPEECH when they eventually landed on it. He found that if the change from SPAACH to SPEECH happened 12 or more characters to the left of SPAACH, the time subsequently spent on SPEECH was just the same as if SPEECH had been there all along. Hardly surprising. More interesting is what happened when the change happened between around seven and 12 characters to the left of SPAACH: Although people did not consciously notice the change, the time subsequently spent on SPEECH was longer than if SPEECH had been there all along—presumably because information had been extracted about SPAACH which subsequently proved incompatible with the information that was actually discovered when the eyes landed on SPEECH. The time spent on SPEECH was greater still if, instead of SPAACH, the 'rogue' word had been something like BLAART. In general, the more letters that were shared between the rogue word and SPEECH, the shorter the subsequent fixation times on SPEECH. So although a nonword would not be recognized as such on that earlier fixation (seven to 12 characters away), it appears that information about its letters would be used to help in the recognition of the real word when it was eventually reached. Presumably, those letters caused the representation of the word to become activated, but only partially, on that earlier fixation. When the eyes subsequently landed on the word itself, it had already been partially activated, and so recognition was faster.

Although *content* words within the 15 character window are not recognized before being fixated, subsequent research has shown that very short words, or very predictable words, are often recognized whilst the eyes are fixating on a preceding word. One consequence of this is that these short predictable words are often skipped—the eyes do not land on them at all.

One final question before we leave eye movements and techniques for studying their effect on reading: when the eyes land on a word, where do they land? Do they land generally in the same place—the beginning, perhaps, or the middle? And if they do, would it matter if they sometimes missed the target? The answer to both these questions is 'yes'. In a series of elegant studies, Kevin O'Regan, working in Paris, asked people to fixate on a particular point on the computer display. A word would then appear which could either be centred around that point, or shifted to one side or another. He could then work out how the time to recognize the word changed depending on where, within the word, the eyes were fixating when that word appeared. He found that there was an optimum position at which the recognition time was least, somewhere just to the left of the centre of the word. The actual optimum position changed depending on the specific word—it was closer to the middle the shorter and more frequent the word. But, in general, it was just to the left of centre. Interestingly, this coincides with where the eyes tend to land during normal reading (and of course, this depends on the kind of script being read, and whether it is read left-to-right or right-to-left). But how can the eyes 'know' to land on this optimum viewing position if they do not yet know what the word is, and consequently, where that word's optimum viewing position is to be found? The answer, of course, is that they cannot, which is why they aim for what, in the general case, is the optimum position. If it turns out that where they actually land is not good enough (i.e. does not allow the word to be recognized), they make a corrective movement to the other side of the word, so maximizing the chances of successful recognition.

What should be clear by now, if nothing else, is that how the eyes move during reading is a different story from the one about how letters come to be invested with meaning and how that meaning is subsequently recovered. Both are clearly essential to the reading process. Although it is possible to talk about the two as if they are quite separable processes, they are not. For example, how far the eyes move during a saccade is a function of the script that is used—the more information vested in a single character, the shorter the jump. The same is true for the duration of a single fixation, and for the extent of the area from which information is extracted during that fixation. Eye movements are controlled, at least in part, by the processes involved in the extraction of meaning from the visual image. They each rely on the other.

A final (written) word

Most of us take our ability to read as much for granted as our ability to use a telephone, watch television, or dial out for pizza. We forget all too easily that until relatively recently, most of the world's population were illiterate. Many people still are. This is not the place to list the obvious advantages of being literate. But there is one consequence that is worth discussing here and, somewhat poetically, it brings us right back to where we started, with hieroglyphics.

A property of hieroglyphic scripts, and Chinese also, is that there exist phonetic characters which, as in the alphabetic scripts, represent individual sounds. In this way, one can take the character for a word like 'peach' and tack the symbol for the /s/ sound on the front, to create the new word 'speech'. The invention of this kind of composite script was an important landmark in the evolution of writing systems, as it marked a shift from the written word as representing meaning directly, to the written word as representing spoken words. It also paved the way for the eventual invention of the more fully sound-based scripts such as the syllabaries and the alphabets. But whereas it seems obvious, to us, that one can tack an /s/ onto 'peach' to create a new word, or take the /s/ off 'speech' to get back to 'peach', it turns out that pre-literate children, and illiterate adults, do not find this an easy and natural thing to do. The same is true of certain dyslexic children—see Chapter 12. They appear to lack the awareness that words can be broken down into individual sounds, and that these sounds can be added to, or taken away, or re-combined, to create new words.

José Morais at the Free University in Brussels, working with Portuguese and Brazilian illiterates, found that whereas they had some appreciation of rhyme, and some awareness of the syllabic structure of a word, they were very poor at tasks which involved taking a sound off one word to create another. It is now generally accepted that the awareness that words are made up of individual sounds smaller than the syllable develops in large part as a consequence of learning to read and, specifically, learning to read an alphabetic script. This is not to say that all illiterates have no such awareness—some do. But on the whole, the 'average' illiterate, and the 'average' pre-literate child, will not be nearly so proficient at playing these sound manipulation games as the average literate. In this respect, learning to read alphabetically has consequences for the way in which we perceive the words we hear.

It is the fact that the concept of phonemes is not a natural one that makes the invention of phonetic symbols in hieroglyphics such an achievement. Flying is unnatural also, and it too is an achievement, but the invention of flying machines pales into insignificance compared to the invention of phonetic writing systems. Indeed, there is probably no other invention that comes close to the written word. On second thoughts, there is no 'probably' about it.

The Greek philosopher Socrates (c. 470–399 BC) believed, apparently, that the invention of writing (credited in Greek legend to Prometheus, the giver of fire) could only do harm to people—it would 'implant forgetfulness into their souls . . . [they would be] calling things to remembrance no longer from within themselves, but by means of external marks' (Plato's *Phaedrus*, 275B). It is ironic, but in keeping with his beliefs, that it is only through writing that anything of Socrates is known today. Indeed, it is only through writing that almost all that is known today is known at all. Socrates may well have been right, but mankind owes much to those external marks on which it so relies.

When it all goes wrong

Og vjev gostv qesehseqj xet e tasqsoti, onehopi xjev ov natv ci moli vu xeli aq upi nuspoph, uqip vji pixtqeqis, epf fotduwis vjev ov xet emm moli vjev. Puv katv upi qesehseqj, iwisz qesehseqj. Us onehopi optvief vjev zua xuli aq epf xisi apecmi vu tqiel.

If that first paragraph was a surprise, imagine what it must be like to wake up one morning, open the newspaper, and discover that it was all like that. Not just one paragraph, every paragraph. Or imagine instead that you woke up and were unable to speak, or that what came out was not what you intended. Or that the first words you heard sounded like some of them were in a foreign language. Many of us have had anxiety dreams in which we open an exam paper to discover that it is written in a language we do not understand. And yet, within the dream, we know we are supposed to understand it. Those of us that have these dreams can recall the feeling of panic, of fear. Some people never wake up from that dream, because it is not a dream—it is their reality.

When brains go wrong, the ability to use language may well go wrong too, but it does not always. In fact, it is surprising how much can go wrong in the brain before language is affected. Chemical imbalances in the brain may affect the transmission of impulses from one neuron to another, leading to a range of disorders such as Parkinson's disease, schizophrenia, and severe depression, each due to different imbalances affecting different parts of the neural circuitry. But aside from any difficulties with articulation (as in Parkinson's), none of these disorders is primarily associated with deficits in the language faculty. For language to go, in adulthood at least, parts of the brain have to go too.

The situation in childhood is somewhat different. Children who sustain damage to the parts of the brain that, when damaged in adulthood, lead to quite severe language deficits, do not suffer the same deficits. They may not suffer any deficit at all. Sadly, this does not mean that children's brains are immune to the effects of damage. But at least with respect to the language faculty, significant recovery is possible— young brains are much more adaptable than older ones. This does not mean, though, that there are no long-lasting childhood language disorders. Dyslexia is a case in point. Little is known about its physical basis; more is known about its functional basis (that is, about which of the individual abilities that make up the language faculty are affected). Of course, this is not to say that there is no physical basis to dyslexia— ultimately, any behaviour is rooted in the neurophysiology and neurochemistry of the brain, and there is some evidence that neurophysiological differences do exist between dyslexics and non-dyslexics. We shall come back to dyslexia a little later. But because the brain is the organ which generates language, we shall start with what happens when something goes overtly wrong with that organ.

Damaged brains

The two most common causes of cell death in the brains of otherwise healthy adults are stroke and head injury. A stroke occurs when a blood vessel in the brain becomes blocked by a clot, or bursts because of a weakening of its walls. In either case, nearby cells die because of a failure in the blood supply and, in the case of a rupture, the physical damage that is caused by the leaked blood. Often, stroke leads to quite localized areas of cell death. Head injury generally leads to more widespread cell death, but the effects of both stroke and head injury can none the less be quite similar. They include impairments of one or more of the following: movement and/or sensation, vision, memory, planning and problem solving, and language. There may also be marked effects on mood and personality.

It has been known since the mid-nineteenth century that the two halves of the brain control different sides of the body—the left hemisphere controls the right side of the body, and the right controls the left. The two hemispheres are connected, and generally split the workload—except in the case of language, where the left hemisphere has primary responsibility. Consequently, a language deficit is a good pointer to left-hemisphere damage. And more specifically, to damage to the left side of that hemisphere.

Damage to the right hemisphere rarely causes any language impair-

ments of the kind that arise following left–hemisphere damage. However, right–hemisphere damaged patients may fail to recognize whether
a speaker is happy, sad, surprised, or angry on the basis of his or her tone
of voice. They may themselves be unable to convey such feelings by
voice alone, and their speech can sound quite 'mechanical' as a
consequence. This is not just a general deficit in their ability to
recognize changes in tone or pitch—some patients can tell on the basis
of such differences alone whether a sentence such as 'She's not coming
to the party' is intended as a statement, a command, or a question. What
is impaired in these cases is not, primarily, the language faculty.

The fact that impairments specific to the language faculty are associated with damage to a part of the left hemisphere leads to the natural
suggestion that that part of the brain is specialized for language.
Whether that means that that part of the brain is genetically pre-
programmed with language-specific functions (as opposed to general
functions that could in principle serve more than just language) is
another matter. It is well established that different parts of the brain are,
in effect, wired up in different ways. Consequently, these different parts
of the brain inevitably function in different ways, and so encode
different kinds of information.

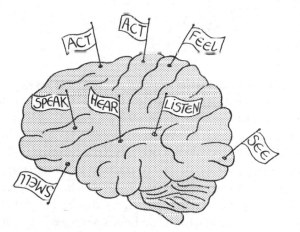

It is possible that the wiring in the language areas of the brain is well-
suited to the kinds of associative processes that language requires. But
again, it is very much an open question whether they are well-suited to
language because our genes 'have language in mind' when specifying
the neuroanatomy of the brain, or whether language has evolved so as
to take advantage of a neuroanatomy whose genetic basis is, so to speak,

agnostic with respect to its ultimate use. There is a clear evolutionary
advantage in being able to communicate, but whether evolution has had
time to encode a genetic basis for language structures, such as grammar,
is unclear. Presumably, there is a part of our brains that encodes the
knowledge and experience relevant for riding a bicycle. But when that
particular bit of neuroanatomy was laid down, was it laid down with
bicycles in mind? Probably not.

Riding a bicycle may or may not involve the same areas of the brain in
different people. We do know, though, that aspects of our ability to spell
(and specifically, to spell regularly and irregularly spelled words) are
encoded in the same areas. But writing has not been around long enough
for evolution to have encoded in our DNA anything at all that could be
specific to spelling, let alone the distinction between regular and irregular spellings. And anyway, not all languages have irregular spellings,
and not all languages are alphabetic (see Chapter 11). So the relevant
neuroanatomy cannot have been laid down with spelling in mind.

The knowledge we have about something—its meaning—will
necessarily reside across many different parts of the brain, so as to
include visual information, information about the sounds associated
with that thing (or the word for that thing), information about its feel,
its smell or taste, its function, and other aspects of the contexts in which
it occurs. Some things may require stronger associations with one part

than with others—the visual areas of the brain, for instance, or the motor areas, which mediate movements and manipulation. Not surprisingly, therefore, the deficits that arise following damage to these different parts can be very varied indeed.

It is surprisingly difficult to identify the form these deficits take. One problem is that there are two quite distinct ways in which these deficits can be described. A classification based on symptoms alone would hide the fact that any one symptomatology could arise from a number of causes. If a patient was unable to say the word 'tiger' when shown one, they might have lost the ability to recognize tigers. Or perhaps they could recognize tigers and knew the word 'tiger', but were simply unable to say it. Why they might be unable to say it is another matter. So going by gross symptoms alone is not enough. An alternative would be to classify the deficits according to which components of the language faculty have been impaired. In effect, that is what we just did when distinguishing between the two 'tiger' deficits. But identifying which components have been impaired is rarely easy. Patients who have suffered some form of brain damage rarely exhibit a deficit that is restricted to just one mental process. Often, different processes are affected to differing degrees, making it hard to disentangle which processes have been affected, and to what extent. Most patients with a deficit in production will have some kind of deficit in comprehension and vice versa. Many patients who have a deficit in their spoken language will also have a deficit in their written language. Do these patients have a single underlying deficit, or do they suffer from multiple impairments that have co-occurred only coincidentally? Often, it is hard to know.

In the descriptions that follow, some of the main kinds of deficit will be described, in terms of both their symptoms and the components that appear to be affected. Deficits which affect spoken language are called *aphasias*. Deficits affecting the ability to understand written language are called *dyslexias*. These two kinds of deficit will be described separately, although as just mentioned, they rarely occur one without the other. And any one patient described as having one particular deficit probably has some other deficit too. But first, a final word on what 'a deficit' means. It is rare for a deficit to completely abolish a particular ability. A patient who is described as being able to read aloud written words whilst being unable to understand them may be able to understand *some* words, but many fewer than he or she could have been expected to before the event that caused the damage. Generally, the published descriptions of these patients do include information about the severity of the deficit.

Failures of understanding

One of the rarest deficits that manifests itself as a failure of understanding is certainly one of the oddest. Patients suffering from *pure word deafness* are unable to understand words spoken to them. But they can read, write, and speak normally. Some patients report that what they hear sounds as if it is in some unrecognizable language. Some (but not all) of these patients can repeat or write down the words they hear even though they do not understand them. In one such case, the patient would write down what she heard, and only by reading what she had written could she understand what had been said to her. In another case, the patient could, despite not understanding the words spoken to him, guess which were real and which were made up. Because the real and made up words differed by just one phoneme, the 'deafness' could not have been due to any failure in recognizing speech sounds (such failures do sometimes occur). These cases suggest that at least part of the neural circuitry that was activated on hearing a word was intact, but that the connections to the circuitry that encoded the meaning had been lost. The meaning was still there, though, otherwise these patients would not have been able to read, write, or speak.

WORD DEAFNESS

An equivalent deficit has been found in reading—one patient was unable to understand many of the written words shown to her, but she could read them aloud perfectly. When she did, she would only then understand the word she had just seen. It did not matter whether the word was regularly or irregularly spelled—her pronunciation would be perfect. When not reading aloud, she could tell which written words were real and which were made up, even though she understood neither. This is another case where the associations from the form of a word (in this case, its visual form) to the circuitry encoding its meaning have been lost.

So being deaf to the meaning of a spoken word, or blind to the meaning of a written word, does not mean that the meaning itself has been lost. These patients have no problem, when wanting to express that meaning, in finding the right words with which to do so.

Failing to find the right words

These patients with word deafness or blindness could not make the link between the name of an object and the object itself (that is, its meaning). This inability was quite specific to either seeing, or hearing, that name. An equivalent deficit, in production, occurs when a patient cannot make the link between an object they are looking at, or perhaps thinking about, and the object's name. Patients suffering from this naming deficit will recognize an object if it is shown to them, and will know that they are being shown a picture of a tiger, for instance, but they will be incapable of saying 'tiger'. Instead, they will either say nothing, or will provide a description rather than the word itself, or will come out with the wrong word, which, depending on the deficit, might be related in meaning—for example, 'lion' for 'tiger'. Some of these patients have absolutely no problem saying a word when it is written down for them, or when it is defined for them—they just cannot say it when shown the object to which it refers. One patient could even write the names of the objects that she could not say. How might these naming deficits come about?

When we look at something, the information we receive via our eyes is just a kind of sensory trigger that sets off some neural circuitry associated with the meaning of whatever we are looking at (this was covered in more detail in Chapter 9). A written word is also a trigger, as is a spoken word, or a definition. But each of these triggers is likely to stimulate a different neural circuitry—a definition will evoke a very different kind of experience, for instance, than whatever is evoked when the physical form of the object is experienced. The taste of an egg, for example, evokes a very different kind of experience from the sight of an egg, and yet each is clearly 'egg', as is the description 'it is laid by hens'. In effect, these triggers evoke different aspects of the meaning of the same thing. They evoke different meaning circuits. And each of these circuits needs to be connected to the circuitry responsible for saying the appropriate word. These connections constitute the association between the different aspects of meaning and speaking.

Naming deficits result when some of the connections have been lost between the neural circuitry that is stimulated by seeing an object (the aspect of meaning concerned with what the thing looks like) and the neural circuitry associated with saying the name of that object. Other connections might still be intact. So if patients experience an object in a different way, perhaps by feeling it, or hearing a description of it, they may be able to name it if the neural circuitry that has been stimulated by that experience is still connected to the circuitry associated with saying the appropriate name. And because only some connections are affected, these patients may be able to name some things, but not others.

The fact that only some of the connections may be affected explains why deficits are rarely all or none—much depends on how extensive the damage has been. It might also explain the surprising finding that some patients are worst at naming certain kinds of thing—living things, man-made things, or fruit and vegetables, for instance. In all likelihood, these *selective deficits* arise because the meaning of an object (what it looks like, what it is for, how it should be used, and so on) requires many different associations across many different parts of the brain—parts that encode physical form, or function, or movement and manipulation.

Certain kinds of thing may rely for their meaning more on one part than another (man-made objects, for example, tend to have function, whereas animals do not). So we store everything we know about an object across different parts of the brain, with each part encoding some different aspect of that object. If connections to one of these parts are lost, whichever aspect of an object is stored in that part will not be able to trigger a naming response. For example, the function of something (a potato-peeler, perhaps) may not be enough, now, to trigger the appropriate naming response. The result may then be a deficit that affects the patient's ability to name certain kinds of object, or even, depending on which connections have been damaged, to recognize those objects.

The deficits described so far have all been quite specific, affecting the connections either between the form of a word and its meaning, or between the meaning of a word and its pronunciation. But the meanings themselves have been spared. Imagine the frustration of knowing what you want to talk about, but being unable to find the words with which to do it. But these are the rarer cases—it is more common for patients to exhibit a range of fairly general deficits, some of which are due to damage to the connections to and from meaning, and some of which are due to damage to the neural circuitry that encodes meaning itself.

Beyond individual words I

Whatever the cause of the deficit, it is inevitable that patients who have problems understanding single words will also have problems understanding sequences of words. Similarly, patients who have problems saying individual words will inevitably have problems producing sequences of them. However, there are deficits in sentence production and comprehension which go beyond what could be expected on the basis of just single-word deficits.

Traditionally, these deficits have been divided into those that affect production, and those that affect comprehension. However, it is quite rare to find a deficit in one and not in the other. Broadly speaking (there is no other way when it comes to the complexities of acquired language disorders!), many patients with disordered spoken language (aphasia) produce slow hesitant speech. Some have particular problems with grammatical function words ('the', 'by', 'was', and so on) and inflections

('-ing', '-s', '-ed', and so on), tending to miss them out completely. Here is one example:

> *Two . . . ah, doctors . . . and ah . . . thirty minutes . . . and yes . . . ah . . . hospital. And, er Wednesday . . . nine o'clock . . . and er Thursday, ten o'clock . . . doctors. Two doctors . . . and ah . . . teeth. Yeah . . . fine.*

More often than not, these patients also have a comprehension deficit. One of the diagnostic features of this comprehension deficit is particularly interesting. Whereas these patients would understand sentences such as 'The dog bit the boy' or 'The boy was bitten by the dog', they would have problems understanding 'The dog was bitten by the boy'. It seems that they tend to interpret such sentences according to what would be a plausible scenario. Dogs tend to bite boys, not the other way around. Basically, it looks as if these patients' brain injury has severely limited their ability to use grammar.

Things are not quite this simple, because a few of the patients who are severely impaired in their ability to use grammar in production have no corresponding comprehension deficit. Similarly, some patients with this particular comprehension deficit do not have the corresponding production deficit. In short, it looks as if the production and compre-hension of grammatical structure can be affected independently.

Reconciling the findings with earlier theory

This last claim is controversial and, if true, it would compromise the account in Chapter 10 of how grammatical conventions are applied during the understanding and production of language. There, it was suggested that the associations that form when learning to understand language serve the production of that language also. In one case, sequences of certain kinds (including words and their inflections) would evoke meanings of certain kinds. In the other, meanings of certain kinds would evoke sequences of certain kinds. But if the same set of associations could both *decode* grammatical information and, when run in the reverse direction, *encode* it, we should find that patients who have a decoding deficit also have an encoding one. But we have just seen that this is not always the case.

This is an example of how research into what can go wrong with language can feed into theories of how language works normally. We now need to modify the theory to take into account the fact that different associative links are used during the encoding and decoding processes. Somehow, these two processes, which are basically just mirror-images of one another, would have to become embodied, during learning, in two distinct sets of associative links. But how?

Imagine that each time we hear a sentence, we simultaneously and unconsciously produce it. Associations will develop between the input sequences and their corresponding meanings. But if the meanings must become associated with the covertly produced output, then these associations will necessarily become a kind of mirror image of those between input and meaning. In effect, going from input to meaning will require one kind of process embodied in one set of associations, whilst going from meaning to input-as-covert-output will require the embodiment of the reverse process but on another set of connections. Technically, the two sets of associations will not be exact mirror-images because the neural activity in response to the input will spread through the neural circuitry, and in doing so will change. This means that the neural activity that has to be associated with the input-as-covert-output will not be quite the same as the neural activity which that input evoked to begin with. But, despite this, there is a sense in which the two sets of associations are complementary.

This description is very speculative, but in the next chapter we shall come across networks of artificial neurons which do the equivalent. They associate input sequences with patterns of (artificial) neural activity corresponding to meaning, and associate those meaning-like patterns with output sequences that are just copies, more or less, of the input.

Beyond individual words II

A second broad category of deficit that goes beyond individual words is marked by very fluent and grammatical speech, complete with grammatical function words and inflections, but often containing completely inappropriate content words (the words that convey the main meaning, such as the nouns, verbs, and adjectives). Sometimes, patients with this deficit produce nonsense words instead of real words, a little like Lewis Carroll's *Jabberwocky*. In one case, for instance, a patient was asked to describe a scene which included a bull chasing a boy-scout past a table on which was a saucepan and a knife, and next to which was a stool. The description of this scene included the following:

> *A buk is cherching a boy . . .*
> *a table with orstrum and a three-legged stroe*

These patients are often severely impaired in their understanding of spoken sentences, and so are unaware of what they themselves have uttered. The deficit suffered by these patients is the converse of the deficit described earlier in which patients could retrieve content words, but could not organize them into grammatical sentences. Here, patients cannot retrieve the appropriate content words, but can organize what they erroneously retrieve into grammatical sequences.

It looks, then, as if the application of grammatical conventions and the selection of the words to which those conventions should apply are functionally separable (see Chapter 10). Unfortunately, this state of affairs is muddied somewhat by the fact that the symptomatology of any individual patient is not always as straightforward as the descriptions given here would predict. As soon as one stops making gross generalizations, and starts looking at individual cases, things become much less clear-cut.

This last complication is true of all acquired language disorders. Which is why it is not easy to categorize the deficits into anything but the broadest of categories, each of which represents a range of deficits and a range of severities. This is true irrespective of whether we are dealing with impaired spoken language, or impaired written language, to which we turn next.

Deficits in reading: acquiring dyslexia

The deficits described so far have been aphasias—predominantly affecting spoken language. *Dyslexias* affect the ability to comprehend written language. To distinguish the kind of dyslexia due to brain damage from the kind that has its origins in childhood, the first kind is often referred to as an *acquired dyslexia*, and the second as a *developmental dyslexia*.

There are various kinds of acquired dyslexia. In *deep dyslexia*, it is common for patients, when asked to read a word out loud, to make errors such as 'kindness' for SYMPATHY or 'orchestra' for SYMPHONY. They see one word, but produce another that is related in meaning. Sometimes, they make errors based on visual similarity instead—they might say 'symphony' when shown SYMPATHY. Things get really complex when they make both kinds of error simultaneously—'orchestra' for SYMPATHY. It looks as if something has gone very wrong with the associations that link the visual form of each word with its meaning.

DEEP DYSLEXIA

Patients suffering from this deficit tend to exhibit a range of symptoms, including an inability to read aloud nonsense words, and for there to be fewer problems with words that are easy to visualize (e.g. CLOCK) than with words that are harder to visualize (e.g. CLICK). Perhaps as a consequence of this, deep dyslexics tend to do better with nouns than with verbs, with adjectives coming in between, and grammatical function words and inflections being particularly problematic. But could a single underlying deficit lead to such a wide range of symptoms? Currently, there is no single agreed theory as to the causes of the symptomatology of deep dyslexia. Generally, these patients have very extensive damage to the left hemisphere. One idea is that the kinds of stroke that lead to deep dyslexia disrupt a blood supply that branches off into different areas of the left hemisphere. When cells in those areas die, the associations to and from those areas (and the information they encode) may also be disrupted. There is not just one underlying deficit—rather there are several, each caused, originally, by the same physical damage. Interestingly, networks of artificial neurons (see Chapter 13) can be built which simulate some of the different kinds of association implicated in normal reading. When 'damaged', they exhibit deficits that can be similar to those found in deep dyslexia.

A subset of the symptoms found in deep dyslexia are often found in another kind of dyslexia—*phonological dyslexia*. Here, the defining characteristic is that patients are unable to read aloud nonsense words (e.g. GLIM), although they have problems understanding certain real words as well. As we shall see, there is reason to care about a deficit in which patients cannot read words which do not exist. One widely accepted explanation of phonological dyslexia is that these patients have somehow lost information about the letter-to-sound correspondences that would allow them to read aloud nonsense words. It is called a phonological dyslexia because the deficit has affected their knowledge of how letters translate into the sounds, or *phonology*, of their language.

PHONOLOGICAL
DYSLEXIA

In the previous chapter we saw that skilled adults tend to access the meaning of a word directly from its visual form, and not by sounding out the word according to letter-to-sound correspondences and subsequently retrieving its meaning on the basis of sound-to-meaning correspondences. However, adults do resort to such correspondences for infrequently occurring words. And these are exactly the real words that phonological dyslexics have problems understanding. We shall return shortly to why such dyslexics have lost those letter-to-sound correspondences. But first, it is useful to contrast these dyslexics with yet another kind—*surface dyslexics*.

The defining characteristic of patients with surface dyslexia is that they are very bad at reading irregular words (such as YACHT, PINT, and REIGN). But they *are* good at reading nonsense words. The explanation is that these dyslexics rely heavily on their knowledge of letter-to-sound correspondences, and have lost the direct association between the visual form of a word and its meaning. This is the converse of the phonological dyslexics, who seem to have lost their knowledge of the letter-to-sound correspondences and so rely more on that direct route to meaning.

SURFACE DYSLEXIA

How do these deficits come about? The simplest explanation is that each route involves a different set of associations. One route is between letters and the phonemes they represent, then between those phoneme sequences and the meanings associated with them. The other is between entire letter sequences and meaning (embodying the direct association

between the visual form of a word and its meaning). Each set of associations is likely to involve different areas of the brain—the associations with meaning will involve the different areas associated with the different aspects of meaning, and the letter-to-sound associations will involve the areas associated with hearing and producing sounds. Localized damage to one area of the brain could in principle destroy associative connections leading to one (other) part of the brain or another, giving rise to one kind of dyslexia or another.

Patients rarely exhibit a pure dyslexia. It is more common for them either to retain some abilities more than others (a partial deficit), or to exhibit a blend of different dyslexias and/or aphasias. Some phonological dyslexics seem to have a more general phonological impairment—they are bad at separating spoken words into their component sounds, or knowing that /k/ and /at/, for instance, make 'cat'. In these cases, the deficit is not specific to letter-to-sound correspondences.

Often, dyslexia is accompanied by a deficit in spelling, but this does not always happen, and sometimes, a deficit in spelling can be found in the absence of a deficit in reading. The acquired spelling disorders, or *dysgraphias*, can be quite similar to the acquired dyslexias. *Deep dysgraphics* make semantic errors when writing words, although once they have written the word, they may notice their own mistake. *Phonological dysgraphics* cannot spell nonwords, and *surface dysgraphics* cannot spell many irregular words (they regularize their spellings). One patient had both a dysgraphia and a naming deficit—when shown, for example, a picture of a lion he said 'leopard' but wrote down TIGER. The words he produced were related in meaning, more or less. Visual similarity was not the problem, as he would make the same kinds of mistakes with, for example, very different looking vegetables. Some dysgraphias, though, have nothing to do with associations between words and their spellings, and have instead to do with the physical side of writing, and lead to problems in choosing the appropriate letters (letters may be omitted or added), or physically writing the letters (individual strokes may be omitted or added).

Dyslexia as a childhood disorder

If different disorders have the same name, are they in fact the same? Confusingly, the answer is 'no'. There have been various attempts to draw comparisons between the acquired and the developmental dyslexias, but these have proved extremely controversial. We shall come to some of the comparisons in a while. But first, what is this other kind of dyslexia?

Developmental dyslexia is a disorder of development and, specifically, the development of certain skills required for reading. As such, it is perhaps best viewed in terms of how the acquisition of these skills has broken down, and against a background of what we know about the normal acquisition of such skills. In fact, children are classified as dyslexic through comparison with other children whose development has proceeded more normally: if a child is at least 18 months to two years older than children with comparable reading skills, and there are no other obvious factors involved (the child is of normal intelligence, normal educational background, has normal eyesight, normal speaking skills, and so on), he or she is classified as dyslexic.

If dyslexia is diagnosed relative to the reading skills of other children, perhaps the only 'deficit' is that dyslexics have progressed more slowly than expected, and simply need more time. But it is not just a matter of time. If it were, the only worry would be the knock-on effect of poor reading ability inside and outside the classroom. But such knock-on effects aside, what is the prognosis for dyslexics if no remedial help is given? Come to that, is remedial help successful? And what kind of remedial help is required?

Before answering any of these questions, we need first to know what the underlying deficit is. Although this has proved a controversial topic, the general consensus is that dyslexic children fail to attain some of the basic *phonological skills* that underlie reading. Phonology refers, simply, to the sounds of the language, and the way in which these sounds are put together to form meaningful units. Typically, dyslexic children have problems playing word games which involve stripping the phonemes off spoken words to create new words (e.g. stripping the /s/ from 'speech'), blending sequences of phonemes to create new words (e.g. adding the /s/ onto 'peach'), or spotting which words rhyme and which do not (e.g. spotting the odd one out in the spoken versions of 'speech, grouch, bleach'). They also find letter-to-sound correspondences hard to master and have to rely heavily on developing a sight vocabulary of words they can recognize directly, without needing any such correspondences. This means they find new words extremely difficult, and consequently that reading alone, without help with those new words (or words that are still not familiar enough), is an almost impossible task. And whereas non-dyslexic children who have acquired a good knowledge of letter-to-sound correspondences will often regularize their spellings, and spell words phonetically (e.g. YOT instead of YACHT), dyslexic children's spelling errors will often be phonetically unrelated to what they are aiming for, and may include completely inappropriate letter-to-sound mappings.

Does the deficit simply impair the letter-to-sound mappings that are required in an alphabetic language like English? One reason for the controversy regarding the nature of the deficit is that some dyslexic children (probably less than one in five) are unable to gain a sight vocabulary but instead use letter-to-sound mappings to spell out each word laboriously. These children seem to have the opposite problem from most dyslexic children, who have poor letter-to-sound mappings and rely on a sight vocabulary. So there is not, after all, a single deficit common to all children classified as dyslexic. There are superficial similarities between the symptoms of these two kinds of developmental dyslexia and the acquired dyslexias (specifically, surface dyslexia—poor sight vocabulary—and phonological dyslexia—poor letter-to-sound correspondences). But it is very unclear whether these similarities reflect the same underlying problems in acquired and developmental dyslexias, or whether they just look similar because some children rely more on a sight vocabulary, and others more on letter-to-sound correspondences. In any case, by the time these children are assessed, many will have developed different strategies for coping with their problem, so complicating their symptomatology.

The majority of dyslexics do none the less exhibit a fairly stable pattern of symptoms. This is borne out also by studies which have determined which factors can predict whether a particular child will have dyslexia. One of these predictors, assessed when the child is still pre-literate and has not yet started to read, is the child's awareness and sensitivity to the internal sound structure of spoken words (assessed using the word games mentioned earlier). Clearly, sensitivity to this structure is important when learning an alphabetic script. Another predictor is the ability to name the letters of the alphabet when shown them. When assessed in five year-olds, this is possibly the best predictor of which children will be diagnosed as dyslexic by the age of eight. Five is a crucial age in many of these studies, because five year-olds are only beginning to read, and so any evidence of dyslexia can only set in later. Why letter-naming should be such a good predictor is something we shall return to. But letter-naming and phonological skill are also good predictors of reading ability in non-dyslexic children. So some researchers have questioned whether dyslexics are just at one end of a continuum of reading ability. We know that individual readers vary considerably in their reading skill. Some children (and adults) place more reliance on letter-to-sound correspondences, whilst others place more reliance on whole-word reading, mapping the visual form directly onto meaning (see Chapter 11 for further details). So are the children who have difficulty acquiring the letter-to-sound mappings doing anything that is qualitatively different from what other children do? To the extent that they rely more on a sight vocabulary, yes. But to the extent that having a sight vocabulary is normal, no.

Whether dyslexics are qualitatively different or not does not really matter. One way or another, they have a reading problem (and often, a writing problem too). Which means that, one way or another, something has to be done to help. What has to be done depends in part on when it is done. If problems are identified at around the age of five or six, preventative measures, such as training the child to become more phonologically aware by playing word games can be effective. But even later on, when the child is around eight or nine years-old, intervention can certainly improve matters. Children's ability to generalize to new, regularly spelled words can be improved by focusing on their phono-logical skills using those word games, and on their letter-to-sound correspondences. Their ability to develop a sight vocabulary which can generalize to new, similar, words can be improved by highlighting similarities between different words, and focusing on subparts of words—contrasting, for example, BEACH and TEACH. So intervention does improve matters (just as it does with non-dyslexic children, in fact). But that is not to say that it will be equally effective for all dyslexics.

The effectiveness of an intervention depends in part on the severity of the impairment. In one study, by Richard Olson and colleagues in Boulder, Colorado, children were given extra reading instruction by computer. Each time the children encountered a word that they could not recognize, the computer would either break the word up into its component syllables (e.g. CHIL-DREN) and speak each syllable individually using a speech synthesizer, or it would break the word up into smaller chunks than syllables, corresponding to everything up until the vowel (the *onset*—the 'SP' in 'SPEECH') and everything from the vowel onwards (called the *rime*—the 'EECH' in 'SPEECH'). For CHILDREN, this would result in the spoken sequence corresponding to CH-IL-DR-EN. The reason for these two kinds of *segmentation* was that a number of studies, primarily by Rebecca Treiman at the Wayne State University in Detroit, have shown that children do not naturally split the words they hear into their component phonemes, but find it easier to split them into syllables, and to split syllables into onsets and rimes. It turned out that children who were very impaired responded better to the syllable-based segmentation, whereas children who were only mildly impaired responded better to the onset/rime segmentation. Not surprisingly, the more aware a child is of the fine internal structure of a spoken word, the more he or she will respond to a remedial programme that assumes some sensitivity to that structure. Broadly speaking, children will benefit most from programmes that focus on the finest detail of internal structure that they are sensitive to. It is exactly this kind of sensitivity that early intervention can improve.

A possible cause of childhood dyslexia

The fact that dyslexic children have poor phonological skills, but benefit when given phonologically related remediation, supports the view that their deficit is phonological. Presumably, the reason such children fail to develop good letter-to-sound mappings is that their neural encoding of the sound patterns of their language has not developed in quite the same way as it does in non-dyslexic children. And this means that associations to the corresponding neural circuitry (from the letter circuitry, for instance) cannot themselves develop in the same way.

It turns out, though, that there is another factor that contributes to dyslexia, which is related to that earlier observation that one of the best predictors of dyslexia (and of reading skill generally) is the ability of the child to name letters—children who are better at this will make better readers and are less likely to be dyslexic. Of course, better letter-naming reflects a greater awareness of the alphabet, which in turn means a greater awareness of what an alphabet is for. But there is another possibility. Alphabet shapes are just arbitrary symbols. The names given to those symbols are, to all intents and purposes, equally arbitrary. Being able to name the letters means having been able to associate an arbitrary symbol with an arbitrary sound. And that is exactly what letter-to-sound correspondences are about.

A variety of studies have explored the ability of dyslexic children to associate symbols with sounds. Typically, dyslexic children perform more poorly than non-dyslexic ones when they have to learn nonsense names for arbitrary shapes. But this effect is specific to verbal stimuli. If you were to ask children to learn which figures go together, for instance, and taught them to associate one figure with another, then you would find that dyslexics would perform no worse than other children. So associations themselves are not the problem, it is associations to sounds that are the problem. But if this is the case, why do these children not have problems learning the names of the everyday things around them? After all, these objects are also just arbitrary shapes, even if they are not drawn out on paper. Evidently dyslexic children do somehow manage to learn those names, and are not so delayed that they stand out as having a general naming problem. On the other hand, they tend to be slower than non-dyslexics when they have to rapidly name objects. This difference can be found even in adult dyslexics. None the less, dyslexics *are* able to name objects, and do somehow overcome the problems they have associating them with spoken sounds.

We experience the objects around us in many different ways, ensuring that the meaning of each object is encoded over numerous neural circuits that each encode different aspects of that meaning (this was discussed earlier in relation to the naming deficits). So there are multiple associations between these different aspects of meaning and the same single name. But the correspondence, for instance, between a letter and a sound does not involve such multiple associations—a letter has no other meaning than its name or its sound. When learning the names of everyday objects perhaps the association problem is overcome by the sheer variety of associations between the object (or rather, the experience of that object) and its name. Support for this idea comes from the finding that children's ability to name letters improves if they also have to trace the letters, which presumably adds another level of experience.

The existence of a selective impairment that affects only certain kinds of association and not others, or only certain kinds of neural encoding (for sounds) but not others, suggests that the neural wiring that would normally serve those associations or encodings is not quite right. Perhaps the wiring has been laid down in a way that does not readily support those kinds of associative processes. Because the wiring is, in part, specified genetically, the problem should have a genetic basis, and it does. If you have a dyslexic parent, there is a high chance that you will be dyslexic too. One fact about dyslexia that *is* clear is that it is heritable.

But dyslexia is not the only language problem in childhood that is heritable. Just as acquired language disorders can affect either spoken language or written language, or both, so in childhood, there are disorders which are not confined to the written language.

Language-specific impairments in childhood

There is a syndrome commonly referred to as specific language impairment (SLI), which is not confined, like dyslexia, just to reading, although it is often accompanied by a deficit in reading. A child will be classified as having SLI if there are no other obvious deficits (they have normal vision, normal hearing, a normal IQ in tests that do not require verbal skills, and so on). It is unclear, though, whether SLI should really be thought of as a syndrome or, instead, as an umbrella term that is applied to any deficit that affects language use. Numerous studies have attempted to establish the cause of the deficit and, unsurprisingly, many have been found. Some SLI children have difficulty discriminating between rapidly changing speech sounds, although standard hearing tests would show their hearing to be entirely normal. Other children seem to have a problem with grammatical function words and inflections, similar to some of the acquired aphasias described earlier.

Their speech is slow and laborious, and their comprehension is often poor. Yet other children fall somewhere in between.

In the mid-1980s, Myrna Gopnik at McGill University in Montreal reported an entire family, spanning several generations, with a high incidence of SLI amongst its members. The pattern of incidence suggested that SLI had been transmitted genetically from one generation of the family to the next. This finding, coupled with the claim that the family had the version of SLI which affected use of grammar, led to all sorts of speculations about the existence of a 'grammar gene'. There are two reasons to be cautious about such speculation. First, it seems that not all the individuals in this family suffered from the same brand of SLI. But, more importantly, perhaps there is no more a grammar gene, or a language gene come to that, than there is a reading gene. After all, dyslexia is heritable, but reading has only been around a few thousand years, so it is inconceivable that evolution has had time to encode anything specific to reading within our genetic make-up. So whatever it is that determines genetically whether or not we are dyslexic is not reading-specific. Similarly, whatever it is that determines genetically whether or not we are likely to suffer some other language-specific impairment may not even be language-specific. It may just be specific to the kinds of wiring that happen to be well suited to the associative process that underlie our use of language.

Other childhood impairments

A very different problem that can arise in childhood is a stutter. Ordinarily, a stutter is considered a speech impediment. There is no equivalent disorder involving any other kind of muscular movement—it is articulation-specific. But it can also be specific to a particular language, and in at least one case, a stammerer stuttered badly when speaking one language, but not when speaking another. Many adults who stutter badly during normal conversation can sing, or speak in a 'funny voice' without stuttering at all (the author P. G. Wodehouse wrote a short story based on such a case).

There are different kinds of stutter, and they probably each have a different cause. Some theories have proposed that a stutter arises when the right hemisphere has taken more control than usual over the articulators (the lips, tongue, and so on). Other theories propose that it has to do with faulty feedback between the signal that initiates the articulation, and the signal received when the articulation happens (if normal adults are asked to speak aloud whilst hearing their own voice played back over headphones after a slight delay, they too stutter). Most theories agree that it has something to do with mis-timing during the articulation process. The fact that only a small proportion of stutterers are female (around 20%) suggests, once again, a genetic component.

Another impairment that can affect articulation is not language-specific at all—children with a hearing impairment often have impaired articulation. When learning to speak, it is inevitable that, if what you hear and attempt to imitate is distorted, what you speak will be distorted too. Possibly the most common kind of hearing impairment in children is temporary. Children with otherwise normal hearing, but who are prone to ear infections, may suffer from glue ear. Here, the middle ear (the part on the inside of the ear-drum) fills up with a sticky fluid that prevents the normal transmission of the vibration of the ear-drum to the inner ear, where nerve fibres respond to the vibration. Often, glue ear is first noticed because the child has an obvious hearing impairment. But sometimes it is noticed because the child's speech is not as clear as would be expected. Often, there are considerable knock-on effects in school. Fortunately, glue ear can be treated relatively easily, and most children catch up quite quickly once the problem has been eliminated.

Sadly, not all impairments to language are so easily treated.

Almost anything that one can imagine going wrong with language *can* go wrong. And some things one would not imagine could go wrong *do*. The range of impairments is vast, and often, especially following brain injury, language is not the only faculty that has been impaired. It is all very well to describe, clinically and unemotionally, the nature of these impairments, but imagine waking up one day and discovering that it had happened to you. Or imagine growing up and losing out at school because you could not take notes easily, or could not understand the teacher, or could not express yourself adequately. Imagine your child having to grow up that way. None of us who are unimpaired can imagine what it is like to hear people speaking but be unable to understand them, or to know what we want to say but be unable to say it. For most of us, the ascent of our own personal Babel is unimpeded, and we should be thankful for that.

Wiring-up a brain

The average adult human brain weighs around 1.3 kg, and contains 10 billion or so nerve cells. Each nerve cell, or neuron, can connect to, and so stimulate, anything between a few hundred and perhaps 100 000 other nerve cells. And each neuron can itself receive connections from up to that same number again. Extend this to all 10 billion cells, and it is surprising that anything as vast and complex could work at all. But evidently it does. Because there is little else in the brain apart from neurons, we have no choice but to accept that they, and the manner in which they interconnect, are responsible for the mental feats of which we are capable. But there is nothing particularly special about neurons: if you stimulate one enough, it will stimulate the other neurons to which it is connected. Yet from this come our mental faculties. There is one further property of the brain that is crucial—even in an adult brain the wiring between the neurons is constantly changing. If it could not change, we could never learn.

We are not born knowing the language we shall end up using. We learn that language. Just as we learn about the world within which we shall use it. The meanings which we evoke with the words of our language are simply patterns of neural activity. These patterns reflect the accumulated experience of the contexts in which those words are used, and as such they have gradually changed with those experiences (see Chapter 9 for further details). But for patterns of neural activity to change, the patterns of neural connectivity and neural transmission that underlie those patterns of activity must also change. Ultimately, it is these changes that allow us to learn from experience. And learning from experience underlies just about everything we do. So how do these changes come about?

Neurons are a little like sunflowers. The flower corresponds to the body of the neuron. The stem is the main length of the neuron down which neural impulses are transmitted to a mass of roots. These connect to other neurons (via the equivalent of the sunflowers' 'petals') to which those impulses are transmitted.

Despite the complexities of the neurochemical processes that underlie neural transmission, there are just three principles at work. The first, and most obvious, is that neurons send impulses to the other neurons to which they are connected. The rate at which impulses are sent corresponds, in a sense, to the 'strength' of the signal. The second is that an impulse from one neuron can either make it more likely that another neuron will generate an impulse of its own, or less likely. Which of these it is depends on the kind of connection (it can be an *excitatory* connection, or an *inhibitory* one). The third principle is perhaps the most important. The connections can change in response to the surrounding neural activity—new ones can grow, especially in the first two to three years of life, although it happens in adulthood too; existing ones can die back (again, this is probably more common in younger brains); and the sensitivity of each connection can change, so that a neuron will need to receive either a stronger or a weaker signal across that connection before it generates its own impulse.

But from these three principles, are we any closer to understanding how a brain can wire itself up for language (or for anything else, come to that)? This is where artificial brains come in.

Inside an artificial neural network

Artificial neural networks exhibit the same three principles introduced in the preceding section. But the neurons are quite different. For a start, the most common neural networks (the 'artificial' will be omitted from now on) are simulated. A computer program keeps track of which neurons there ought to be, what each should currently be doing, which should be connected to which, and so on. These simulated neurons are a lot simpler than their real counterparts. The purpose of these neural networks is not to simulate the precise workings of the brain. What matters is that a signal is passed from one neuron to each of the others it connects to, or the fact that the sensitivity of a connection can change. There is no attempt to model the process by which it changes.

Artificial neurons are very much simpler than real ones. The computer works out how much stimulation a neuron should receive, and allocates that neuron a number to reflect how *active* it should be. Real neurons are similar—the rate at which they generate neural impulses, the strength of the signal, changes as a function of how much stimulation they receive. This number, the neuron's *activation*, is calculated on the basis of how active each of the neurons feeding into it is, and how 'strong' each of these connections is. The *connection strength* reflects the fact that the sensitivity of real neural connections can vary. It is a little like the volume knob on an amplifier. The higher the volume, the louder the signal. But the difference is that in these artificial networks, the connection strength is just a number. If it is positive, it is an *excitatory* connection. If it is negative, it is an *inhibitory* connection. If it is zero, then that is the same as if there were no connection between those two neurons.

That, briefly, is the underlying physiology of a neural network. The fact that a computer keeps track of what is going on within an artificial neural network, and does all the working out, is immaterial. We could

instead build an artificial neural system which consisted of physically
distinct artificial neurons, with complex interconnections that enabled
the neurons to, in effect, add, subtract, and multiply (equivalent
interconnections exist within the brain). It is just much easier to have a
computer simulate all this. But the important point is that the computer
is simply doing what a real network could in principle do for itself.

How networks work

The easiest way to figure out how neural networks work is to go
through an example. There are many different kinds, and we shall take
as our example one that could be used, for instance, to learn letter-to-
sound correspondences. Typically, the neurons in these networks are
separated into distinct groups. In our example we shall use just three
such groups. One is going to act as the 'eyes' of the network—patterns
of activity across the neurons in that group will represent the letter that
the network is 'seeing'. Another group is going to represent the
phonemes that the network is supposed to output (perhaps to a speech
synthesizer). The third group will be intermediaries between the letter
neurons and the phoneme neurons.

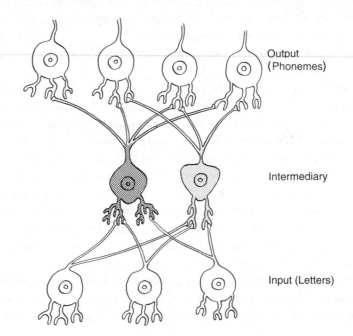

Output (Phonemes)

Intermediary

Input (Letters)

In real brains, there would probably be thousands of neurons in the chain, but the advantage of artificial neural networks is that they can be very much simpler than real brains. The only route from the letter neurons to the phoneme neurons in this example network is via the intermediary neurons. In principle, we could allow a more direct route, but we shall not do so here. Another thing we shall not allow in this example are direct connections from one letter neuron to another, or between the phoneme neurons.

That is the basic anatomy of the network. How does it work? We can start off by assuming that it has not yet learned anything. We must also assume that when the network 'sees' a letter, the computer activates the letter neurons, giving each neuron a particular amount of activation. Each letter of the alphabet would have its own unique activation pattern. We shall return shortly to why the computer allocates one pattern, rather than another, to any one letter.

We can now work through what happens when the network sees an L. First, the letter neurons will each be activated, by different amounts, according to the pattern of activation that has been allocated to that letter. Next, the computer will look at each neuron in the intermediary set of neurons, work out how much stimulation each one is receiving from all the letter neurons that connect to it (taking into account each connection's strength), and activate it accordingly. For each neuron, it takes the activation value of all the neurons connecting to it, multiplies each of those values by the appropriate connection strength, adds the results of all these multiplications, enters the grand total into an equation which converts it to a number between 0 and 1, and sets the neuron's activation to this final value. Once it has done this for all the intermediary neurons, it does the same thing again for the phoneme neurons connected to the intermediary neurons. In this way, the pattern of activation across the letter neurons spreads, via the intermediary neurons, to the phoneme neurons.

The final pattern that develops across the phoneme neurons will mean absolutely nothing. The network has not learnt anything yet, and the connection strengths are all just random. So the activation pattern across the phoneme neurons would also be random. But if the network had learnt what it was intended to learn (and we shall come to how it would do this shortly), the pattern across the phoneme neurons when the network was seeing the letter L would have been a pattern that was supposed to correspond to the phoneme /l/. It would be a pattern that the computer had previously allocated to that phoneme, in much the same way that it had allocated one pattern to the letter L, another to M, and so on. The learning process would have taken a random set of connection strengths, and would have managed to change them so that a particular pattern across the letter neurons (the pattern for L) would spread through the network and cause a particular pattern across the phoneme neurons (the pattern for /l/).

There is an important consequence of this last fact. If the connection strengths start off as random, they will scramble up the pattern allocated to L when they transmit it to the intermediary neurons. Whether it is one pattern or another makes absolutely no difference—it will still be scrambled. But if the network can learn to change the connection strengths so that it activates a specific pattern across the phoneme neurons in response to a specific pattern across the letter neurons, even when the connection strengths started off as random, it would not matter what pattern was initially allocated to any individual letter, as long as it was different from the pattern allocated to any other letter. This is just as well when it comes to thinking about our own brains and the activation patterns that they start out with. As long as our senses are consistent, it does not matter what patterns of neural activity they cause, so long as the same sensation gives rise to the same pattern of activity, and there is some way of changing the neural connectivity from its initial (potentially random) state to its final (most definitely non-random) one. Exactly how this happens in the artificial case is described next.

How (some) networks learn

The way in which networks like the one in our example learn is surprisingly simple. But before seeing how they learn it is as well to consider what they learn. The sensitivity of each connection within the network determines the precise pattern of activation that forms across the phoneme neurons in response to a particular pattern of activation across the letter neurons. So if you want the network to produce a particular phoneme pattern in response to a particular letter pattern, you have to get the connections just right. And that is what networks learn to do. They can learn to set the sensitivities of their own connections so that, eventually, the network can encode many different letter–phoneme pairings using the same set of neural connections.

Only one extra detail needs to be added to allow this to happen—when a pattern is input to the network across the letter neurons, something has to be able to tell the network what pattern of activation it should output across the phoneme neurons. What happens is that the computer looks at the activation value of each of the output (phoneme) neurons and compares it with what it should have been if the right activation pattern had been produced. It then modifies the strength of each connection leading to that neuron by a very small amount that is dependent on how close it got to the right pattern. It does this for each connection leading to each of the output neurons. It then does the same thing for each connection leading to each of the intermediary neurons. It works out (in effect) what the activation pattern across these neurons should have been in order to get something a little more similar to the correct activation at the output neurons. It then works out how each one of these neurons did compared to how it should have done, and modifies the strength of each connection leading to each neuron, but again, only by a very small amount. It sounds complicated, but it just requires some fairly simple mathematics (which computers are good at). This whole process is repeated for each pairing of input and output patterns presented to the network, with each presentation causing the connection strengths to change very slightly. Eventually, as the network learns those input–output pairings, the changes to those connection strengths become even more slight, until they stop altogether when the network gets each pairing right.

David Rumelhart, Geoffrey Hinton, and Ronald Williams at the University of California in San Diego first described this learning procedure in the mid-1980s. Although it is very unlikely that real brains systematically modify the sensitivity of their neural connections in exactly the same way, we do know that those sensitivities do change (to the point where the connections may even disappear). The principles, if not the methods, are the same.

Coping with the sequential structure of language

The problem with language is that things happen one after the other. The neural network that we have been looking at is severely limited because, although it can learn to associate one thing with another, the things it learns about are static, unchanging patterns. What is needed is a network which can take a single pattern across one set of neurons (representing, for instance, the visual image of a word) and associate that with a sequence of patterns, one after the other, across another set (representing the sequence of phonemes that need to be uttered, one after the other, to say that word). Or, better still, a network which can take a sequence of patterns across one set of neurons (representing, perhaps, the incoming speech signal) and generate another sequence of patterns across another set of neurons (representing, perhaps, the developing meaning of that signal).

Our example network has a further limitation that is in some respects even more serious. In order to learn anything, it needs the equivalent of a teacher who can tell it that the current activation pattern is not quite right, and can tell it the correct pattern that it should be aiming for. But except for when we are explicitly taught to read, and are explicitly taught such things as letter-to-sound correspondences, nobody teaches us what the correct activation patterns should be in response to what we hear. Could we design a network which did *not* rely on an explicit teacher?

In the late 1980s, Jeffrey Elman, working at the University of California, San Diego, developed a neural network that addressed both these drawbacks. He borrowed an idea that had previously been developed by a colleague of his, Michael Jordan. Jordan had demonstrated that a very simple extension to our example network could learn to output a sequence of things, one thing after another, when given just a single input pattern. The network acted as if it had a queue, or buffer, containing activation patterns waiting to be output, with something directing which pattern should come next (see Chapter 10 for the application of queues in language production). Jordan's extension gave the network the equivalent of a memory for what it had output so far. Fortunately, his new network could use the same learning procedure as before. Elman extended Jordan's technique so that the network would also be able to take as input a sequence of things. Better still, he got rid of the need for any explicit teaching. This is how the 'Elman net' works:

Imagine that at the first tick of a clock an activation pattern spreads from the input neurons to the intermediary neurons. At the second tick it spreads from the intermediary neurons to the output neurons. On the third tick, a new input (the next element in the sequence) feeds through from the input neurons to the intermediary neurons, and so on. Elman added an extra step. At the first tick, as before, activation would spread from the input neurons to the intermediary neurons. At the second tick, two things would happen. Activation would still spread from the intermediary neurons to the output neurons. But it would also spread to a new set of neurons (*copy neurons*) that were wired-up so that they would duplicate the activation pattern across the intermediary ones—each copy neuron received activation from just one intermediary neuron, and a connection strength of one ensured that the copy neuron would take on the activation value of the intermediary neuron it was connected to. But each copy neuron had connections back to each of the intermediary neurons. So on the third tick, the intermediary neurons would receive both new activation from the input neurons, and a copy of the previous pattern of activation across those inter-mediary neurons. The pattern of activation across the intermediary neurons would therefore embody both the network's reaction to the new input, and the network's reaction to the previous input. And of course, that reaction was also a reflection of the reaction before that, and before that. The network therefore had a memory of how it had reacted to previous inputs, and how they were sequenced through time. And because it had a memory of its previous reactions, each output could be determined, in part, by that memory.

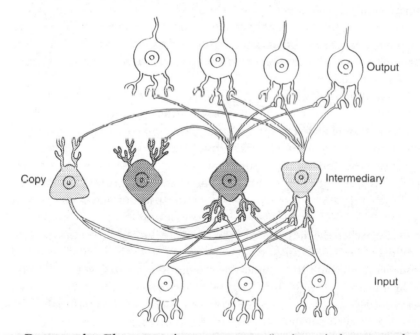

Because the Elman net has a memory for how it has reacted to previous input, it can either take a sequence of things in one order, and output one thing, or take those same things in a different order, and output something else (whether a static pattern or a sequence of changing patterns). We shall see an example of what the net was capable of in the next section. But a final innovation was Elman's realization that his network could be taught without an explicit teacher. He designed his network so that it would predict what its next input would be.

Neural networks and the prediction task

Whereas our earlier network could learn to associate one pattern with another, the Elman net can learn to associate a changing sequence of patterns with another changing sequence of patterns. The prediction task is just a variant on the idea that one sequence can be associated with another. Each element in an input sequence causes the network to output something. That output is compared with the next input, and the strengths modified according to the discrepancy. In principle, then, the Elman net can be trained to predict, on the basis of what it has seen so far of an input sequence, what the next element in that sequence is likely to be. But how useful is this? Surely we are not exposed to sequences of words, for instance, which allow us to predict with any certainty what the next element is going to be? In fact, we are. Here is what Elman did.

Using a limited vocabulary, Elman generated around 10 000 very short sentences. Each word, like each letter in our earlier example network, was allocated its own unique activation pattern. So a sentence, when presented to the network, would cause a sequence of activation patterns across the input neurons that corresponded to the sequence of words making up the sentence. These would spread through the network and cause a sequence of activation patterns across the output neurons. The network's task was to predict, after each word in the sentence, what the next word was going to be. Each output pattern would be compared against the pattern allocated to the next word in the input sequence, and the connection strengths changed (ever so slightly) according to how different the two patterns were. This was repeated many times for each of the 10 000 sentences. Not surprisingly, the network never managed to predict, with any great success, what the next word would ever be—something like 'the boy' could be followed by any number of different verbs, for instance, but the network would not be able to predict which verb. So why all the excitement?

Elman knew full well that the network could not be expected to predict with any accuracy the next word in any sequence. But after repeated exposure to the many different sentences, it did none the less learn to output, at each step through the sequence, a complex pattern that represented the variety of different words that might occur next. If, for example, the boy ate a sandwich in one sentence, and a cake in another, the network would predict, after 'The boy ate', that the next word would be 'sandwich' or 'cake'. It would do this by outputting the pattern of each one of these words simultaneously, superimposed on one another to form a composite pattern.

Elman was also interested in something else the network did. If a pattern of activation across the input neurons represented a particular word, what did the patterns of activation that developed across the intermediary neurons represent? With successive exposure to different sequences (or the same sequence, come to that), the learning procedure changed all the connection strengths linking the input neurons to the intermediary ones. The same input pattern would therefore lead to different intermediary patterns as the learning progressed. So different patterns evolved during (and as a consequence of) that learning. If activation patterns can be equated with representations, that means that the network had evolved its own, internal, representations. But of what?

In order to answer this question, Elman waited until the network had reached a point where the changes were very slight indeed, and, in effect, there was nothing more it could learn from successive exposure to the sentences it was being trained on—it was not getting any better. He then used a statistical procedure to analyse all the intermediary activation patterns that were produced in response to each input word. This allowed him to see which words caused similar patterns of activation across those intermediary neurons, and which caused different patterns. He found that all the nouns produced similar activation patterns, and the verbs did so too, but the two sets of patterns were quite distinct. Crucially, the patterns input to the network across the input neurons were just arbitrary patterns. Some might have been similar through chance, but others were quite different. But this did not stop the network from learning to distinguish between the noun patterns and the verb patterns.

In addition to being able to distinguish between nouns and verbs, the network also learned to distinguish between *transitive* and *intransitive* verbs ('chase' vs. 'sleep'), and between *animate* nouns ('boy', 'lion', 'monster') and *inanimate* nouns ('sandwich', 'plate', 'glass'). It distinguished also between animals and humans, and between things that were edible and things that were not. In each case, words within one category would cause patterns of activation across the intermediary neurons which were similar, but which would be quite different from the patterns caused by words from another category. How could any of this come about?

The only information available to the network was in the form of activation patterns across its input neurons. For each word (that is, for each activation pattern), it had information about what had come beforehand in the sequence, and what had come after. And that is exactly the information that distinguishes nouns from verbs—they occur in different contexts. For instance, in the sentences that Elman used, verbs would be preceded by nouns, and nouns sometimes by verbs, but never by nouns. Similarly, certain nouns would occur in the context of certain verbs but not in the context of certain other verbs: inanimate nouns could only occur before certain kinds of verb, edible nouns after certain kinds of verb, and so on. In fact, all the distinctions that the network made were based solely on the fact that different kinds of word occurred in different kinds of context. The network's memory meant that it could 'spot' that certain kinds of word occurred in certain similar kinds of context, whereas certain other kinds of word occurred in different kinds of context.

This still fails to explain how the network spotted anything at all. It would need some mechanism that would cause it to form representations that were defined by the contexts. This is where the prediction task comes in. The first step in the argument to explain all this is that the network did learn to predict which words could come next. And because the different words that can occur in the same position within a sentence must have the same *syntactic category* (e.g. noun, verb), the output patterns would necessarily come to reflect exactly those categories, with finer distinctions being made for subcategories that appeared in some contexts but not others—hence the distinction between animates and inanimates, transitives and intransitives, and so on. So the output neurons reflected the syntactic category of the next word in the input. But something must also have reflected, for the right category to be predicted, the syntactic categories that had come earlier in the sequence. That is what the intermediary neurons did. In Elman's sequences, the best predictor of the next word was the immediately preceding word (in fact, the current word being 'seen' by the network), so the most obvious characteristic that was encoded by those neurons was the syntactic category of that word. In effect, this reflected the range of words that could occur in that position in the sentence.

The general principle at work here is that the intermediary neurons encode whatever property of the input sequences allows the correct (or best) predictions to be made at the output neurons. This happens because the connection strengths within the network change as a function of how good the prediction has been. If the intermediary neurons manage to encode a property of the input sequences that is highly predictive of the correct output, the strengths will be changed only very slightly, if at all. But if the intermediary neurons have failed to encode any property that is predictive of the correct output, the strengths will be changed quite substantially, across the many exposures that the network receives. And because the network's memory is encoded in those connection strengths, anything that is not predictive will, in effect, be forgotten.

So the Elman net does not use its memory to store a faithful reproduction of everything that it has ever encountered. If 'sandwich' and 'cake' had occurred in *exactly* the same contexts, they would have given rise to the same internal representations (that is, patterns of activation across its intermediary neurons). But in real language, different words tend to occur in different contexts, and Elman's simulations attempted to capture this. 'Sandwich' and 'cake' occurred in subtly different contexts and gave rise to subtly different representations, but whatever could be predicted by 'sandwich' that was the same as whatever could be predicted by 'cake' was encoded, by the network, in that part of the representation that was common to both words. This explains why all the words of the same syntactic category evoked, in Elman's network, similar activation patterns across the intermediary neurons—the overlap between the individually distinct patterns conveyed information that applied to each word in that category, or, in other words, the appropriate generalizations.

One final property of these networks: if the network sees a word like 'the', it can predict that the next word will be a noun (e.g. 'cake') or an adjective (e.g. 'big'). So a composite pattern will be output that reflects both these possibilities. However, if, in the network's experience, it is more common for a noun to follow words like 'the' than it is for an adjective to follow them, the pattern will reflect the difference in the frequency of occurrence. This is a straightforward consequence of the manner in which the connection strengths are changed slightly each time the network encounters each word. If there are lots of nouns in that position, they will pull the strengths in one direction. If there are lots of adjectives, they will pull in another. The final balance depends simply on how many pulls there are in each direction. So, not only does the output of the network reflect the range of predictions that are possible at each point in the sequence, it also reflects the likelihood of each of those predictions.

That, briefly, is the Elman net. We do not know whether the real neural networks operating in our brains do the same kinds of thing. Probably, they do not. But in all likelihood, some of the principles are the same. The remainder of this chapter will look at how networks exhibiting the same properties as the Elman net might explain some of the phenomena that the preceding chapters have introduced. Much of what follows is conjecture, but it is conjecture based on observable fact.

On the meaning of meaning

In the Elman net, the information that was stored about each word— whether it was specific information or general information shared with similar words—was about the contexts in which each word could occur. 'Cake' appeared after verbs like 'eat', not 'chase'. 'Dog' followed verbs like 'chase', but not verbs like 'eat'. Yet they both followed verbs. With this limited information, the network made subtle distinctions between edible things, inedible things, animals, and humans. It made distinctions that we might normally think of as having something to do with the words' meanings.

In Chapter 9, the meaning of something was defined as the knowledge about the contexts in which that something could occur. By this criterion the Elman net had acquired an element of meaning. It was very limited, because the only context it had available to it, and on which basis it could distinguish between different words, was the linguistic context. But imagine that the network could receive information more generally about the contexts in which those words would ordinarily be used. The network might have neurons that received information from a retina, or from an ear. The network would not know that these different inputs corresponded to different kinds of information, just as it did not know that the input in Elman's original simulations reflected words in a language (and just as our own neurons do not know what their input reflects). But the network still did a good job of categorizing the words in ways which, as defined by that language, were meaningful. With additional inputs, reflecting other aspects of the contexts in which those words would ordinarily be experienced, the network ought to be able to do an even better job. The nature of the prediction task means that only aspects of the context that are predictive of the current word would be encoded.

One of the puzzles in Chapter 4 was to explain how a child would know which aspects of the context to associate with the sounds he or she heard. That puzzle is effectively solved if the only aspects selected are those that are predictive, or predicted by, those sounds. And this, according to the descriptions given in Chapter 9, is exactly what is required in order to capture the meaning of something. In fact, meaning is nothing more than that very encoding. In principle then, even an artificial neural network could achieve such an encoding—it could achieve meaning.

Who did what, and to whom

All this talk of neural activation, the encoding of experience, and prediction, is a far cry from the earlier talk (in Chapter 8) of participants, roles, and the assignment of one to the other. On the face of it, it looks as if we have ended up with an analysis of how we derive meaning that is quite different from that earlier role-assignment approach. In fact, we have simply ended up with a different vocabulary for describing the same process.

One of the puzzling properties of the way in which we go about assigning roles (to use that vocabulary) is that we apparently assign them without waiting for the grammatical information that would unambiguously signal which assignments should be made. We assume that, in the sequence 'The woman that Bertie presented the wedding ring . . . ', the woman is being given the wedding ring even before we encounter the grammatical information, later on in the sentence, that would tell us whether this was right. It need not be. The sentence could be 'The woman that Bertie presented the wedding ring to his fiancée in front of was his cousin'—yes this is a difficult sentence, but if we blindly obeyed the principles of grammar, we should not assign any role to the woman until we reached the gap between 'of' and 'was'. It looks from the evidence (see Chapter 8) as if there is some sort of need to allocate each participant a role as soon as one becomes available. We are even prepared to make preliminary role assignments which must subsequently be revised. Why? This is where the more recent talk of neural encoding and prediction comes in.

When we encounter a sentence like 'A balding linguist ate a very large fish', our experience of similar linguistic contexts ('an X Y'd')

correlates with our experience of X doing the Y'ing (as opposed to X
being Y'd). When the verb 'ate' is encountered in this sentence, a
pattern of neural activity ensues which reflects this experience. And in
so doing, it reflects, in effect, the assignment of the 'eater' role to the
linguist. When 'a very large fish' is encountered, the ensuing pattern of
neural activity reflects the assignment of the 'being eaten' role to the
fish. So that is how the neural equivalent of role-assignment works. But
each pattern of neural activity also constitutes a prediction of what the
successive patterns will be. In a world in which linguists ate fish 75% of
the time, and spaghetti the remaining 25%, the patterns of neural
activity after 'ate' would reflect these differences. They would, in effect,
predict one assignment as being more likely than the other, before the
sentence unambiguously signalled which was the correct assignment. Of
course, we do not live in such a world, but this example demonstrates
that if, after 'ate', there was a strong likelihood that one thing, rather
than another, would fill the being-eaten role, then this would be
reflected in the pattern of neural activity at that point.

In sequences of the form 'The X that . . .' (as in 'The woman
that . . .'), the X will be assigned a role by something later on in the
sentence, in the relative clause. The X could in principle fill any of the
roles that become available when the next verb is encountered. And
because the predictions that are made at each step in a sentence reflect
what is possible given our experience, it follows that the neural activity
evoked by the sequence 'The woman that Bertie presented the wedding
ring . . .' will reflect the possibility that the woman is the recipient of the
wedding ring. And because, in our experience, the thing that occupies
the same position as 'the woman' in this sentence is almost always
assigned one of the roles associated with the next verb, the possibility
that the woman is the recipient in this case is very strong. The neural
activity would reflect the strength of this possibility. It would reflect, in
effect, that particular role-assignment, before the point in the sentence
that would unambiguously signal that this was the correct role assignment. The relationship between meaning, prediction, and experience,
makes such 'early' role assignments an inevitability.

Time flew like an arrow

The link between prediction and meaning ensures that only certain
aspects of our experience (or a network's) become encoded as the

meaning of something. It also ensures that when a particular combination of contextual factors is encountered, certain predictions will be more likely, and so more influential, than others. This has consequences for the way in which ambiguities are resolved. An example from Chapter 7 involved eating pizza with your friends, your fingers, your favourite topping, your favourite wine, or your customary enthusiasm. The image that is conjured up by hearing that your friend ate pizza with his favourite film star probably does not involve that film star being poured into a glass, being used to cut through the pizza, or being sprinkled on top. We are usually quite unaware of these other possibilities. Why? Because past experience prevents the corresponding predictions from being made.

Chapter 7 ended with the observation that many factors can influence our interpretation of ambiguous sentences. Sometimes it might be the plausibility of the role-assignments. At other times it might be the frequency of the occurrence in the language at large of one kind of interpretation rather than another (or perhaps, of one kind of grammatical structure rather than another). At other times it might be the fit with the context. Each of these different factors will cause the network (real or artificial) to predict some aspect of its future input.

These factors are influential only insofar as they are predictive. Some factors may be more predictive than others. For example, the frequency of occurrence of a particular syntactic sequence in the language at large may be much more predictive of what will happen next than any other factor. But on occasion, and depending on the context, some other factor may be more predictive. The patterns of activation that encode these predictions will be superimposed one on the other, and depending on the precise circumstances (the preceding input) one pattern may dominate. What counts is not the kind of information that constitutes each factor, but simply how predictive it is.

Words and how we found them

An Elman-like network with sufficiently rich input could derive meaning from sequences of words. At least, that is the conjecture. But why should the linguistic input to this hypothetical network be confined just to sequences of words? As far as the original Elman net was concerned, it was simply experiencing different activation patterns across its input neurons. It could not know what those patterns correlated with in the world beyond its neurons. In Elman's original experiments, the activation patterns across the input neurons did represent whole words. But, although we perceive what we hear as sequences of words, each word is itself a sequence of phonemes, and phonemes can themselves be broken down into subtly different acoustic patterns. If an Elman-like net was given these acoustic patterns as input, what would happen?

By trying to predict what will come next, an Elman-like net will learn to encode information that is predictive of the kinds of context in which an input sequence might occur. If it is a sequence of phonemes (or of the acoustic patterns that make up each phoneme) the network will learn to encode information about the contexts in which those sequences might ordinarily occur. It would be able to predict the range of phonemes (or equivalent) that could continue a sequence—in effect, the range of words that are compatible with the sequence of phonemes heard so far. And as the network 'heard' progressively more of any one sequence, the number of possible continuations would fall, and the network would progressively activate patterns that reflected more strongly the remaining predictions. But there is more. With the right kinds of input (more than just the linguistic input), and sufficient exposure to the language, the network could in principle learn not simply what the next phoneme was likely to be, but more generally it could learn about the context in which that entire sequence would occur—in effect, the meaning of the word composed of those phonemes. So as more of each word was heard, the network's internal activation patterns would reflect more strongly the meaning of each word that was still compatible with the input. Eventually, when no other continuation was possible, they would reflect just the one meaning.

The description given in Chapter 6 of this process included the idea that a sequence of phonemes stimulates a neural circuit much like a sequence of numbers opens a mechanical combination lock, with successive tumblers falling into place one number after another. This analogy is in fact inappropriate. The different neural circuits are not physically separable in the same way that different combination locks are. One can think of each word that is input to the network as activating a separate neural circuit, but it is the same neurons each time, just with different activation patterns across them. It is the same connections also.

The process by which we recognize spoken words is complicated, as we saw in Chapter 6, by the fact that the same word will often be pronounced using different phonemes, depending on the surrounding words. So the sequence corresponding to 'Hand me that thin book' might on occasion sound more like 'hameethathimboo'. One possible solution, mentioned in that chapter, was that we use rules which define the circumstances in which a phoneme of one kind should be interpreted as a phoneme of another. We would then recover the meaning of the re-interpreted sequence—something that sounded like 'thim' would be re-interpreted as 'thin' if the following phoneme had been a /b/ (as in 'book'). A rule of this kind is nothing more than a statement of the contextual conditions in which a particular meaning should be associated with one sequence of phonemes rather than another. This is exactly the kind of thing that networks can learn. If 'thim' had been experienced in exactly the same contexts as had been experienced with 'thin', except that the following phoneme was a /b/, the network would inevitably activate a pattern across its intermediary neurons that reflected this experience. As long as 'thim' was encountered before a /b/, the network would activate a pattern across its intermediary neurons that was, to all intents and purposes, the same as that for 'thin'.

To the extent that linguistic rules are simply generalizations about the contexts in which one can predict one thing to happen or another, a network exhibiting the same properties as an Elman net ought to be able to encode information that is equivalent to those rules. In fact, it is difficult to see how else a set of rules could be encoded within the neural circuitry.

Words and what we learnt to do with them

In this final section, we move away from what an Elman-like net could in principle do, back to what Elman's net actually did.

Many linguists and psycholinguists believed that the acquisition of grammatical knowledge would not be possible if the only input to the learning device was the language itself. The basic problem was that grammatical knowledge was believed to exist as rules about the relative positioning of syntactic categories (things like 'noun' and 'verb') within the sentences of the language. But if you did not know about syntactic categories, how could you generate these rules? Even if you knew about which syntactic categories existed in your language, how would you know which words belonged to which category? The only solution to this problem (so the argument went) was to assume that some of the knowledge that was necessary for learning about grammar was innate (see Chapter 4). Several researchers suggested instead that because those linguistic rules were simply generalizations about which words could occur where in the sentence, all the child needed to do was calculate the equivalent—in other words, calculate the individual positions of each word relative to each other word in the language. The problem, at the time, was how the learning device would avoid learning irrelevant facts. Knowing that a noun might appear four words before a verb, or seven words after 'a' or 'the' would not be very helpful. In any case, it would be impossible to store in memory every possible fact about every possible position in which every possible word could occur. The Elman net demonstrated a simple solution.

The only information that Elman's network encoded was information that was predictive of the next word. In effect, it did simply calculate the position of each word relative to each other. It kept the information that was predictive, and discarded the information that was not. It encoded the information it kept as a combination of information that was specific to each word, and information that constituted generalizations that applied to whole groups of words. And as we saw earlier in this chapter, by developing those generalizations, the network developed the equivalent of syntactic categories and knowledge about which order they could appear in. It acquired grammar.

It might appear that there is little these networks cannot do. But an inherent problem with many artificial neural networks is that they can be quite unpredictable. Their mathematical properties do not guarantee that two networks with, for example, different numbers of neurons, will behave in exactly the same way. Much of the previous discussion is therefore limited to speculation until such time as the appropriate networks are built, and trained on the appropriate kinds of input. But even if this happened, and they did all the things we hoped they could do, there would still be a lot they could not do. They would not play. They would not have the same drives or desires as their human counterparts. They would not sit on the kitchen floor and lick the cake mixture off the spoon. They would not interact with their environment. They would not develop physically. Would that matter, though? To the extent that these are all parts of the child's experience, yes. To the extent that artificial neural networks are being built which mimic aspects of neural development, or which can learn to interact with their environment in appropriate ways, perhaps not.

Elman's prediction task is appealing because as tasks go, it has obvious evolutionary advantages—watching a moving object, catching a fly, chasing a beetle, and fleeing a foe all require the organism to predict, from one moment to the next, what is about to happen. But although it has obvious appeal, is it really enough to explain the phenomena that we have been dealing with here? Probably not. Even a frog can track a moving object, catch a fly, chase a beetle, or flee a cat. But can it talk? Does it understand? True, it does not grow up in the same environment that we do, but attempts to bring up even chimpanzees in the home environment have failed to produce a human chimpanzee. Their language is at best limited, and there is considerable controversy surrounding the claim that such chimpanzees can acquire even the smallest rudiments of grammatical knowledge. Perhaps what differs across the species is the sophistication and subtlety of prediction that each species is capable of. At the least, the difference must have something to do with differences in the sophistication, subtlety, and development, of their neural networks. It is therefore instructive to consider the principles, predictive or otherwise, that might be shared between natural and artificial neural networks. To echo a by-now familiar theme, the methods may well be different, but the principles may well be similar. And if we understand those principles, we necessarily understand better whatever lies at Babel's summit.

The descent from Babel

Depending on which books you read, language evolved as a form of social grooming (much likes apes picking at each other's nits), or as a form of social cooperation. Perhaps it evolved as an extension of the animal calls that other species exhibit, or as an extension of the various gestures that we (and other animal species) are capable of. No one can be sure *why* language evolved. There is something compelling about the argument that language evolved because a people with even a rudimentary language, and the ability to socially organize themselves through that language, would be better able to defend themselves, hunt, share out the food, reproduce, and so on. If this were right, the evolution of language would be little more mysterious than the evolution of hunting in packs, or migrating in groups, or living in family units. They each involve essentially social activities that improve the survival of the species. And the only reason monkeys did not evolve language of the complexity and richness of our own is that they did not need to. They adapted to their environment in a fundamentally different way than *Homo habilis* did (so-called because of his use of tools, around 2 million years ago). Being adapted physically to the environment was not the only way in which the survival of a species could be ensured. Had we not been able to organize ourselves socially (and linguistically), we would not have progressed, in evolutionary terms, so remarkably. By the time modern man came along (about 100 000 years ago), language was already, perhaps, quite firmly established.

Evolving languages

It is generally accepted that languages, like the different races of humans, evolved from a common origin. The first hint that this may be the case arose in the eighteenth century when an Englishman, Sir William Jones, was appointed as a judge in Calcutta. Much Hindu law was written in Sanskrit which, at that time, was no longer spoken, except as part of religious ceremonial. As Jones learnt more about it, he started to notice similarities between words in Sanskrit, Greek, Latin, German, Italian, Spanish, French, Czech, Icelandic, Welsh, English, and several other of what are now known as the *Indo-European* languages. Example words from these languages are 'matar', 'meter', 'mater', 'Mutter', 'madre', 'madre', 'mère', 'matka', 'móDir', and 'mam', which all mean 'mother', and 'nakt', 'nux', 'nox', 'Nacht', 'notte', 'noche', 'nuit', 'noc', 'nótt', and 'nos', which all mean 'night'.

At current estimates, approximately half the world's population speak a descendent of the original Indo-European language. And by looking at which words are common across all the descendants of that language, and which are different (and hence refer to concepts that developed after the languages had split), historical linguists have deduced that the original Indo-European civilization developed in a cold forest region of eastern Europe, away from a coast (there is no common word for 'sea'), about 5000 years ago. Dogs and horses were domesticated, and they farmed animals such as sheep and cows (the domestication of animals and crops happened about 5000 years before). These people also had words for wild animals such as bears and wolves. They probably knew about copper, but not about any other metals. Around 2500 BC the civilization broke up (for any number of possible reasons, such as paucity of food, climactic change, or social disintegration) and a mass migration took place in many different directions. It was these migrations that formed the basis for the different individual Indo-European languages that exist today, Lithuanian being considered the oldest.

The Indo-European languages are not the only languages to be found in Europe. Finnish and Hungarian are *Uralic* languages, whilst Basque shows no similarity whatsoever to any other language. It is now thought that the ancestors of all the European languages, together with the *Afro-Asiatic* languages (which include the Semitic and Egyptian languages), the *Altaic* languages (including Turkish and Mongolian) and some of the languages of southern India are descendants of a language that goes back 10 000 to 13 000 years. That language, together with the Australasian languages, the North American Indian languages, and in fact all the other languages of the world, is itself perhaps a descendant of an ancestral language that goes back many thousands of years before then. These descendants may even have developed after the initial migration, around 100 000 years ago, out of Africa. As different populations settled in different areas, so their languages began to diversify.

Estimates regarding the age of our languages' ancestors are pure conjecture, because there were, of course, no written records earlier than around 3500 BC. Most of these estimates are based on a mixture of linguistic and archaeological information. Languages can be compared with one another in terms of features they do or do not share. They may have similar words, or use similar sounds, or similar ways for expressing grammatical information. There are many different ways of plotting the relationships between the different languages (geographical proximity is a useful guide also). On the basis of these relationships, historical linguists can work backwards and infer the ancestral languages that could have given rise to the languages we see today. Dating those ancestral languages, and when their 'offspring' diverged, relies primarily on archaeological information about the patterns of migration that have taken place through the ages.

Recently, attempts have even been made to bring genetics into the equation. Geneticists have been able to develop family trees of racial groups based on similarities and differences in the DNA, and to estimate the ancestral lineage that led to the present day. They have even estimated, on the basis of what is known about the rate of genetic mutation, that the roots of that tree—our common ancestors—date from between 150 000 and 200 000 years ago. According to the geneticist Luigi Cavalli-Sforza, the shape of the gene tree is not too dissimilar from the shape of the language tree.

This last observation (admittedly, a somewhat controversial one) does not mean that differences in language are caused by differences in DNA. An Englishman is no more or less pre-programmed to speak an Indo-European language than he is to speak one of the Australasian languages. All it means is that when people migrate, they take both their genes and their language with them.

A relatively recent example of one such migration took place around 1000 years ago, when the Gypsies first left their ancestral homeland. Originally, it was thought that the Gypsies had come from Egypt (from which the word 'gypsy' is derived). But linguistic comparisons of Romany (the language of the Gypsies) with the Afro-Asiatic languages, and with Sanskrit and the subsequent Indian languages, showed quite unambiguously that Romany, and its speakers (and their genes), had originated in India.

So, for whatever reasons, and over however many years, the world's populations migrated, settled, and migrated again, until they reached the point, now, where they speak over 5000 different languages.

The diversity of language

Ninety-five percent of the world's population speak fewer than 100 languages. Twenty percent speak just one language (Chinese). Five percent speak one or other of the remaining 5000 or so languages. A country that is just a few hundred square miles can be the home to several different languages each of which is unintelligible to a speaker of one of the others. The island of New Guinea is host to some 700 languages. Even in Europe the same situation holds. Ask someone what language is spoken in Italy, and he or she will probably say 'Italian'. Yet the inhabitants of two villages separated by only 15 miles may have dialects that are as different from one another as French is from Spanish. 'Italian' is in fact just one of the many dialects to be found in Italy, which are, effectively, different languages. 'Italian' originated in Tuscany (around Florence) and achieved literary prominence following the publication of works by Dante in the fourteenth century.

Most of us are familiar with languages like French, Italian, Spanish, or German. French and Italian share a lot with English in terms of grammar. One needs barely more than a dictionary to translate a sentence from one of these languages into another. German is somewhat different because its verbs can appear at the ends of its sentences (see Chapter 8). Even so, it tends to do pretty much the same sorts of things as English. A language like Malay, though, is quite different. For example, plurals are usually dealt with simply by repeating the singular form. Whereas speakers of English say 'books', speakers of Malay say 'book book' (actually, they say 'buku-buku') and 'child child' ('anak-anak'). Some words do have different plural forms though. The equivalent to 'eyes' is not 'eye eye'—that means 'police'!

Other languages go to other extremes. French and Italian use *gender* (nouns are masculine or feminine). German adds a third gender—*neuter*. Swahili adds a fourth, fifth, and sixth. Finnish, on the other hand, has no gender and unlike English, no articles (like 'a' or 'the'). But it makes up for this in other ways. Like German, Finnish is a *case-marked* language (see Chapter 7). For German this means that a different article is used depending on the role that the noun plays in the sentence (such as the subject of the sentence, the indirect object, or whatever). German has just four cases, Latin had one more—but Finnish, which uses different inflections to indicate case, has fifteen.

So the different languages of the world have quite different ways of dealing with grammar. They can also use quite different sounds. Languages like Hottentot (also referred to as Nama), from South West Africa use clicks, which are made by clicking the tongue away from the roof of the mouth. Languages like Thai and Mandarin Chinese use differences in pitch to distinguish between words that would otherwise sound the same—they are *tone languages* (see Chapter 11). And whereas English words can select from around 12000 syllables, Chinese words can select from only around 400. So some languages have smaller repertoires of sounds than others. English, for instance, uses around 44 different phonemes. Hawaiian uses just 12 (five vowels and seven consonants).

Different languages also have different written forms (see Chapter 11). Quechua was the language of the Incas, who flourished in the late fifteenth century. Although the language is still spoken today, mainly in Peru, the Incas themselves never developed a writing system. Records were kept in the form of knotted cords (called quipu) which represented numerical information such as records of census counts, goods in storage, and distances. The Aztecs, who flourished in Mexico between the fourteenth and sixteenth centuries, spoke Nahuatl, which is still spoken today in parts of Mexico. They used a pictographic script until the Spaniards introduced the Roman script as part of their conquest of the region. Pictographic scripts are more primitive even than the hieroglyphic scripts that developed around 3500 BC. None the less, in Southern China, the Nakhi language still uses one. The majority of languages, though, use alphabetic scripts. Some of these alphabets, and the scripts they use (that is, the symbols they use to represent each phoneme), can be traced to the invention of a single person. The Armenian alphabet, for instance, was invented at the beginning of the fifth century by a missionary called Mesrop Mashtots. The Russian Cyrillic alphabet dates from the ninth Century, and was invented by a Greek missionary called Cyril and his brother!

One of the more recently invented scripts is used by speakers of Cherokee (an American Indian language). Cherokee has a *syllabary*, with one symbol for each of its 86 syllables. It was invented by an Indian called Sequoyah, who believed that an essential ingredient of the white man's power was his written language. In 1821, after several years' work, he 'published' his syllabary. He borrowed many of the characters for his syllabary from English, but because he was unable to read English, they took on a completely different pronunciation—w is pronounced as /la/, z as /no/, and h as /ni/, for instance. So quick was its uptake amongst the Cherokee people that the first Cherokee newspaper appeared only a few years later.

Single-handedly developing, and 'marketing', an entire writing system is certainly a quite extraordinary feat. Single-handedly saving an entire language from extinction is another.

The extinction of language

It is estimated that of the 5000 or so languages currently spoken, half will become extinct over the next 50 years. Many of these languages are spoken by only a handful of people, and as those people disappear, so will their languages.

Hebrew ceased as a spoken language over 2000 years ago. Its existence continued only through religious ritual and prayer. In the late nineteenth century, Eliezer ben Yehuda, a Lithuanian studying in Paris, dedicated himself to reviving Hebrew. He emigrated to Palestine, and recreated Hebrew as a language for contemporary use (he is credited with coining 4000 new words that were needed to bring the language back into what was by then the twentieth century). But Hebrew was a

...y language indeed. It was of such historical and religious interest that there was enormous support for ben Yehuda's work. No such luck for some of the North American Indian languages, or the Australian Aboriginal languages, or the hundreds of other languages around the world that are slowly being cleared to make way for the languages of television, film, books, and newspapers.

To lose a language is to lose an entire history. Much folklore is passed down through the generations by word of mouth only. When those mouths stop talking, that folklore is lost. Some Australian Aboriginal folklore has its roots, apparently, in events that happened at least 10 000 years ago, when Tasmania and the Australian landmass were still joined. There are folk memories of a time when the land that is now submerged was walked upon by the ancestors of today's aboriginal people. Lose a language, and you lose that past, and everything that its speakers' ancestors struggled to achieve.

Looking towards Babel: the final view

As adults, language is probably the most effortless thing we do. But understanding how we *do* language is as difficult as doing language is easy. The psycholinguistic ascent, which attempts to bring us closer to that understanding, is nowhere near as smooth, as effortless, or even as complete, as the ascent that each baby embarks on as they make their way to adult language use.

None the less, we have caught brief glimpses here of what the views would be like as we made that psycholinguistic ascent—from how babies learn something about their language before they are even born, to how adults derive meaning from the words they hear, or express meaning using the words they say.

A theme that has been common to the various stages of our psycholinguistic ascent has been that how we learn language underlies everything we do with language. Ultimately, language serves no other purpose than to convey meaning. And yet meaning is nothing more than the experience we have accumulated from infancy onwards. In order to understand what is going on, and why, in your brain or mine as we speak or listen, we need to understand how these brains of ours accumulate experience, how they encode it, how they react to it, and how they predict it. Meaning relies on what we have learned, and what we can predict from that learning.

If the meaning evoked by a sequence of words did not constitute, amongst other things, a prediction of what was likely to happen next, we would never look round when someone shouted 'Look out!'. We would still touch the stove when told 'It's hot'. We would be unable to conjure up, using words alone, images of things that were absent. And if we could not represent, within the neural structures of our brains, what was about to happen, we would be unable to encode what we were about to say—we would be unable to utter, one-by-one, the words that would express the meaning we wished to convey. So being able to encode what is about to happen, or might be about to happen, is an essential ingredient in the language recipe, not to mention the evolutionary recipe.

So, finally, what *is* language? In the end, there is just one view from Babel. Language, quite simply, is a window through which we can reach out and touch each other's minds. Anyone can reach through it—regardless of race, regardless of belief. It is the most intimate act we can ever perform. We must be sure, always, to keep that window open.

Bibliography

For each chapter, references are provided to (1) general non-specialist reading covering similar topics; (2) academic articles and reviews describing the key findings discussed in the chapter; and (3) academic articles containing other material relevant to the chapter.

General reading for the non-specialist on language as a whole, as well as a selection of academic textbooks, are referred to under the first chapter.

Chapter 1: Looking towards Babel

General reading

Crystal, D. (1987). *The Cambridge encyclopedia of language*. Cambridge: Cambridge University Press.

Miller, G. A. (1991). *The science of words*. New York: Scientific American Library.

Pinker, S. (1994). *The language instinct: The new science of language and mind*. London: Allen Lane, The Penguin Press.

Psycholinguistic textbooks

Caplan, D. (1992). *Language: Structure, processing, and disorders*. Cambridge, MA: MIT Press/Bradford Books.

Caron, J. (1992). *An introduction to psycholinguistics*. Hemel Hempstead: Harvester Wheatsheaf.

Carroll, D.W. (1994). *Psychology of language* (2nd edn). Pacific Grove: Brooks/Cole.

Harley, T. (1995). *The psychology of language: From data to theory.* Hove: Erlbaum (UK) Taylor & Francis.

Taylor, I., & Taylor, M. M. (1990). *Psycholinguistics: Learning and using language.* Englewood Cliffs, NJ: Prentice-Hall.

Whitney, P. (1998). *The psychology of language.* Boston: Houghton Mifflin Company.

Chapter 2: Babies, birth, and language

General reading

Mehler, J., & Dupoux, E. (1994). *What infants know: The new cognitive science of early development.* Cambridge, MA: Blackwell.

Key findings

Bertoncini, J., & Mehler, J. (1981). Syllables as units in infant speech perception. *Infant Behaviour and Development,* **4**, 247–260.

DeCasper, A. J., Lecanuet, J.-P., Busnel, M. C., Granier-Deferre, C., & Maugeais, R. (1994). Fetal reactions to recurrent maternal speech. *Infant Behaviour and Development,* **17**, 159–164.

DeCasper, A. J., & Spence, M J (1986). Prenatal maternal speech influences newborns' perception of speech sounds. *Infant Behaviour and Development,* **9**, 133–150.

Mehler, J., Jusczyk, P. W., Lambertz, G., Halsted, N., Bertoncini, J., & Amiel-Tison, C. (1988). A precursor of language acquisition in young infants. *Cognition,* **29**, 143–178.

Other sources

Bertoncini, J., Bijelac-Babic, R., Jusczyk, P. W., Kennedy, L. J., & Mehler, J. (1988). An investigation of young infants' perceptual representations of speech sounds. *Journal of Experimental Psychology: General,* **117**, 21–33.

Cooper, R. P., & Aslin, R. N. (1989). The language environment of the young infant: Implications for early perceptual development. *Canadian Journal of Psychology,* **43**, 247–265.

Goodman, J. C., & Nusbaum, H. C. (Eds.) (1994). *The development of speech perception.* Cambridge, MA: MIT Press/Bradford Books.

Jusczyk, P. W. (1985). The high-amplitude procedure as a methodological tool in speech perception research. In G. Gottlieb &

N. A. Krasnegor (Eds.), *Infant methodology*, pp. 195–222. Norwood, NJ: Ablex.

Jusczyk, P. W. (1993). How word recognition may evolve from infant speech perception capacities. In G. T. M. Altmann & R. C. Shillcock (Eds.), *Cognitive models of speech processing: The second Sperlonga workshop*, pp. 27–55. Hove: Lawrence Erlbaum Associates.

Jusczyk, P. W. (1997). *The discovery of spoken language*. Cambridge, MA: MIT Press/Bradford Books.

Mehler, J., Dupoux, E., & Segui, J. (1990). Constraining models of lexical access: The onset of word recognition. In G. T. M. Altmann (Ed.), *Cognitive models of speech processing*, pp. 236–262. Cambridge, MA: MIT Press.

Chapter 3: Chinchillas do it too

General reading

Mehler, J., & Dupoux, E. (1994). *What infants know: The new cognitive science of early development*. Cambridge, MA: Blackwell.

Key findings

Eimas, P. D., & Miller, J. L. (1980). Contextual effects in infant speech perception. *Science*, **209**, 1140–1141.

Eimas, P. D., Siqueland, E. R., Jusczyk, P., & Vigorito, J. (1971). Speech perception in infants. *Science*, **171**, 303–306.

Kuhl, P. K., & Miller, J. D. (1975). Speech perception by the chinchilla: Voiced–voiceless distinction in alveolar plosive consonants. *Science*, **190**, 69–72.

Liberman, A. M., Harris, K. S., Hoffman, H. S., & Griffith, B. C. (1957). The discrimination of speech sounds within and across phoneme boundaries. *Journal of Experimental Psychology*, **54**, 358–368.

McGurk, H., & MacDonald, J. (1976). Hearing lips and seeing voices. *Nature*, **264**, 746–748.

Stevens, E. B., Kuhl, P. K., & Padden, D. M. (1988). Macaques show context effects in speech perception. *Journal of the Acoustical Society of America*, **84**, 577–578.

Summerfield, Q. (1981). Articulatory rate and perceptual constancy in phonetic perception. *Journal of Experimental Psychology: Human Perception and Performance*, **7**, 1074–1095.

Werker, J. F. (1989). Becoming a native listener. *American Scientist*, **77**, 54–59.

Other sources

Goodman, J. C., & Nusbaum, H. C. (Eds.) (1994). *The development of speech perception*. Cambridge, MA: MIT Press/Bradford Books.
Miller, J. L. (1987). Rate-dependent processing in speech perception. In A. W. Ellis (Ed.), *Progress in the psychology of language*. pp. 119–157. Hillsdale, New Jersey: Lawrence Erlbaum Associates.
Miller, J. L., & Eimas, P. D. (1983). Studies on the categorization of speech by infants. *Cognition*, **13**, 135–165.
Miller, J. L. & Eimas, P. D. (Eds.) (1995). *Handbook of perception and cognition, Vol. 11: Speech, language and communication*. New York: Academic Press.
Werker, J. F. (1993). Developmental changes in cross-language speech perception: Implications for cognitive models of speech processing. In G. T. M. Altmann & R. C. Shillcock (Eds.), *Cognitive models of speech processing: The second Sperlonga workshop*, pp. 57–78. Hove: Lawrence Erlbaum Associates.
Werker, J. F., & Pegg, J. E. (1992). Infant speech perception and phonological acquisition. In C. Ferguson, L. Menn, & C. Stoel-Gammon (Eds.), *Phonological development: Models, research and implications*, pp. 285–311. Parkton, MD: York Press.

Chapter 4: Words, and what we learn to do with them

General reading

Aitchison, J. (1994). *Words in the mind: an introduction to the mental lexicon*, (2nd edn). Oxford: Blackwell.
Pinker, S. (1994). *The language instinct: The new science of language and mind*. London: Allen Lane, The Penguin Press.

Key findings

Bates, E., Dale, P. S., & Thal, D. (1994). Individual differences and their implications for theories of language development. In P. Fletcher & B. MacWhinney (Eds.), *The handbook of child language*, pp. 96–151. Oxford: Basil Blackwell.

Curtiss, S. (1977). *Genie: A psycholinguistic study of a modern-day 'wild child'*. London: Academic Press.

Fisher, C., Hall, D. G., Rakowitz, S., & Gleitman, L. (1994). When it is better to receive than to give: Syntactic and conceptual constraints on vocabulary growth. *Lingua*, **92**, 333–376. Reprinted in L. Gleitman & B. Landau (Eds.) (1994), *The acquisition of the lexicon*. Cambridge, MA: MIT Press/Bradford Books.

Fernald, A., & Simon, T. (1984). Expanded intonation contours in mothers' speech to newborns. *Developmental Psychology*, **20**, 104–113.

Gleitman, L. (1994). The structural sources of verb meanings. In P. Bloom (Ed.), *Language acquisition: Core readings*. pp. 174–221. Hemel Hempstead: Harvester Wheatsheaf.

Hirsh-Pasek, K., & Golinkoff, R. M. (1991). A new look at some old themes. In N. Krasnegor, D. Rumbaugh, M. Studdert-Kennedy, & R. Schiefelbusch (Eds.), *Biological and behavioural aspects of language acquisition*, pp. 301–320. Hillsdale, NJ: Lawrence Erlbaum Associates.

Hirsh-Pasek, K., Kemler Nelson, D. G., Jusczyk, P. W., Cassidy, K. W., Bruss, B., & Kennedy, L. (1987). Clauses are perceptual units for young infants. *Cognition*, **26**, 269–286.

Kelly, C. A., & Dale, P. S. (1989). Cognitive skills associated with the onset of multiword utterances. *Journal of Speech and Hearing Research*, **32**, 645–656.

Markman, E.M. (1994). Constraints children place on word meanings. In P. Bloom (Ed.), *Language acquisition: Core readings*, pp. 154–173. Hemel Hempstead: Harvester Wheatsheaf.

Morgan, J. L., Meier, R. P., & Newport, E. L. (1987). Structural packaging in the input to language learning: Contributions of prosodic and morphological marking of phrases to the acquisition of language. *Cognitive Psychology*, **19**, 498–550.

Naigles, L. (1990). Children use syntax to learn verb meanings. *Journal of Child Language*, **17**, 357–374.

Petitto, L. A., & Marentette, P. F. (1991). Babbling in the manual mode: Evidence for the ontogeny of language. *Science*, **251**, 1397–1536.

Pinker, S. (1987). The bootstrapping problem in language acquisition. In B. Macwhinney (Eds.), *Mechanisms of language acquisition*, pp. 399–441. Hillsdale, NJ: Lawrence Erlbaum Associates.

Shore, C., O'Connell, B., & Bates, E. (1984). First sentences in language and symbolic play. *Developmental Psychology*, **20**, 872–880.

Other sources

Bates, E., & Goodman, J. C. On the inseparability of grammar and the lexicon: Evidence from acquisition, aphasia and real-time processing. *Language and Cognitive Processes* (in press).

Bloom, P. (Ed.) (1993). *Language acquisition: Core readings.* Hemel Hempstead: Harvester Wheatsheaf.

Bowerman, M. (1990). Mapping thematic roles onto syntactic functions: Are children helped by innate linking rules? *Linguistics*, **28**, 1253–1289.

Chomsky, N. (1968). *Language and mind.* New York: Harcourt Brace.

Cooper, W. E., & Sorensen, J. M. (1977). Fundamental frequency contours at syntactic boundaries. *Journal of the Acoustical Society of America*, **62**, 683–692.

Fernald, A. (1984). The perceptual and affective salience of mothers' speech to infants. In L. Feagans, C. Garvey, & R. Golinkoff (Eds.), *The origins and growth of communication*, pp. 5–29. Norwood, NJ: Ablex.

Fletcher, P. & MacWhinney, B. (Eds.) (1995). *The handbook of child language.* Oxford: Basil Blackwell.

Gleitman, L., Gleitman, H., Landau, B., & Wanner, E. (1988). Where learning begins: Initial representations for language learning. In F. Newmeyer (Eds.), *The Cambridge linguistic survey, Vol. III*, pp. 150–193. Cambridge, MA: Harvard University Press.

Gleitman, L., & Landau, B. (Eds.) (1994). *The acquisition of the lexicon.* Cambridge, MA: MIT Press/Bradford Books.

Gleitman, L. R., & Wanner, E. (1982). Language acquisition: The state of the state of the art. In E. Wanner & L. R. Gleitman (Eds.), *Language acquisition: State of the art*, pp. 3–48. New York: Cambridge University Press.

Jackendoff, R. (1993). *Patterns in the mind.* Hemel Hempstead: Harvester Wheatsheaf.

Kemler Nelson, D. G., Hirsh-Pasek, K., Jusczyk, P. W., & Wright Cassidy, K. (1989). How the prosodic cues in motherese might assist language learning. *Journal of Child Psychology*, **16**, 55–68.

Landau, B., & Gleitman, L. R. (1985). *Language and experience: Evidence from the blind child.* Cambridge, MA: Harvard University Press.

MacWhinney, B. (Ed.) (1987). *Mechanisms of language acquisition.* Hillsdale, New Jersey: Lawrence Erlbaum Associates.

Morgan, J. (1986). *From simple input to complex grammar.* Cambridge, MA: MIT Press.

Morgan, J. L., & Demuth, K. (Ed.) (1996). *Signal to syntax.* Mahwah, NJ: Lawrence Erlbaum Associates.

Petitto, L. A. (1992). Modularity and constraints in early lexical acquisition: Evidence from children's first words, signs, and gestures. In M. R. Gunnar & M. Maratsos (Eds.), *Modularity and constraints in language and cognition,* pp. 25–58. Hove: Erlbaum.

Pinker, S. (1984). *Language learnability and language development.* Cambridge, MA: Harvard University Press.

Pinker, S. (1989). *Learnability and cognition.* Cambridge, MA: MIT Press.

Pinker, S. (1995). Language acquisition. In L. R. Gleitman & M. Liberman (Eds.), *Language: An invitation to cognitive science,* pp. 135–182. Cambridge, MA: MIT Press/Bradford Books.

Pinker, S. (1995). Why the child holded the baby rabbits: A case study in language acquisition. In L. R. Gleitman & M. Liberman (Eds.), *Language: An invitation to cognitive science,* pp. 107–133. Cambridge, MA: MIT Press/Bradford Books.

Weist, R. M. (1989). Time concepts in language and thought: Filling the Piagetian void from two to five years. In I. Levin and D. Zakay (Eds.), *Time and human cognition,* pp. 63–118. Amsterdam: Elsevier Science Publishers.

Chapter 5:   Organizing the dictionary

General reading

There are, surprisingly, no non-specialist readings on this topic.

Key findings

Cutler, A., Mehler, J., Norris, D., & Segui, J. (1983). A language-specific comprehension strategy. *Nature,* **304**, 159–160.

Dupoux, E. (1993). The time course of prelexical processing: The syllabic hypothesis revisited. In G. T. M. Altmann & R. C. Shillcock (Eds.), *Cognitive models of speech processing: The second Sperlonga meeting,* pp. 81–114. Hove: Lawrence Erlbaum Associates.

Marslen-Wilson, W., & Warren, P. (1994). Levels of perceptual representation and process in lexical access: words, phonemes, and features. *Psychological Review,* **101**, 653–675.

Mehler, J., Domergues, J. Y., Frauenfelder, U., & Segui, J. (1981). The syllable's role in speech segmentation. *Journal of Verbal Learning and Verbal Behaviour*, **20**, 298–305.

Other sources

Cutler, A., Mehler, J., Norris, D., & Segui, J. (1986). The syllable's differing role in the segmentation of French and English. *Journal of Memory and Language*, **25**, 385–400.

Cutler, A., Mehler, J., Norris, D., & Segui, J. (1989). Limits on bilingualism. *Nature*, **340**, 229–230.

Cutler, A., Mehler, J., Norris, D., & Segui, J. (1992). The monolingual nature of speech segmentation by bilinguals. *Cognitive Psychology*, **24**, 381–410.

Cutler, A., & Norris, D. (1988). The role of strong syllables in segmentation for lexical access. *Journal of Experimental Psychology: Human Perception and Performance*, **14**, 113–121.

Chapter 6: Words, and how we (eventually) find them

General reading

Aitchison, J. (1994). *Words in the mind: an introduction to the mental lexicon* (2nd edn). Oxford: Blackwell.

Key findings

Gaskell, M. G., & Marslen-Wilson, W. D. (1996). Phonological variation and inference in lexical access. *Journal of Experimental Psychology: Human Perception and Performance*, **22**, 144–158.

Marslen-Wilson, W. D. (1973). Linguistic structure and speech shadowing at very short latencies. *Nature*, **244**, 522–523.

Marslen-Wilson, W. D. (1987). Functional parallelism in spoken word recognition. *Cognition*, **25**, 71–102. Reprinted in U. H. Frauenfelder & L. K. Tyler, (Eds.) (1987). *Spoken word recognition*. Cambridge, MA: MIT Press/Bradford Books.

Marslen-Wilson, W. D., & Tyler, L. K. (1975). Processing structure of sentence perception. *Nature*, **257**, 784–786.

Marslen-Wilson, W. D., & Tyler, L. K. (1980). The temporal structure of spoken language understanding. *Cognition*, **8**, 1–71.

Shillcock, R. (1990). Lexical hypotheses in continuous speech. In G. T. M. Altmann (Ed.), *Cognitive models of speech processing: Psycholinguistic and computational perspectives*, pp. 24–49. Cambridge, MA: MIT Press/Bradford Books.

Swinney, D. A. (1979). Lexical access during sentence comprehension: (Re)considerations of context effects. *Journal of Verbal Learning and Verbal Behaviour*, **18**, 645–659.

Tabossi, P. (1993). Connections, competitions, and cohorts. In G. T. M. Altmann & R. C. Shillcock (Eds.), *Cognitive models of speech processing: The second Sperlonga meeting*, pp. 277–294. Hove: Lawrence Erlbaum Associates.

Tanenhaus, M. K., Leiman, J. M., & Seidenberg, M. S. (1979). Evidence for multiple stages in the processing of ambiguous words in syntactic context. *Journal of Verbal Learning and Verbal Behaviour*, **18**, 427–441.

Zwitserlood, P. (1989). The locus of the effects of sentential-semantic context in spoken-word processing. *Cognition*, **32**, 25–64.

Other sources

Altmann, G. T. M. (1990). Cognitive models of speech processing: An introduction. In G. T. M. Altmann (Ed.), *Cognitive models of speech processing: Psycholinguistic and computational perspectives*, pp. 1–23. Cambridge, MA: MIT Press.

Aranoff, M. (1976). *Word formation in generative grammar*. Cambridge, MA: MIT Press.

Marslen-Wilson, W. (1990). Activation, competition, and frequency in lexical access. In G. T. M. Altmann (Eds.), *Cognitive models of speech processing: Psycholinguistic and computational perspectives*, pp. 148–172. Cambridge, MA: MIT Press.

Marslen-Wilson, W., Tyler, L. K., Waksler, R., & Older, L. (1994). Morphology and meaning in the English mental lexicon. *Psychological Review*, **101**, 3–33.

Marslen-Wilson, W. D. (Ed.) (1989). *Lexical representation and process*. Cambridge, MA: MIT Press.

Marslen-Wilson, W. D. (1993). Issues of process and representation in lexical access. In G. T. M. Altmann & R. C. Shillcock (Eds.), *Cognitive models of speech processing: The second Sperlonga meeting*, pp. 187–210. Hove: Lawrence Erlbaum Associates.

Chapter 7: *Time flies like an arrow*

General reading

Pinker, S. (1994). *The language instinct: The new science of language and mind.* London: Allen Lane, The Penguin Press.

Key findings

Altmann, G. T. M., Garnham, A., & Dennis, Y. (1992). Avoiding the garden path: Eye movements in context. *Journal of Memory and Language*, **31**, 685–712.
Altmann, G. T. M., & Steedman, M. J. (1988). Interaction with context during human sentence processing. *Cognition*, **30**, 191–238.
Frazier, L. (1987). Sentence processing: A tutorial review. In M. Coltheart (Ed.), *Attention and performance XII: The psychology of reading*, pp. 559–586. Hove: Erlbaum.
Hamburger, H., & Crain, S. (1982). Relative acquisition. In S. A. Kuczaj (Ed.), *Language development*, pp. 245–274. Hillsdale, NJ: Lawrence Erlbaum Associates.
MacDonald, M. C., Pearlmutter, N. J., & Seidenberg, M. S. (1994). The lexical nature of syntactic ambiguity resolution. *Psychological Review*, **101**, 676–703.
Trueswell, J. C. (1996). The role of lexical frequency in syntactic ambiguity resolution. *Journal of Memory and Language*, **35**, 566–585.

Other sources

Altmann, G. T. M. (Ed.) (1989). *Parsing and interpretation. A special issue of Language and Cognitive Processes.* Hove: Lawrence Erlbaum Associates.
Altmann, G. T. M. (1996). Accounting for parsing principles: From parsing preferences to language acquisition. In T. Inui & J. McClelland (Eds.), *Attention and performance XVI*, pp. 479–500. Cambridge, MA: MIT Press.
Clifton, C., Frazier, L., & Rayner, K. (Ed.). (1994). *Perspectives on sentence processing*. Hillsdale, NJ: Lawrence Erlbaum.
Crain, S., Thornton, R., Boster, C., Conway, L., Lillo-Martin, D., and Woodams, E. (1996). Quantification without qualification. *Language Acquisition*, **3**, 83–153.

Crain, S. and Fodor, J. D. (1993). Competence and performance in child language. In E. Dromi (Ed.) *Language and cognition: A developmental perspective*, pp. 141-171. Norwood, NJ: Ablex.

Crain, S. (1991). Language acquisition in the absence of experience. *The Behavioral and Brain Sciences*, **4**, 597–650.

Frazier, L., & Clifton, C. (1995). *Construal*. Cambridge, MA: The MIT Press/Bradford Books.

Mitchell, D. C. (1994). Sentence Parsing. In M. A. Gernsbacher (Ed.), *Handbook of psycholinguistics*, pp. 375–409. San Diego: Academic Press.

Rayner, K., Carlson, M., & Frazier, L. (1983). The interaction of syntax and semantics during sentence processing: Eye movements in the analysis of semantically biased sentences. *Journal of Verbal Learning and Verbal Behaviour*, **22**, 358–374.

Spivey-Knowlton, M., Trueswell, J., & Tanenhaus, M. (1993). Context and syntactic ambiguity resolution. *Canadian Journal of Experimental Psychology*, **47**, 276–309.

Tanenhaus, M. K. (1988). Psycholinguistics: An overview. In F. J. Newmeyer (Ed.), *Linguistics: The Cambridge Survey. Volume III*, pp. 1–37. Cambridge: Cambridge University Press.

Tanenhaus, M. K., & Trueswell, J. C. (1995). Sentence comprehension. In J. L. Miller & P. D. Eimas (Eds.), *Handbook of perception and cognition, Vol. 11: Speech, language and communication*, pp. 217–262. San Diego: Academic Press.

Trueswell, J. C., Tanenhaus, M. K., & Garnsey, S. M. (1994). Semantic influences on parsing: Use of thematic role information in syntactic disambiguation. *Journal of Memory and Language*, **33**, 285–318.

Chapter 8: Who did what, and to whom

General reading

Pinker, S. (1994). *The language instinct: The new science of language and mind*. London: Allen Lane, The Penguin Press.

Key findings

Boland, J. E., Tanenhaus, M. K., & Garnsey, S. M. (1990). Evidence for immediate use of verb-based 'control' information in sentence processing. *Journal of Memory and Language*, **29**, 413–432.

Boland, J. E., Tanenhaus, M. K., Garnsey, S. M., Carlson, G. N. (1995). Verb argument structure in parsing and interpretation: Evidence from wh-questions. *Journal of Memory and Language.* **34**, 774–806.

Garnsey, S. M., Tanenhaus, M. K., & Chapman, R. M. (1989). Evoked potentials and the study of sentence comprehension. *Journal of Psycholinguistic Research*, **18**, 51–60.

Grimshaw, J., & Rosen, S. T. (1990). Knowledge and obedience: The developmental status of Binding Theory. *Linguistic Inquiry*, **21**, 187–222.

Kutas, M., & Hillyard, S. A. (1983). Event-related brain potentials to grammatical errors and semantic anomalies. *Memory and Cognition*, **11**, 539–550.

Kutas, M., & Hillyard, S. A. (1984). Brain potentials during reading reflect word expectancy and semantic association. *Nature*, **307**, 161–163.

McDaniel, D. (1990). Binding principles in the grammars of young children. *Language Acquisition*, **1**, 121–138.

Tanenhaus, M. K., Boland, J. E., Mauner, G. N. & Carlson, G. (1993). More on combinatory lexical information: Thematic effects in parsing and interpretation. In G. T. M. Altmann & R. C. Shillcock (Eds.), *Cognitive models of speech processing: The second Sperlonga meeting*, pp. 297–319. Hove: Lawrence Erlbaum Associates

Tanenhaus, M. K., Garnsey, S. M., & Boland, J. E. (1990). Combinatory lexical information and language comprehension. In G. T. M. Altmann (Ed.), *Cognitive models of speech processing: Psycholinguistic and computational perspectives*, pp. 383–408. Cambridge, MA: MIT Press/Bradford Books.

Other source

Tanenhaus, M. K., & Trueswell, J. C. (1995). Sentence comprehension. In J. L. Miller & P. D. Eimas (Eds.), *Handbook of perception and cognition, Vol. 11: Speech language and communication*, pp. 217–262. San Diego: Academic Press.

Chapter 9: On the meaning of meaning

General reading

Aitchison, J. (1994). *Words in the mind: an introduction to the mental lexicon* (2nd edn). Oxford: Blackwell.

Key findings

Garnham, A. (1981). Mental models as representations of text. *Memory & Cognition*, **9**, 560–565.
Garnham, A. (1985). *Psycholinguistics: Central topics*. London: Routledge.
Johnson-Laird, P. N. (1983). *Mental models*. Cambridge: Cambridge University Press.

Other sources

Clark, H. H., & Haviland, S. E. (1977). Comprehension and the Given-New contract. In R. O. Freedle (Ed.), *Discourse production and comprehension*. pp. 1–40. Ablex.
Jackendoff, R. (1993). *Patterns in the mind*. Hemel Hempstead: Harvester Wheatsheaf.
Stevenson, R. J. (1993). *Language, thought, and representation*. Chichester: John Wiley and Sons.

Chapter 10: Exercising the vocal organs

General reading

This is another important topic that has not been dealt with in any general non-specialist readings.

Key findings

Baars, B. J., Motley, M. T., & MacKay, D. (1975). Output editing for lexical status from artificially elicited slips of the tongue. *Journal of Verbal Learning and Verbal Behaviour*, **14**, 382–391.
Beattie, G. W., Cutler, A., & Pearson, M. (1982). Why is Mrs Thatcher interrupted so often? *Nature*, **300**, 744–747.

Ford, M. (1982). Sentence planning units: Implications for the speaker's representation of meaningful relations underlying sentences. In J. Bresnan (Eds.), *The mental representation of grammatical relations*, pp. 797–827. Cambridge, MA: MIT Press.

Gee, J. P., & Grosjean, F. (1983). Performance structures: A psycholinguistic and linguistic appraisal. *Cognitive Psychology*, **15**, 411–458.

Levelt, W. J. M., Schriefers, H., Vorberg, D., Meyer, A. S., Pechmann, T., & Havinga, J. (1991). The time course of lexical access in speech production: A study of picture naming. *Psychological Review*, **98**, 122–142.

Schriefers, H., Meyer, A. S., & Levelt, W. J. M. (1990). Exploring the time course of lexical access in language production: Picture–Word interference studies. *Journal of Memory and Language*, **29**, 86–102.

van Turennout, M., Hagoort, P., & Brown, C. (1997) Electrophsyiological evidence on the time course of semantic and phonological processes in speech production. *Journal of Experimental Psychology: Learning, Memory, and Cognition*, **23**, 787–806.

Other sources

Fodor, J. A., Bever, T. G., & Garrett, M. F. (1974). *The psychology of language: An introduction to psycholinguistics and generative grammar.* New York: McGraw-Hill.

Foss, D. J., & Hakes, D. T. (1978). *Psycholinguistics: An introduction to the psychology of language.* Englewood Cliffs, NJ: Prentice-Hall.

Levelt, W. J. M. (1989). *Speaking: From intention to articulation.* Cambridge, MA: MIT Press/Bradford Books.

Levelt, W. J. M. (Ed.) (1993). *Lexical access in speech production.* Cambridge, MA: Blackwell Publishers.

Levelt, W. J. M. (1995). The ability to speak: From intentions to spoken words. *European Review*, **3**, 13–23.

Meyer, A. S. (1990). The time course of phonological encoding in language production: The encoding of successive syllables of a word. *Journal of Memory and Language*, **29**, 524–545.

Meyer, A. S. (1991). The time course of phonological encoding in language production: Phonological encoding inside a syllable. *Journal of Memory and Language*, **30**, 69–89.

Schriefers, H., Zwitserlood, P., & Roelofs, A. (1991). Morphological decomposition vs. left-to-right matching. *Journal of Memory and Language*, **30**, 26–47.

Chapter 11:   The written word

General reading

Ellis, A. W. (1993). *Reading, writing and dyslexia: A cognitive analysis* (2nd edn). Hove: Lawrence Erlbaum Associates.

Key findings

McConkie, G. W., & Rayner, K. (1975). The span of the effective stimulus during a fixation in reading. *Perception & Psychophysics*, **17**, 578–586.
McConkie, G. W., & Rayner, K. (1976). Asymmetry of the perceptual span in reading. *Bulletin of the Psychonomic Society*, **8**, 365–368.
Morais, J., Bertelson, P., Cary, L., & Alegria, J. (1986). Literacy training and speech segmentation. *Cognition*, **24**, 45–64.
Morais, J., Cary, L., Alegria, J., & Bertelson, P. (1979). Does awareness of speech as a sequence of phones arise spontaneously? *Cognition*, **7**, 323–331.
O'Regan, J. K., & Lévy-Schoen, A. (1987). Eye-movement strategy and tactics in word recognition and reading. In M. Coltheart (Ed.), *Attention and Performance XII: The psychology of reading*, pp. 363–383. Hove: Lawrence Erlbaum Associates.
Rayner, K. (1975). Parafoveal identification during a fixation in reading. *Acta Psychologica*, **39**, 271–282.
Share, D. L. (1995). Phonological decoding and self-teaching: *sine qua non* of reading acquisition. *Cognition*, **55**, 151–218.
Van Orden, G. C. (1987). A rows is a rose: Spelling, sound, and reading. *Memory & Cognition*, **15**, 181–198.

Other sources

Gough, P. B., Ehri, L. C., & Treiman, R. (Eds.) (1992). *Reading acquisition*. Hillsdale, NJ: Lawrence Erlbaum Associates.
Just, M. A., & Carpenter, P. A. (1980). A theory of reading: From eye fixations to comprehension. *Psychological Review*, **57**, 329–354.
Morais, J., Content, A., Cary, L., Mehler, J., & Segui, J. (1989). Syllabic segmentation and literacy. *Language and Cognitive Processes*, **4**, 57–67.
Rayner, K., & Polatsek, A. (1989). *The psychology of reading*. Englewood Cliffs, NJ: Prentice-Hall.

Rayner, K., Sereno, S. C., Morris, R. K., Schmauder, A. R., & Clifton, C. (1989). Eye movements and on-line language comprehension processes. *Language and Cognitive Processes*, **4**, SI 21–50.

Snowling, M. J. (1996). Contemporary approaches to the teaching of reading. *Journal of Child Psychology and Psychiatry*, **37**, 139–148.

Chapter 12: When it all goes wrong

General reading

Ellis, A. W. (1993). *Reading, writing and dyslexia: A cognitive analysis* (2nd edn). Hove: Lawrence Erlbaum Associates.

Sacks, O. (1986). *The man who mistook his wife for a hat*. London: Duckworth.

Key findings

Ellis, A. W., & Young, A. W. (1988). *Human cognitive neuropsychology*. Hove: Lawrence Erlbaum Associates.

Franklin, S., Howard, D., & Patterson, K. (1994). Abstract word meaning deafness. *Cognitive Neuropsychology*, **11**, 1–34.

Gopnik, M. (1990). Genetic basis of grammar defect. *Nature*, **347**, 26.

Hulme, C. (1981). *Reading retardation and multi-sensory teaching*. London: Routledge & Kegan Paul.

Lambon Ralph, M. A., Sage, K., & Ellis, A. W. (1996). Word meaning blindness: A new form of acquired dyslexia. *Cognitive Neuropsychology*, **13**, 617–639.

Miceli, G., & Capasso, R. Semantic errors as evidence for the independence and the interaction of orthographic and phonological word forms. *Language and Cognitive Processes* (in press).

Olson, R. K., & Wise, B. W. (1992). Reading on the computer with orthographic and speech feedback. *Reading and Writing*, **4**, 107–144.

Van Riper, C. (1982). *The nature of stuttering* (2nd edn). Englewood Cliffs, NJ: Prentice-Hall.

Vargha-Khadem, F., Watkins, K., Alcock, K., Fletcher, P., & Passingham, R. (1995). Praxic and nonverbal cognitive deficits in a large family with a genetically transmitted speech and language disorder. *Proceedings of the National Academy of Sciences of the USA*, **92**, 930–933.

Other sources

Badecker, B., & Caramazza, A. (1985). On consideration of method and theory governing the use of clinical categories in neurolinguistics and cognitive neuropsychology: The case against agrammatism. *Cognition*, **20**, 97–125.

Caplan, D. (1992). *Language: Structure, processing, and disorders.* Cambridge, MA: MIT Press/Bradford Books.

Castles, A., & Coltheart, M. (1993). Varieties of developmental dyslexia. *Cognition*, **47**, 149–180.

Code, C. (Ed.) (1991). *The characteristics of aphasia.* Hove: Lawrence Erlbaum Associates.

Gopnik, M., & Crago, M. B. (1991). Familial aggregation of a developmental language disorder. *Cognition*, **39**, 1–50.

Parkin, A. J. (1996). *Explorations in cognitive neuropsychology.* Oxford: Blackwell.

Plaut, D., & Shallice, T. (1994). *Connectionist modelling in cognitive neuropsychology: A case study.* Hove: Lawrence Erlbaum Associates.

Plaut, D. C., McClelland, J. L., Seidenberg, M. S., & Patterson, K. E. (1996). Understanding normal and impaired word reading: Computational principles in quasi-regular domains. *Psychological Review*, **52**, 25–82.

Snowling, M. (1987). *Dyslexia: A cognitive developmental perspective.* Oxford: Blackwell.

Snowling, M. J. (1995). Phonological processing and developmental dyslexia. *Journal of Research in Reading*, **18**, 132–138.

Chapter 13: Wiring-up a brain

General reading

There are, again surprisingly, no non-specialist readings which describe work on neural networks.

Key findings

Elman, J. L. (1990). Finding structure in time. *Cognitive Science*, **14**, 179–211.

Elman, J. L. (1990). Representation and structure in connectionist models. In G. T. M. Altmann (Ed.), *Cognitive models of speech processing: Psycholinguistic and computational perspectives*, pp. 345–382. Cambridge, MA: MIT Press/Bradford Books.

Jordan, M. I. (1986). *Serial order: A parallel distributed processing approach* Report No. 8604. Institute of Cognitive Science, University of California, San Diego.

Other sources

Bechtel, W., & Abrahamsen, A. (1991). *Connectionism and the mind.* Cambridge, MA: Basil Blackwell.

Cottrell, G. W., & Plunkett, K. (1994). Acquiring the mapping from meaning to sounds. *Connection Science*, **6**, 379–412.

Ellis, N., & Humphreys, G. (1997). *Connectionist models in psychology.* Hove: Erlbaum (UK) Taylor & Francis.

Elman, J. L. (1993). Learning and development in neural networks: The importance of starting small. *Cognition*, **48**, 71–99.

Elman, J. L. (1995). Language as a dynamical system. In R. F. Port & T. V. Gelder (Eds.), *Mind as motion*, pp. 195–225. Cambridge, MA: MIT Press/Bradford Books.

Elman, J. L., Bates, E. A., Johnson, M. H., Karmiloff-Smith, A., Parisi, D., & Plunkett, K. (1996). *Rethinking innateness: A connectionist perspective on development.* Cambridge, MA: MIT Press/Bradford Books.

Rumelhart, D. E. and McClelland, J. L. (1986) *Parallel distributed processing: Explorations in the microstructure of cognition.* Cambridge, MA: MIT Press/Bradford Books.

Chapter 14: The descent from Babel

General reading

Aitchison, J. (1996). *The seeds of speech: Language origin and evolution.* Cambridge: Cambridge University Press.

Crystal, D. (1987). *The Cambridge encyclopedia of language.* Cambridge: Cambridge University Press.

Dunbar, R. (1996). *Grooming, gossip and the evolution of language.* London: Faber and Faber.

Key finding

Cavalli-Sforza, L. L., Piazza, A., Menozzi, P., & Mountain, J. L. (1988). Reconstruction of human evolution: Bringing together genetic, archaeological and linguistic data. *Proceedings of the National Academy of Sciences of the USA*, **85**, 6002–6006.

Other sources

Flood, J. (1995). *Archaeology of the dreamtime: the story of prehistoric Australia and its people*, (Revised edition). Sydney: Angus & Robertson.

Katzner, K. (1986). *The languages of the world*. London: Routledge.

Moseley, C. and Asher, R. E. (1994). *Atlas of the world's languages*. London: Routledge.

Index

Jabberwocky 117
James, William 153
Japanese 25, 86, 112, 162–3, 169, 173–4
Javanese 50
Johnson-Laird, Philip 125
Jones, Sir William 227
Jordan, Michael 212
Jusczyk, Peter 17, 22

kanji 163
katakana 162
knotted cord 230
Kuhl, Patricia 28
Kutas, Marta 111

language, evolution of 226
Latin 227
learnability 44, 48
letter-naming 199, 201–2
Levelt, Willem 157–8
lexical access 5, 7, 68–77, 80–2
    acoustic mismatch 73–7
    see also mental lexicon
lexical decision 71, 73, 79
lexical entry 77–8
    activation of 177
    see also lexical access
lexical search, see lexical access
Liberman, Alvin 24
linguistics 3–4, 99–100, 116
literacy 178–9
Lithuanian 227
logogram 54, 163, 169, 174
look-and-say 165
loudness 12, 141

MacDonald, Janet 23
Malay 230
Markman, Ellen 38
Marslen-Wilson, William 61, 69–70, 72–3,
    75
Mashtots, Mesrop 231
Maynard Smith, John 160
McConkie, George 175
meaning 33–4, 66–7, 69, 71, 73, 77–81,
    87, 97–100, 102, 117–37, 184, 188–9,
    205
    acquisition of 36–41
    in neural networks 218–19
    of words 120–2
    of written words 166, 170–3, 178

Mehler, Jacques 13–15, 17–18, 57
melody 157
memory 126, 129
mental lexicon 22, 64, 68, 71, 78, 80, 87
    access code 55–61, 63
    see also lexical access
mental model 126–31, 136, 140, 142
mental representation 99–100, 129
Meyer, Antje 158
migration 227
Miller, James D. 28
Miller, Joanne 30
mind 121
Mongolian 227
monkeys, Macaque 31
Morais, José 179
Morgan, James 48–50
morpheme 66
morphology 66–8, 88
Morton, John 70

Nahuatl 230
Naigles, Letitia 40
Nakhi 231
naming deficits 187–9
neural activity 120–2, 127–9, 134–5,
    145–7, 153, 155, 158, 168, 173, 205
neural circuitry 70–1, 77, 81, 120, 153–5,
    188, 201
neural connection 120, 146, 155, 188, 206
neural network 207–18
    coding sequential structure 211–13
    copy neurons 212
    learning in 210–11
neuron 120, 205–7
New Guinea 229
non-nutritive sucking 5–6, 13, 15
North American Indian 227
noun 36–7, 39, 40–1, 45, 86

object 43, 86, 146
Olson, Richard 200
optimum viewing position 177
O'Regan, Kevin 177
Oxford English Dictionary 65, 76, 80, 119

papyrus 160
past tense 51, 67
pause 156–7
Pavlov 121, 135
Philippines 52